Essential College English

Essential College English

A Grammar and Punctuation Workbook for Writers

Fifth Edition

Norwood Selby
Surry Community College

 LONGMAN

An Imprint of Addison Wesley Longman, Inc.

New York • Reading, Massachusetts • Menlo Park, California • Harlow, England
Don Mills, Ontario • Sydney • Mexico City • Madrid • Amsterdam

Acquisitions Editor: Steven Rigolosi

Development Editor: Jennifer Krasula

Marketing Manager: Melanie Goulet

Supplements Editor: Donna Campion

Project Manager: Donna DeBenedictis

Design Manager: Rubina Yeh

Text and Cover Designer: Sandra Watanabe

Technical Desktop Manager: Heather A. Peres

Electronic Page Makeup: Sandra Watanabe

Senior Print Buyer: Hugh Crawford

Printer and Binder: The Maple-Vail Book Manufacturing Group

Cover Printer: Coral Graphic Services, Inc.

Library of Congress Cataloging-in-Publication Data

Selby, Norwood
    Essential College English : a grammar and punctuation workbook
for writers / Norwood Selby. — 5th ed.
        p. cm
    Includes index.
    ISBN 0-321-03808-8 (pbk.)
    1. English language—Grammar problems, exercises, etc. 2. English
language—Punctuation Problems, exercises, etc. I. Title
    PE1112 .S37 1999
    428.2—dc21   99-16378
                                                                CIP

Please visit our website at http://www.awlonline.com

ISBN 0-321-03808-8

12345678910—MA—02010099

Brief Contents

Contents

C h • p t e r **3**

80 Phrases

C h • p t e r **4**

104 Clauses

C h • p t e r **5**

126 Sentence Types, Sentence Variety, and Sentence Combining

C h • p t e r **6**

C h • p t e r **7**

C h • p t e r **8**

Chapter 12

290 Semicolons

Chapter 13

300 Apostrophes

Chapter 14

312 Quotation Marks

Chapter 15

324 Capitalization and Italics

Preface

E_ssential College English_ has been in print since 1982 and has sold more than 100,000 copies. Its purpose remains the same: to provide students with an understandable explanation of the basic rules of grammar and punctuation. Though some people question the usefulness of teaching grammar, there is no question that the business world expects correctly written correspondence. _Essential College English_ explains correct usage in simple terms.

The book can be used as a developmental text or as a supplemental text in composition courses. However it is used, it provides essential information that every writer needs. I hope you find _Essential College English_ an enjoyable and informative text. Over the years I have received much positive feedback from students and faculty alike. I hope your experience with the text is equally beneficial.

Organization

Part I of _Essential College English_ follows a logical progression of the rules of basic grammar. Chapter 1 discusses subjects, verbs, and complements—the main components of a sentence. Chapter 2 defines individual parts of speech, while Chapters 3 and 4 explain how these parts can be put together to form phrases and clauses. Chapter 5 introduces the types of sentences that make writing interesting. Special emphasis is given to the concept of sentence combining, including a wealth of practice exercises. Chapter 6 addresses the issues of subject-verb and pronoun-antecedent agreement.

Chapters 7 and 8 move into descriptions of common errors in sentence composition. Students learn how to identify and correct sentence fragments, fused sentences, and comma splices. Part I concludes with chapters on pronoun case reference and the formulation and use of adjectives and adverbs.

Part II covers the ground rules for punctuation, dedicating chapters to each major form of punctuation (commas, semicolons, apostrophes, and quotation marks). It concludes with chapters on capitalization and italics, abbreviations and numbers, and an overview of other punctuation marks.

New in the Fifth Edition

- **Writer's Tips** and two **Writing Assignments** in each chapter give students more writing practice.
- Chapter 5, **"Sentence Structure, Sentence Variety, and Sentence Combining,"** includes increased coverage of sentence combining.
- **Examples** include a wider representation of ethnic names and topics, reflecting the diversity of today's student population.
- All **grammatical rules are either boxed or printed in boldface,** making it easier to find and refer to them.
- Many **exercises** have been rewritten to reflect current trends.
- **Checklists,** which summarize important and complex grammar rules, appear throughout the text as quick reference points for students.
- The **design** has been completely updated to produce a book that is visually appealing and easy to use.

Continuing Features

- Each chapter includes a large number and variety of practice exercises. **Practice Sentences** provide the opportunity to practice grammatical rules immediately after they are discussed. **Editing Practice** offers practice in locating and correcting grammatical errors in written materials.
- Extensive review exercises are included at the end of each chapter. **Mastery Tests** measure comprehension of the material discussed in each chapter. **Editing Tests** measure ability to locate and correct grammatical errors.
- Traditional principles of basic, sentence-level grammar and usage are explained in **concise, clear language** throughout the text.

The Teaching and Learning Package

Each component of the teaching and learning package has been carefully crafted to ensure that the course is a rewarding experience for both instructors and students.

INSTRUCTOR'S MANUAL/TEST BANK.

This supplement contains a diagnostic grammar test, individual chapter tests, a diagnostic punctuation and grammar test, and answers to all tests and text-book exercises. 0-321-04445-2

THE WRITER'S TOOLKIT.

This CD-ROM offers a wealth of tutorial, exercise, and reference material for writers needing grammar support. It is compatible with either a PC or Macintosh platform and is flexible enough to be used either occasionally for practice or regularly in class lab sessions. The Writer's ToolKit is included free with this text.

The Longman Basic Skills Package

In addition to the book-specific supplements, a series of other skills-based supplements is available for both instructors and students either free or at greatly reduced prices.

For Additional Reading and Reference

THE DICTIONARY DEAL.

Two dictionaries can be shrinkwrapped with any Longman Basic Skills title at a nominal fee. *The New American Webster Handy College Dictionary* (0-451-18166-2) is a paperback reference text with more than 100,000 entries. *Merriam Webster's Collegiate Dictionary*, Tenth Edition (0-87779-709-9), is a hardcover reference with a citation file of more than 14.5 million examples of English words drawn from actual use.

PENGUIN QUALITY PAPERBACK TITLES.

A series of Penguin paperbacks is available at a significant discount when shrinkwrapped with any Longman Basic Skills title. Some titles available are: Toni Morrison's *Beloved* (0-452-26446-4), Julia Alvarez's *How the Garcia Girls Lost Their Accents* (0-452-26806-0), Mark Twain's *Huckleberry Finn* (0-451-52650-3), *Narrative of the Life of Frederick Douglass* (0-451-52673-2), Harriet Beecher Stowe's *Uncle Tom's Cabin* (0-451-52302-4), Dr. Martin Luther King Jr.'s *Why We Can't Wait* (0-451-62754-7), and plays by Shakespeare, Miller, and Albee. For a complete list of titles or more information, please contact your Addison Wesley Longman sales consultant.

80 Readings, SECOND EDITION.

This inexpensive volume contains 80 brief readings (1–3 pages each) on a variety of themes: writers on writing, nature, women and men, customs and habits, politics, rights and obligations, and coming of age. Also included is an alternate rhetorical table of contents. 0-321-01648-3.

100 THINGS TO WRITE ABOUT.

This 100-page book contains 100 individual assignments for writing on a variety of topics and in a wide range of formats from expressive to analytical. Ask your Addison Wesley Longman sales representative for a sample copy. 0-673-98239-4

Electronic and Online Offerings

THE LONGMAN ENGLISH PAGES WEBSITE.

Both students and instructors can visit our free content-rich website for additional reading selections and writing exercises. From the Longman English pages, visitors can conduct a simulated Web search, learn how to write a résumé and cover letter, or try their hand at poetry writing. Stop by and visit us at **http://longman.awl.com/englishpages.**

THE BASIC SKILLS ELECTRONIC NEWSLETTER.

Twice a month during the spring and fall, instructors who have subscribed receive a free copy of the Longman Basic Skills Newsletter in their E-mail. Written by experienced classroom instructors, the newsletter offers teaching tips, classroom activities, book reviews, and more. To subscribe, visit the Longman Basic Skills website at **http://longman.awl.com/basicskills,** or E-mail **Basic Skills.**

DAEDALUS ONLINE.

Addison Wesley Longman and The Daedalus Group are proud to offer the next generation of the award-winning Daedalus Integrated Writing Environment. Daedalus Online is an Internet-based collaborative writing environment for students. The program offers prewriting strategies and prompts, computer-mediated conferencing, peer collaboration and review, comprehensive writing support, and secure, 24-hour availability. For educators, Daedalus Online offers a comprehensive suite of online course management tools for managing an online class, dynamically linking assignments, and facilitating a heurisitic approach to writing instruction. For more information, visit **http://www.awlonline.com/daedalus,** or contact your Addison Wesley Longman sales representative.

Researching Online, THIRD EDITION.

A perfect companion for a new age, this indispensable new supplement helps students navigate the Internet. Adapted from *Teaching Online,* the instructor's Internet guide, *Researching Online* speaks directly to students, giving them detailed, step-by-step instructions for performing electronic searches. Available at a nominal charge when shrinkwrapped with any Longman Basic Skills text. 0-321-05802-X

Teaching Online: Internet Research, Conversation, and Composition, SECOND EDITION.

Ideal for instructors who have never surfed the Net, this easy-to-follow guide offers basic definitions, numerous examples, and step-by-step information about finding and using Internet sources. Free to adopters. 0-321-01957-1

For Instructors

Competency Profile Test Bank, SECOND EDITION.

This series of 60 objective tests covers ten areas of English competency including fragments, comma splices and run-ons, pronouns, commas, and capitalization. Each test is available in remedial, standard, and advanced versions. Available as reproducible sheets or on computer diskettes. Free to instructors. Paper: 0-321-02224-6. IBM: 0-321-02633-0. Macintosh: 0-321-02632-2.

Diagnostic and Editing Tests, SECOND EDITION.

This collection of diagnostic tests helps instructors assess students' competence in Standard Written English for the purpose of placement or to gauge progress. Available as reproducible sheets or in computerized versions. Free to instructors. Paper: 0-321-02222-X. IBM: 0-321-02629-2. Macintosh: 0-321-02628-4.

ESL Worksheets, SECOND EDITION.

These reproducible worksheets provide ESL students with extra practice in areas they find the most troublesome. A diagnostic test and posttest are provided, along with answer keys and suggested topics for writing. Free to adopters. 0-321-01955-5

80 Practices.

A collection of reproducible, ten-item exercises that provide additional practices for specific grammatical usage problems such as comma splices, capitalization, and pronouns. Includes an answer key. Free to adopters. 0-673-53422-7

CLAST Test Package, FOURTH EDITION.
These two 40-item objective tests evaluate students' readiness for the CLAST exams. Strategies for teaching CLAST preparedness are included. Free with any Longman English title. Paper: 0-321-01950-4 IBM: 0-321-01982-2 Macintosh: 0-321-01983-0

TASP Test Package, THIRD EDITION.
These 12 practice pretests and posttests assess the same reading and writing skills covered in the TASP examination. Free with any Longman English title. Reproducible sheets: 0-321-01959-8 IBM: 0-321-02623-3 Macintosh: 0-321-02622-5

Teaching Writing to the Non-Native Speaker.
This booklet examines the issues that arise when non-native speakers enter the developmental classroom. Free to instructors, it includes profiles of international and permanent ESL students, factors influencing second-language acquisition, and tips on managing a multicultural classroom. 0-673-97452-9

For Students

Visual Communication: A Writer's Guide.
This unique new offering introduces document design principles that writers can apply across different genres of writing including academic papers, résumés, business letters, Web pages, brochures, newsletters, and proposals. Emphasizing audience and genre analysis, the guide shows how readers' expectations influence and shape a document's look. Practical discussions of space, type, organization, pattern, and graphic elements are featured, along with planning worksheets, design samples, and exercises. 0-321-05071-1

Using WordPerfect in Composition AND *Using Microsoft Word in Composition.*
These two brief guides assume no prior knowledge of WordPerfect or Word. Each guide begins with word-processing basics and gradually leads into more sophisticated functions. Shrinkwrapped free with any Longman Basic Skills text. WordPerfect: 0-673-52448-5 Microsoft Word: 0-673-52449-3

Learning Together: An Introduction to Collaborative Theory.
This brief guide to the fundamentals of collaborative learning teaches students how to work effectively in groups, how to revise with peer response, and how to coauthor a paper or report. Shrinkwrapped free with any Longman Basic Skills text. 0-673-46848-8

A Guide for Peer Response, SECOND EDITION.
This guide offers students forms for peer critiques including general guidelines and specific forms for different stages in the writing process. Also appropriate for freshman-level courses. Free to adopters. 0-321-01948-2

Acknowledgments

I would like to thank the following instructors for their valuable feedback on this new edition of *Essential College English:*

Jackie Atkins, Pennsylvania State University, Du Bois
Jeffrey Carroll, University of Hawaii at Manoa
Marlys Cordoba, College of the Siskiyous
Judy Covington, Trident Technical Community College
Joanne Ernst, Manatee Community College
Jane Flesher, Chippewa Valley Technical College
Trish Ireland, Grand Valley State University
Rodney Keller, Ricks College
Mimi Markus, Broward Community College
Ed Nagelhout, University of Nevada, Las Vegas
Twila Papay, Rollins College
Mary Sue Ply, Southeastern Louisiana University
Kathryn Roosa, San Jacinto College
Lauren Sewell, University of Tennessee at Chattanooga
Holly Young, Arkansas State University at Beebe

NORWOOD SELBY

part 1

Grammar

Subjects, Verbs, and Complements

You are beginning a study of your language. What you learn will help you better understand how the English language works and give you more confidence in yourself when communicating with others. Think about how important communication is in all phases of day-to-day life and how you can benefit from having confidence in your use of language. If you couldn't communicate, how could you get a date, order a pizza, or pass your English course? Without communication you would be isolated.

As you know by this point in your education, every field of study has names for things. Automobile mechanics know not only what a carburetor is but what the names of the parts are that make up a carburetor. Physicians know the names of bones, muscles, nerves, etc. The names given to things make it easier for people talking about a subject to know exactly what is being discussed. Language also has names for things, such as the terms *subjects*, *verbs*, and *complements* mentioned in the title of this chapter. These terms provide a kind of shorthand that allows us to learn more easily. Once we are familiar with the concepts the terms represent, we can better understand and more easily analyze the writing. Do not allow yourself to be bothered by the various terms you will encounter. Just consider them tools to use in learning about language. Other terms could just as easily be used and, in fact, often are. There is nothing sacred about the terminology.

In this book we break the study of language down into basic steps. Study each step until you feel you understand it before moving on to the next.

Subjects and Predicates

> An English sentence contains both a **subject** and a **predicate**. A sub-
> ject is what is talked about in a sentence.

<u>John</u> drives a 1966 Mustang.
 John is the subject of the sentence. He is being talked about in the
 sentence.

> A **predicate** says something about the subject.

In the sentence above, *drives a 1966 Mustang* is the predicate. It says something about John.
 A sentence can be composed of just a subject and a predicate.

<u>Mary</u> sews.
 Mary is the subject. She is being talked about in the sentence.
 Sews is the predicate. The word *sews* says something about Mary.

More often, however, a sentence contains more than just a subject and a predicate.

 A tall man with red hair walked into a restaurant.
  The subject of the sentence is *man.* He is being talked about.
  Walked is the predicate in the sentence. It says something about
  the man (subject).

The sentence is said to have a **complete subject** and a **complete predicate.**
The complete subject contains the basic subject *man* (called the **simple subject**) and all the words that relate to the subject. Thus, the complete subject is
A tall man with red hair. *A, tall,* and *with red hair* all relate to *man.* The complete predicate contains the predicate itself, *walked* (called a **simple predicate**) and all the words that relate to it. Thus, *walked into a restaurant* is the
complete predicate. *Into a restaurant* relates to *walked.*

 The fat cat ate the lasagna.
  The complete subject is *The fat cat.*
  The complete predicate is *ate the lasagna.*

 The tired student stretched out for a nap.
  The complete subject is *The tired student.*
  The complete predicate is *stretched out for a nap.*

The key word in the complete predicate is the verb. *Stretched* is the verb in the sentence above because it is the key word that says something about the subject.

Recognizing Verbs

Action Verbs

> **Verbs** are often the most important words in sentences.

When you can recognize them, you are on your way. Everything else in a sentence relates to the verb either directly or indirectly.

> The easiest verbs to recognize are those which show action.

Words such as *run, jump, play, sing,* and *drive* can clearly show action.

The men <u>run</u> three miles every day.
> *Run* is the verb.

The boxer <u>jumps</u> rope for fifteen minutes every day.
> *Jumps* is the verb.

The girl <u>played</u> basketball for thirty minutes.
> *Played* is the verb.

Not all action verbs show physical action. Many verbs in English express mental action; these include *think, believe, imagine,* and *wonder.* They are also action verbs; they just express a different kind of action. As you know, thinking can be hard work; it is an active process.

The executives <u>think</u> about the company's problems every morning.
> *Think* is an action verb.

They <u>believe</u> in the potential of the company.
> *Believe* is an action verb.

PRACTICE SENTENCES 1–1
Identify the action verbs in the following sentences by underlining them.

Example: Cecil and Lupe <u>joined</u> a local community organization.

1. The club sponsored many projects.

2. It sought improvement in all areas of the community.

3. Cecil joined the community cleanup project.

4. He collected soda cans and other types of litter on the streets of the city.

5. Lupe participated in the community face-lift project.

6. She painted the inside and outside of several old buildings.

7. Cecil and Lupe went to lunch one day.

8. They compared notes on their community work.

9. They considered the work too hard.

10. Now they learn about property repairs by watching television.

Linking Verbs

Action verbs are easy to recognize: just look for the word that tells what is being done.

> Some verbs do not show action. Instead they link the subject to another word, phrase, or clause that names or describes it. Thus they are known as **linking verbs.**

The various forms of the verb *be* are the most common linking verbs. The verb *be* is very irregular and takes many forms (for example, *is, was, are, am, were, being,* and *been*). By examining a few examples, you will see how forms of the verb *be* link parts of sentences together.

Jane is tall.
    Is is a linking verb.

The word *is* does not show action. Instead, *is* establishes a connection, or equivalency, between *Jane* and *tall*. It links the woman to an attribute describing her, and so it is known as a *linking verb.*

I am a student.
    Am is a linking verb.

Notice that the verb *am* links the word *I* to the word *student.* It is a linking verb.

PRACTICE SENTENCES 1-2

Identify the linking verbs in the following sentences.

Example: Susan is an English major.

1. In high school Susan became an avid science student.

2. She was in the physics lab every afternoon.

3. In college, however, Susan seemed to lose interest in science.

4. She became aware of the beauty of the English language.

5. She is now very happy with a good novel.

6. Susan also feels the rhythm of a poem by John Keats.

7. Chaucer's *Canterbury Tales* is one of her favorite works.

8. She appears fond of the early form of the English language.

9. Her favorite poet, however, is Emily Dickinson.

10. No doubt, Susan will be an outstanding English teacher.

Though forms of *be* are the most common linking verbs, they are not the only ones. Many verbs that refer to the senses are linking verbs.

Words such as *feel, taste, sound, smell,* and *look* can be linking verbs, though they do not always have to be (see the section on correct usage of adjectives and adverbs, Chapter 10). Other linking verbs are *become, seem,* and *appear.* Here are some linking verbs:

LINKING VERBS

is am was were been being	any form of the verb *be*	feel taste sound smell look become seem appear

---

The pie tastes sour.
   Tastes links *pie* to *sour.*

The girl became a champion fiddler.
   Became links *girl* to *fiddler.*

The man <u>seems</u> confident.

Seems is a linking verb. What does it link?

Auxiliary Verbs

Besides action verbs and linking verbs, there is another type of verb; the auxiliary verb.

> An **auxiliary verb** precedes the main verb and helps it do its job.

The auxiliary verb may make the main verb more precise in describing and telling when things happen. It may indicate obligation, possibility, emphasis, or permission.

The man <u>will complete</u> the project.

The main verb is *complete,* and the auxiliary verb is *will.* The auxiliary verb tells you that the action has not yet been completed. It will be completed, however, sometime in the future.

Ralph <u>has finished</u> his five-year probation.

The main verb is *finished,* and the auxiliary is *has.* The auxiliary verb tells you that the action has been completed.

I <u>have noticed</u> the change in policy.

The main verb is *noticed,* and the auxiliary is *have.* The auxiliary verb tells you that the action has been completed.

You <u>must complete</u> the assignment.

The main verb is *complete;* the auxiliary is *must.* The auxiliary indicates that the act of completing is an obligation.

I <u>do know</u> the answer to that question.

The main verb is *know;* the auxiliary is *do.* The auxiliary emphasizes the act of knowing.

Some common auxiliary verbs are:

AUXILIARY VERBS			
am	did	is	should
are	has	may	was
could	had	might	were
do	have	must	will

Sometimes only one of these auxiliaries will be used with the main verb. Sometimes more than one will be used.

Jane Davis <u>is working</u> behind the counter this afternoon.
I <u>am working</u> behind the counter this afternoon.
You <u>are working</u> behind the counter this afternoon.
Evelyn Smith <u>will be working</u> behind the counter next week.
John Coppleton <u>is being assigned</u> behind the counter next week.

In each of the examples the last word in the word group (*working* and *assigned*) is the main verb. The other words underlined as part of the verb are auxiliaries. The auxiliaries formed from *be* help to identify the time of the action.

Note: Forms of *be* can be auxiliaries of other verbs. A form of *be* is a linking verb if it is the main verb in the sentence. Example: This sentence is short. *Is* is a linking verb that links the word *sentence* to the word *short*. There is no other verb in the sentence, so *is* cannot be an auxiliary verb.

My professor <u>is teaching</u> me English.
   Is is not a linking verb because it is not the main verb in the sentence. It is an auxiliary verb that precedes the main verb *teaching* and tells when the teaching is being done.

Auxiliary verbs do not always occur side by side with main verbs. In fact, when an auxiliary is used to form a question, the auxiliary occurs earlier in the sentence than the main verb.

<u>Are</u> the engines <u>performing</u> properly?
   Are is the auxiliary of the main verb *performing*.

<u>Has</u> the man <u>completed</u> the cabinets?
   Has is the auxiliary of the main verb *completed*.

Sometimes the auxiliaries themselves are separated:

<u>Is</u> the movie <u>being filmed</u> today?
   Is and *being* are auxiliaries of the main verb *filmed*.

You <u>should</u> not <u>have played</u> an ace just then.
   Should and *have* are auxiliaries of the main verb *played*.

When auxiliaries are used to introduce questions, the easiest way to analyze the sentence is by turning the question into a statement:

Question: Are the engines performing properly?
Statement: The engines *are performing* properly. (Now the auxiliary and the main verb are together.)

Question: Has the man completed the cabinets?
Statement: The man *has completed* the cabinets. (Auxiliary and main verb are now together.)

PRACTICE SENTENCES 1-3

Underline the auxiliary verbs in the following sentences.

Example: John Combs <u>is</u> considering the need for a dog house.

1. He <u>has</u> obtained all the wood.

2. He <u>has</u> had all the necessary tools for many years.

3. He <u>has</u> planned an entire day for the project.

4. He <u>will</u> construct the frame first.

5. Then he <u>will</u> attach the floor.

6. After that he <u>will</u> assemble the sides.

7. Next he <u>will</u> work on the roof.

8. Finally he <u>will</u> attach the shingles.

9. The dog <u>will</u> be so proud.

10. But first John <u>must</u> begin the project.

PRACTICE SENTENCES 1-4

Identify the verbs (auxiliaries and main) in the following sentences by underlining them.

Example: I <u>am going</u> to college for a degree in accounting.

1. At first I <u>was planning</u> a career as clerk in a local department store.

2. But I <u>could</u> never <u>earn</u> a good salary in such a position.

3. I <u>would</u> never <u>be promoted</u> in the family-owned business either.

4. So, what <u>can</u> I <u>do</u>?

5. I <u>have</u> always <u>enjoyed</u> working with numbers.

6. In college I <u>could study</u> accounting.

7. An accountant <u>can make</u> a good living.

8. Accountants <u>can help</u> people with their financial problems as well.

9. <u>Would</u> I <u>enjoy</u> a career in accounting?

10. My teachers and my heart <u>are telling</u> me, "Yes."

PRACTICE SENTENCES 1–5

In the blanks provided, write out the verbs in the following sentences.

Example: The courtroom was opened at 9:00 A.M.

Verb <u>was opened</u>

1. The judge listened to the arguments of both attorneys.

Verb_____

2. According to the prosecutor, the judge did not listen to his case.

Verb_____

3. The judge had already decided the issue.

Verb_____

4. On the other hand, the defense attorney was not pleased either.

Verb_____

5. He was not convinced of the judge's objectivity.

Verb_____

6. The judge was used to such opposing viewpoints.

Verb_____

7. He had heard it all before.

Verb_____

8. In fact, the judge did not know anything about the case.

Verb_____

9. He had been out of town for three weeks before the trial.

Verb_____

10. To him the two lawyers had just been actors on a stage.

Verb_____

Recognizing Subjects

The second step in learning the basics of English grammar is to be able to recognize the subject. After you have found the verb, you should then find the subject. The subject is rather easy to recognize. You find it by asking *Who?* or *What?* in front of the verb.

> John swept the sidewalk.
> Who or what swept? **John.**

> Jane considered the problem for three hours.
> Who or what considered? **Jane.**

> The robot set the table.
> Who or what set the table? **robot.**

> The computer saved the company a fortune.
> Who or what saved the company a fortune? **computer.**

> The **subject** is a naming word. The subject of an action verb names
> the doer of the action.

In the sample sentences just presented, John does the action of sweeping, Jane does the action of considering, the robot does the action of setting, and the computer does the action of saving.

PRACTICE SENTENCES 1–6

Find the action verbs in the following sentences. Then ask Who? *or* What? *in front of the verb. The word that answers the question is the subject. Underline it.*

Example: <u>Curt</u> likes fine furniture.

1. He owns several books about furniture styles and periods.

2. Recently he developed an interest in the construction of furniture.

3. This interest led to an interest in woodworking equipment.

4. Now his basement contains numerous tools.

5. Unfortunately his shop has poor ventilation.

6. Sawdust covers everything, including the washer and dryer.

7. His wife prefers to buy her furniture from a store.

8. Curt built a beautiful oak cabinet.

9. The cabinet cost him over $300 to make.

10. His wife saw one just like it in a display window for $195.

As you know, not all verbs are action verbs. Linking verbs do not express action, but they do take subjects. Since a linking verb does not express any action, the subject of a linking verb cannot be the doer of any action.

> Like any other subject, the subject of a linking verb is a naming word. Also like any other subject, the subject of a linking verb can be found by asking *Who?* or *What?* in front of the verb.

Gene Caudill is president of the Exeter Company.
  Who or what is? **Gene Caudill.**

The machine is a constant source of trouble.
  Who or what is? **Machine.**

PRACTICE SENTENCES 1–7

Find the linking verbs in the following sentences. Then ask Who? *or* What? *in front of the verb. The word that answers the question is the subject. Underline it.*

Example: The <u>Corvette</u> is a fine automobile.

1. Nearly every model is a classic.

2. The lines of the car are sleek.

3. The interior is usually leather.

4. For years now the body has been fiberglass.

5. The car is famous for its speed.

6. Owners are in love with the car's power.

7. Is the Corvette a true sports car?

8. It probably is not.

9. It is too big and too heavy.

10. Proud owners are not into such labels, however.

You may have found the subjects in the preceding sentences by just under-lining the first naming word in the sentence. Underlining the first naming word worked in all the sample sentences because those sentences follow the most com-mon order an English sentence takes: subject-verb. However, not all sentences in English follow the subject-verb order. Sentences beginning with the word *there* alter the subject-verb order. Don't mistake the expletive *there* for the subject. It merely indicates that the subject will follow the verb. (An expletive like *there* only serves as a filler and does not contribute to the meaning of the sentence.)

subject
There are four girls on the Little League team.

If you get in the habit of finding the verb and then asking *Who?* or *What?* in front of it, you should have no trouble with sentences that are not in the sub-ject-verb order. In the preceding example sentence, if you know that *are* is the verb and ask *Who?* or *What are?* you will easily see that the subject is *girls*.

subject
Is Robert making a new piece for the machine?

The sentence is not in the subject-verb order. It is in the auxiliary-subject-verb order. If you ask *Who?* or *What is making?* you will see that the answer is *Robert,* the subject. The easiest way to find the subject and verb in such a sen-tence is to turn the question *Is Robert making a new piece for the machine?* into a statement: *Robert is making a new piece for the machine.* Now the sentence is in the subject-verb order.

PRACTICE SENTENCES 1–8

Identify the subjects in the following sentences by underlining them.

Example: I recently purchased a full size pickup.

1. My family was raised in the city.

2. Pickup trucks were not common.

3. My sister once owned a sports car.

4. My brother had a V-8 Jeep.

5. My favorite vehicle had been a VW van.

6. So why did I decide to purchase a pickup?

7. My family moved to a rural area several years ago.

8. Pickups were more common than Cadillacs.

9. A truck bed comes in handy for hauling lumber and other things.

10. My smile broadens at the envy of my neighbor.

Now that you can recognize subjects and verbs, it is time to apply your knowledge. In the following exercise you will be expected to identify both subjects and verbs. You should have no difficulty if you find the verb first and then ask *Who?* or *What?* to find the subject.

PRACTICE SENTENCES 1–9

In the blanks provided, indicate the subjects and verbs, including auxiliary verbs.

Example: Rhonda leads a hectic life.

subject __Rhonda__

verb __leads__

1. Every day she can be found with a car full of children.

subject _____

verb _____

2. She has been selected the neighborhood chauffeur.

subject _____

verb _____

3. The job was fun at first.

subject _____

verb _____

4. Now she does not have time for it.

subject _____

verb _____

5. She is working eight hours a day in an accounting firm.

subject _____

verb _____

6. She was recently hired as a junior accountant.

   subject_____

   verb_____

7. In addition, she has registered for three night classes.

   subject_____

   verb_____

8. Her husband has been helping her.

   subject_____

   verb_____

9. Still, many of the home and family responsibilities fall on her.

   subject_____

   verb_____

10. Obviously Rhonda has made a busy life for herself.

    subject_____

    verb_____

Recognizing Compound Subjects and Compound Verbs

The next step in being able to recognize subjects and verbs is realizing that they may be compounded; that is, two or more subjects or two or more verbs may be joined together by the words *and, or, nor, but.*

John, Bob, and Ralph went to the game together.
   The compound subjects are *John, Bob,* and *Ralph.*

Tony Arrowsmith sings well but dances clumsily.
   The compound verbs are *sings* and *dances.*

Jane said she would either trade the car or sell it.
   The compound verbs are *trade* and *sell.*

PRACTICE SENTENCES 1–10

Identify all the compound verbs in the following sentences by underlining them.

Example: Mr. Jordan <u>manages</u> a business and <u>drives</u> a race car.

1. Cindy practices dentistry and works with local civic clubs.

2. Last semester I read twelve books and wrote three papers.

3. Samantha makes good money and saves nearly half of it.

4. John visited his father and gave him a nice recliner.

5. Carmen completed her nursing program and now makes good money.

6. The children went to the amusement park and played all day.

7. Randy bought a new radio and tuned it to his favorite stations.

8. Nikki has thirteen Barbie dolls and wants seven more.

9. The hunter went to the woods before sunrise and stayed until noon.

10. My sister plays the clarinet in the local orchestra and teaches elementary school.

A compound subject is no more trouble than a compound verb. You still must find the verb first and ask *Who?* or *What?* in front of it.

Bob Smith, Elaine Frank, and John Bartlett are competent engineers.
Who or *What are?* The compound subject is *Bob Smith, Elaine Frank,* and *John Bartlett.*

Television, radios, newspapers, and magazines help to keep people well informed.
Who or *what keep?* The compound subject is *television, radios, newspapers,* and *magazines.*

PRACTICE SENTENCES 1–11

Identify all the compound subjects in the following sentences by underlining.

Example: <u>Kareem</u> and <u>Antonia</u> like to collect things in pairs.

1. A Monet and a Manet are two of their favorite paintings.

2. Kareem and Antonia recently purchased two Edsels.

3. The red sedan and the blue convertible are quite noticeable in their front yard.

4. A golden vase and a silver ladle are their newest additions.

5. The vase and the ladle were purchased from an estate sale.

6. Several years ago Kareem and Antonia went to a gun show.

7. An antique pistol and a collectible rifle were two of their purchases.

8. Pearl handles and an engraved barrel are the characteristics of the Colt pistol.

9. The lever action and the tube magazine identify the Winchester rifle.

10. Kareem and Antonia are still looking for collectible pairs that interest them.

Finally, in some sentences, both subjects and verbs are compound.

Joan Burger and Tony Arrowsmith sing and dance well together.

The compound subject is *Joan Burger* and *Tony Arrowsmith,* and the compound verb is *sing* and *dance.* Of course, sentences with compound subjects and compound verbs can vary from the subject-verb order like any other sentences.

There are three men and four women on the committee.
The compound subject is *men* and *women.* The verb is *are.*

Are Ed Shoenbaum and Lorraine Chute entering or leaving?
Ed Shoenbaum and Lorraine Chute is the subject, and *are entering and leaving* is the verb.

Recognizing Complements

Once you can recognize subjects and verbs, you can move on to the next step in sentence analysis; recognizing complements.

A **complement** is a word that completes the meaning of the subject and the predicate.

The four most important complements are (1) **direct objects,** (2) **indirect objects,** (3) **predicate nominatives,** and (4) **predicate adjectives.**

Direct Objects

Although the direct object is a common element in many sentences, not all verbs take direct objects.

> The **direct object** receives the action of the verb, and so the verb must express action before there can be a receiver of the action.

When a verb has a direct object, the object generally appears in a sentence after the subject and verb. Remember: You find the verb first; then you find the subject. Just as you asked *Who?* or *What? before* the verb to find the subject, you ask *Whom?* or *What? after* the verb to find the direct object.

Mary made a mistake.
Clearly, *made* is the verb in the sentence. Now ask *Who? or What?* in front of the verb: *Who or what made?* Mary. *Mary* is the subject. To find the direct object, ask whom or what after the verb: Mary made *whom* or *what?* Mistake. *Mistake* is the direct object.

The following chart indicates which questions to ask, where to ask them, and which order to ask them in.

Mary made a mistake.

2		1		3
Subject	*(Who?*	← Verb →	*(Whom?*	Direct Object
↓	*What?)*	↓	*What?)*	↓
Mary		made		mistake

Be very careful to ask your questions before the verb when looking for the subject and after the verb when looking for the direct object. Since both subjects and direct objects are naming words, a direct object will answer a subject's question and vice versa. Therefore, if you ask the right question in the wrong place, you will get the wrong answer.

In looking for direct objects you must consider other things besides the questions they answer, however. One of the main points to keep in mind is that not *all* sentences have direct objects. Note the following example:

John swims every day.
John is the subject and *swims* is the verb.
There is no direct object.

Clearly, not all action verbs take direct objects.

Remember, too, that only action verbs can take direct objects. Note the following example:

The animal is a deer.
There cannot be a direct object since the verb is the linking verb *is* and not an action verb.

On the other hand:

This company produces ten cars an hour.
> The verb *produces* is an action verb; it can and does take a direct object: *cars.*

It is easy to remember that only action verbs can take direct objects when you understand what direct objects are. Direct objects receive the action of the verb. Clearly then, as we said earlier, there must be action before there can be a receiver of the action.

In the sentence *Mary made a mistake,* a mistake receives the action of being made. In the sentence *The company produces ten cars an hour,* the cars receive the action of being produced. In the sentence *John loves Beth Henson very much,* Beth Henson receives the action of being loved. In all these sentences the receiver of the action is the direct object. Of course, all of the direct objects answer the question *Whom?* or *What?* asked after the verb:

Mary made <u>what?</u>
> *Mistake* is the direct object.

The company produces <u>what?</u>
> *Cars* is the direct object.

John loves <u>whom?</u>
> *Beth Henson* is the direct object.

Notice that the most common pattern for sentences containing direct objects is subject-verb-object.

>   s.   v.   d.o.
> Mary made a mistake.

>   s.   v.   d.o.
> The company produces ten cars an hour.

>   s.   v.   d.o.
> John loves Beth Henson very much.

PRACTICE SENTENCES 1–12

In the following sentences write d.o. *above the direct objects. Be sure to get in the habit of finding the verb first, then the subject, and then the direct object. Caution: You may find that some of the sentences do not contain direct objects.*

>   d.o.
> **Example:** Susan and Tom play golf every week.

1. Tom drives the ball a long way off the tee.

2. Unfortunately, his ball often misses the fairway.

3. His fairway irons, however, are quite accurate.

4. Tom does not chip the ball well around the greens.

5. But he loves his putter.

6. From ten feet in he putts the ball consistently well.

7. Susan, on the other hand, hits her driver accurately.

8. She is a good irons player also.

9. However, she cannot putt the ball well outside two feet.

10. Together, though, she and Tom make a good team.

Though the most common pattern for sentences containing direct objects is subject-verb-object, do not assume that is the only pattern.

Does John play golf often?
> Notice *does* is an auxiliary, *John* is the subject, *play* is the main verb, and *golf* is the direct object. The pattern is auxiliary-subject-verb-object.

aux.   s.   v.   d.o.
Do computers solve problems quickly?

Like verbs and subjects, direct objects can also be compound.

      d.o.   d.o.   d.o.
John loves golf, tennis, and skiing.

      d.o.   d.o.   d.o.
Jane loves Bob, John, and Roy.

A CHECKLIST FOR DIRECT OBJECTS

A direct object must:
1. Be a naming word.
2. Be in the predicate.
3. Follow an action verb.
4. Answer the question *What?* or *Whom?*

Indirect Objects

After you learn to recognize subjects, verbs, and direct objects, the next sentence part you need to look for is the indirect object. Like subjects and direct objects, indirect objects are naming words.

> You can find an **indirect object** if it is present by asking *To* or *For whom?* or *To* or *For what?* after the direct object.

<small>s.</small>   <small>v.</small>   <small>d.o.</small>
Bruce gave Martha a ring.

    Bruce gave a ring *to* or *for whom? Martha* is the indirect object.

<small>s.</small>   <small>v.</small>   <small>d.o.</small>
The philanthropist gave the museum a million dollars.

    The philanthropist gave dollars *to* or *for what? Museum* is the indirect object.

Remember: The indirect object is the fourth sentence element you try to find. Be sure you ask the right question in the right place.

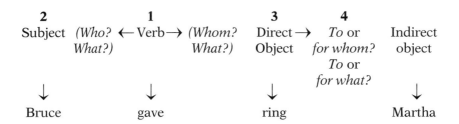

2	1		3	4	
Subject	*(Who?* ← Verb →	*(Whom?*	Direct →	*To* or	Indirect
	What?)	*What?)*	Object	*for whom?*	object
				To or	
				for what?	
↓	↓		↓		↓
Bruce	gave		ring		Martha

Most sentences will not contain indirect objects because only a few verbs can take them. Here are examples of some of the verbs that can take indirect objects: *give, bring, buy, present, throw,* and *award.*

    Even though the indirect object is the fourth sentence part you try to find, it is always located in the sentence before the direct object. The order is subject-verb-indirect object-direct object. Note the following examples:

<small>s.</small>   <small>v.</small>   <small>i.o.</small>   <small>d.o.</small>
The quarterback threw his receiver a perfect pass.

<small>s.</small>   <small>v.</small>   <small>i.o.</small>   <small>d.o.</small>
The committee awarded Sara the prize.

Of course, when the sentence is a question, the order may change.

aux.   s.   v.   i.o.   d.o.
Did the executive buy her office a new typewriter?

But such a sentence fits the pattern of subject-verb-indirect object-direct object if you turn it around into a statement.

            s.   v.   i.o.   d.o.
The executive did buy her office a new typewriter.

One thing to remember when studying indirect objects is that you must mentally supply the words *to* or *for* before the *whom* or *what*. If the sentence has the *to* or *for* expressed, the word cannot be an indirect object.

The quarterback threw a perfect pass (to) his receiver.

Since the *to* is expressed, the word *receiver* cannot be an indirect object. Which of the following sentences contains an indirect object?

1. The team presented the coach a new trophy case.
2. The team presented a new trophy case to the coach.

Sentence 1 contains the indirect object since you mentally supply the missing *to:* The team presented (to) the coach a new trophy case.

A CHECKLIST FOR INDIRECT OBJECTS

An indirect object must:
1. Be a naming word.
2. Be in the predicate.
3. Follow an action verb.
4. Answer the question *To whom? To what? For whom?* or *For what?*

PRACTICE SENTENCES 1-13

Identify the indirect objects in the following sentences by writing i.o. *over the correct word. Caution: Some sentences may not contain indirect objects.*

                        i.o.
Example: Lupe gave Carla a beautiful opal ring.

1. Carla gave Lupe a big hug.

2. He received the hug gladly.

3. Then the florist delivered Carla two dozen roses.

4. Carla was amazed at the gifts.

5. She prepared Lupe a dinner.

6. She fixed him his favorite meal.

7. Carla did not understand Lupe's motives.

8. Did Lupe give her the ring as a proposal?

9. He gave her tokens of his affection.

10. However, he was not interested in marriage.

Predicate Nominatives

As you have noticed, only action verbs can take direct and indirect objects. However, linking verbs take complements. One such complement is the predicate nominative.

> A **predicate nominative** is a naming word (noun or pronoun) that follows a linking verb and renames the subject.

                       p.n.
Jane Martinez is a psychologist.
> *Psychologist* is a naming word that follows the linking verb *is* and renames the subject *Jane Martinez*. *Psychologist* is a predicate nominative.

                  p.n.
John Smith was an explorer.
> *Explorer* is a naming word that follows the linking verb *was* and renames the subject *John Smith*. *Explorer* is a predicate nominative.

Since the predicate nominative is linked to the subject by the verb, sentences containing predicate nominatives have linking verbs rather than action verbs.

               p.n.
The Eagles are a good team.
> The verb *are* links the predicate nominative *team* to the subject *Eagles*.

Of course, not all linking verbs have predicate nominatives, just as not all action verbs have direct objects.

John Tybalt is handsome.

There is no other word in the sentence that renames the subject *John Tybalt*. Therefore, the sentence does not contain a predicate nominative.

 A CHECKLIST FOR PREDICATE NOMINATIVES

A predicate nominative must:
1. Be a naming word.
2. Be in the predicate part of the sentence.
3. Follow a linking verb.
4. Mean the same or rename the subject.

PRACTICE SENTENCES 1–14

In the following sentences, identify the predicate nominatives by underlining them. Caution: Not all sentences contain predicate nominatives.

Example: Joyce is an <u>athlete</u>.

1. She has always been an active individual.

2. She is a jogger and a weight lifter.

3. She became a tennis champion at thirteen.

4. Joyce is one of the top three women golfers in the state.

5. But to her, golf seems too tame.

6. She is now into basketball.

7. She practices four hours a day.

8. She is the top scorer for her team.

9. Joyce is also the only woman on her team.

10. Her teammates are her biggest fans.

Predicate Adjectives

A **predicate adjective** is a word (adjective) that usually follows a linking verb and qualifies, limits, or describes (modifies) the subject.

---

p.a.

Jane is happy.

> *Happy* is an adjective that follows the linking verb *is* and modifies the subject *Jane*. *Happy* describes *Jane*. *Happy* is a predicate adjective.

p.a.

The computer is expensive.

> *Expensive* is an adjective that follows the linking verb *is* and modifies the subject *computer*. *Expensive* is a predicate adjective.

A predicate adjective is linked to the word it modifies by a linking verb. Remember: Both predicate adjectives and predicate nominatives are used with linking verbs.

A CHECKLIST FOR PREDICATE ADJECTIVES

A predicate adjective must:
1. Be an adjective.
2. Be in the predicate part of the sentence.
3. Follow a linking verb.
4. Modify the subject.

PRACTICE SENTENCES 1–15

In the sentences below, underline each predicate adjective. Caution: Some sentences may not contain predicate adjectives.

Example: The Case knife on the shelf is <u>old</u>.

1. It is also very valuable.

2. The pearl handle is genuine.

3. The tang is stamped "Case Bros. Cut. Co., Little Valley, N.Y."

4. Knife collectors are aware of its value.

5. But they must be careful.

6. Older Case knives are often not genuine.

7. Some people in the knife business are not honest.

8. Fortunately, most dealers are very reputable.

9. This knife seems genuine to me.

10. I bought it for $850.

Name _____

Class _____

Section _____ Score: _____

REVIEW EXERCISE 1-A   RECOGNIZING SUBJECTS AND VERBS

In the blanks provided, identify all subjects and verbs in the following sentences.

Example: The divorce rate in the United States is very disturbing.

subject(s) *rate* _____

verb(s) *is disturbing* _____

1. Sociologists are studying the problem.

subject(s)_____

verb(s) _____

2. They are examining the causes.

subject(s)_____

verb(s) _____

3. Are men or women primarily at fault?

subject(s)_____

verb(s) _____

4. Some sociologists blame women for taking advantage of the new no-fault divorce laws.

subject(s)_____

verb(s) _____

5. Women are paying men back for years of irresponsibility and neglect.

subject(s)_____

verb(s) _____

6. Other sociologists have a different view.

    subject(s)_____

    verb(s) _____

7. They feel men are being used and abused.

    subject(s)_____

    verb(s) _____

8. Women are taking advantage of a court system that favors the mother.

    subject(s)_____

    verb(s) _____

9. The divorce rate *must* be reduced.

    subject(s)_____

    verb(s) _____

10. Children are paying the price.

    subject(s)_____

    verb(s) _____

REVIEW EXERCISE 1-B IDENTIFYING TYPES OF COMPLEMENTS

In the following sentences, indicate whether the italicized word is a direct object (d.o.), an indirect object (i.o.), a predicate nominative (p.n.), or a predicate adjective (p.a.) by writing your answer in the space provided.

GROUP 1 **Example:** Danya likes her *job* in the bookstore.

_____*d.o.*_____

1. She has more *responsibility*.

_____

2. She orders the *textbooks* for the entire college.

_____

3. Her boss gave *her* a raise after one month.

_____

4. Danya was very *proud* of herself.

_____

5. She seems a different *person*.

_____

6. Danya has a *system*.

_____

7. Her system is extremely *simple*.

_____

8. She counts the *books* currently on the shelves.

_____

9. Then she consults registration *figures*.

_____

10. This gives *Danya* an accurate estimate of the school's needs.

_____

GROUP 2   **Example:** Eric and Terry gave *Mrs. Jones* a microwave oven.

_____i.o._____

11. The oven was a *Sanyo.*

_____

12. It had many special *features.*

_____

13. They bought the *oven* on special at Wal-Mart.

_____

14. They charged the *Sanyo* to their credit card.

_____

15. To Eric and Terry, Mrs. Jones is a special *person.*

_____

16. She introduced *them* to each other.

_____

17. She gave *them* encouragement.

_____

18. She was *optimistic* about their relationship.

_____

19. She cooked them many *meals* over the years.

_____

20. Now she is a microwave *wizard.*

_____

Name _____

Class _____

Section _____ Score: _____

MASTERY TEST 1-A   SUBJECTS AND VERBS

1. Write two sentences containing verbs that express action.

    a. _____

       _____

    b. _____

       _____

2. Write two sentences containing linking verbs.

    a. _____

       _____

    b. _____

       _____

3. Write two sentences containing compound verbs.

    a. _____

       _____

    b. _____

       _____

4. Write two sentences containing compound subjects.

    a. _____

       _____

    b. _____

       _____

5. Write two sentences containing compound subjects and compound verbs.

   a. _____

   _____

   b. _____

   _____

MASTERY TEST 1-B   COMPLEMENTS

1. Write two sentences that contain direct objects but not indirect objects.

   a. _____

   _____

   b. _____

   _____

2. Write two sentences that contain compound direct objects and no indirect objects.

   a. _____

   _____

   b. _____

   _____

3. Write two sentences that contain direct and indirect objects.

   a. _____

   _____

   b. _____

   _____

4. Write two sentences that contain predicate nominatives.

   a. _____

   _____

   b. _____

   _____

5. Write two sentences that contain predicate adjectives.

    a. _____

       _____

    b. _____

       _____

Writing Effectively

Essential College English is a text intended primarily to help you improve your knowledge of the English language. As you can tell from the subtitle, the emphasis is on grammar and punctuation. However, the main purpose for learning the mechanics of the language is to be able to apply that knowledge in your writing.

One thing you want to work on in your writing is *unity,* making sure that the main point of your composition is developed throughout. If the point of your paper is to inform readers about the need to recycle, don't get sidetracked about the placement of recycling containers in the school gym by the kind of cola you prefer. Similarly, try to improve the *coherence* of your writing and the flow of your essay. Writing that lacks coherence is choppy. It jumps from one sentence to the next. Your composition may be unified, but it still won't flow well. To improve your coherence, you need to use verbal bridges, such words as *however, moreover, also, as well as* and *consequently.*

But the most important thing to consider about your writing is to make sure you *know* what you want to say. An important part of knowing what to say is knowing your audience. Different readers have different expectations. For instance, a letter to your best friend would be different than a letter to the editor of a newspaper.

Sometimes a writer just makes a statement, but never really develops it. If you are going to write about the need for recreational facilities in your community, for example, you should stress this need and what can be done.

Developing your ideas takes practice. You might at first find yourself simply rewriting the same idea in five different ways. This is repetitiveness, not development! To move beyond just repeating an idea over and over, ask yourself these questions:

- What point am I making here?
- How can I more clearly explain or define what I mean by———?
- What specific examples can I use to show my readers what I mean?

You may feel that the first sentence you write must be perfect, but this isn't true. Good writing doesn't happen all at once. Rather, it is a process:

- First, you have to get your ideas on paper.
- Once you have something written, you can revise it to make sure it's clear, organized, and smooth.
- Finally, you proofread carefully for errors in spelling and punctuation, as well as typographical errors (typos).

If you try to do all these steps in one day, your mind may be too tired to catch everything or you might freeze at the sight of that blank page. You may even feel frustrated because you're not sure what to write. But if you know that whatever you first write does not have to be perfect, you'll take some of the pressure off.

One way to practice writing is to use a prewriting journal in which you get words on paper as they come to you without worrying about whether they make sense or are grammatical. You can jot down words you commonly misspell, vocabulary definitions, and topics of interest to you. It is very important to write about what is meaningful to you, to find some sort of connection with your topic. A prewriting journal can help.

Assignment 1-1 Write one paragraph (about half a page) on the following topic: If you had to design a birthday card for your best friend, what would you want it to say? What thoughts would you want your friend to read? How would you express your feelings? Are there certain memories you'd want to refer to? What would you design the cover of the card to look like? Why?

Assignment 1-2 In three paragraphs (about one and a half pages), describe your favorite movie. What kind of movie is it (action, romance, historical, etc.)? What do you like about it (characters, action, dialogue, etc.)? If you had to recommend it to a friend, how would you describe it? Why would you want your friend to see it?

Go Electronic!

For additional readings, exercises, and Internet activities, visit the Longman English pages at:

> http://longman.awl.com/englishpages

If you need a user name and password, please see your instructor.

More Practice with Your Writing and Grammar Skills

For additional practice with your writing and grammar skills, use the Writer's ToolKit CD–ROM included with this text. The ToolKit provides a wealth of computerized tutorials and practice activities.

Parts of Speech

In every field there are names for everything pertinent to that field. Every piece in a telephone has a name. Similarly, everything in a sentence has a name. Each "piece" in a sentence is used as a certain part of speech. The part of speech of a word depends on the way the word is used in a particular sentence. Therefore the same word can be any of several parts of speech. For example:

Blue is my favorite color. (noun)
My father drives a blue truck. (adjective)
Mark is blueing his gun barrel. (verb)

Before you can understand the parts of speech, however, you must be familiar with their definitions. The definitions tell you how the word may be used. If you know the part of speech of every word in a sentence, then you know what every word in that sentence does. There are eight parts of speech:

PARTS OF SPEECH

nouns	adverbs
pronouns	prepositions
adjectives	conjunctions
verbs	interjections

Nouns

> **Nouns** are naming words. They name people, places, things, and ideas: *Robert, England, tire,* and *justice.*

<u>Robert</u> names a person.
<u>England</u> names a place.
<u>Tire</u> names a thing.
<u>Justice</u> names an idea.

Subjects are naming words as well. A noun, however, is merely a way of identifying how a word is used in a sentence. A subject, on the other hand, is a word that tells what is talked about in a sentence. Clearly, most subjects will be nouns. However, there may be many nouns in a sentence that don't tell what is being talked about. For instance:

Bob lent <u>Mary</u> the <u>key</u> to the <u>car.</u>
    Only the noun *Bob* is the subject. But the underlined words *Mary, key,* and *car* are all nouns.

Some nouns name more specifically than others. *Ms. Smith, woman, lady, person, mother, wife,* and *Jane Everette Smith* are all nouns that might identify the same person. *Ms. Smith* and *Jane Everette Smith* both name more specifically than the other words; they are known as proper nouns.

> A **proper noun** is capitalized and names a specific person, place, or thing. *Chicago* is a proper noun and so is *Mississippi River.*

Woman, lady, person, mother, and *wife* are all common nouns.

> A **common noun** names a general class of people or things and is not capitalized. Words such as *city* and *river* are common nouns.

As you can see, nouns are quite versatile. They can also name things as concrete as *sand* and *wood* and as abstract as *freedom* and *justice.*

PRACTICE SENTENCES 2-1
In the following sentences underline all the nouns.

    Example: <u>Chess</u> is an interesting <u>game.</u>

1. The origins go way back in history.

2. The pieces have taken many shapes over the years.

3. Some old sets are valuable.

4. Through the years chess has been a game of strategy.

5. Many experts say to move the pawns in the center first.

6. Next, the knights should be put into play.

7. Perhaps the bishops should be put into play after the knights.

8. Good players try to dominate the center of the board.

9. They do not move the queen too early in the game.

10. The object, naturally, is to capture the opponent's king.

Pronouns

> **Pronouns** are naming words that are used to take the place of nouns. *John* is a noun; *he* is a pronoun. *Team* is a noun; *they* is a pronoun.

Pronouns name in an even more general manner than common nouns. By the way, you probably remember that the subjects, direct objects, and indirect objects you were identifying earlier were also naming words. Subjects, direct objects, and indirect objects are either nouns or pronouns. You may be wondering why pronouns are even needed in English. Perhaps the following paragraph will illustrate why pronouns are used.

> John left John's apartment and got into John's car. John went over to Sally's house. John and Sally listened to Sally's stereo. Sally's parents came in and asked John and Sally to turn the music down low. John got irritated at Sally's father, and John suggested that John and Sally leave Sally's house.

There are no pronouns in that paragraph—but there should be. Pronouns are important in making sentences easier to read. Without them English sentences would be choppy and repetitious.

Since pronouns take the place of nouns, it is not difficult to understand their function. However, many people have trouble identifying pronouns because there are so many kinds. Rather than worrying about all the different kinds, refer to the following list of words commonly used as pronouns:

PRONOUNS

I	we	each
mine	us	this
me	our	these
you	ours	those
your	many	who
yours	few	whom
he	both	whoever
his	several	whomever
him	one	whose
she	some	myself
her	anyone	yourself
hers	anybody	himself
it	everyone	herself
its	everybody	ourselves
they	no one	themselves
them	nobody	all
their	somebody	which
theirs	none	what

PRACTICE SENTENCES 2-2

Underline the pronouns in the following sentences.

Example: Sherrie loves her relatives and thinks of them at Christmas.

1. She gave an uncle in Phoenix a beautiful sweater.

2. The American Indian designs on it just seemed to suit him.

3. She gave each of his children a pair of slippers.

4. Sherrie gave everyone in the family a poinsettia.

5. Aunt Leda received a vase with Greek markings on it.

6. John Keats would have been proud of it.

7. Sherrie shopped in all of the stores in town for her brother's present.

8. Several of the clerks thought she was crazy.

9. "What is a Hula Hoop?" they asked her.

10. The hoop she found was listed as a football-throwing target.

EDITING PRACTICE 2–3

In the spaces provided, rewrite the following paragraph, replacing the unnecessarily repetitious nouns with appropriate pronouns.

Dr. Jones has a daughter named Mary. Mary is the apple of Dr. Jones's eye. When Mary was four years old, Mary's father gave Mary a sixty-four-piece tea set and an expensive Lionel electric train. When Mary was sixteen, Mary's father gave Mary a brand-new Lexus. Unfortunately, Mary's father was disappointed in Dr. Jones's daughter. Mary let one of Mary's friends drive the car, and Mary's friend wrecked the car. Fortunately, no person was hurt. Mary has learned to be more careful with Mary's possessions and with Mary's father's feelings.

_____

_____

_____

_____

_____

_____

_____

_____

_____

_____

_____

_____

_____

_____

_____

_____

Adjectives

> **Adjectives** are words that describe, clarify, or limit (modify) a noun or pronoun. They are usually easy to recognize because they answer the questions *Which one? What kind? How many? Whose?*

One-word adjectives come before the words they modify.

adj. n.
big car
   Which car? big

adj. n.
Siamese cat
   What kind of cat? Siamese

adj. n.
three men
   How many men? three

One kind of adjective is extremely easy to identify: the article. The articles are *a, an,* and *the.* Remember, however, *article* does not name a part of speech. *A, an,* and *the* are adjectives.

PRACTICE SENTENCES 2-4
Underline the adjectives in the following sentences.

Example: The antique shop was an unusual place.

1. The old place had a wooden floor.

2. There were small tables, tall shelves, and entire corner displays throughout the shop.

3. One pine table contained antique glass.

4. Some pieces were valuable while others could have come from a local landfill.

5. One set of shelves contained many radios.

6. No radio was newer than 1945.

7. An amateur radio operator would be in seventh heaven.

8. One corner display was composed entirely of old rifles.

9. There was everything from an antique matchlock to an impeccable flintlock.

10. The antique shop had objects of diverse quality, but it was a fascinating place to visit.

Some adjectives can be confusing. Words such as *his, your, my, her, our, their,* and *its* are as much pronouns as adjectives.

John keeps *his* car in good shape.
The girls made *their* entrance.

In the first sentence *his* is a pronoun taking the place of the noun *John.* At the same time, however, *his* is an adjective modifying the subject *car.* In the second sentence, *their* is a pronoun taking the place of *girls* as much as it is an adjective modifying *entrance.* Some people call words like these *pronominal adjectives;* others call them *adjectival pronouns.* It is not important which part of speech you prefer to call them; the important thing to remember is that they fit the definitions of both pronouns and adjectives at the same time.

PRACTICE SENTENCES 2-5
Underline the adjectives in the following sentences.

Example: The lawnmower is an old Simplicity.

1. The rusty machine barely runs.

2. There is little paint anywhere on the body.

3. The plastic seat has many holes in it.

4. But the Simplicity is dependable and reliable.

5. Besides that, Jasper is too cheap to purchase a new machine.

Verbs

The first thing you did in Chapter 1 was to recognize verbs. By now you should be able to recognize them easily. However, you should know other things about verbs besides how to recognize them. You should realize that verbs are either regular or irregular and that they have tense, voice, number, and mood.

Regular and Irregular Verbs

Look at the following model:

1. I _____ today.

2. I _____ yesterday.

3. I have _____ .

4. I am _____ -ing.

Fill each blank with the appropriate form of the same verb; the forms are known as the principal parts of the verb. The first principal part is called the **simple present.** The second is the **simple past.** The third principal part is called the **past participle;** notice that the third principal part must be preceded by an auxiliary, such as *have.* The fourth principal part is known as the **present participle** and is also preceded by an auxiliary, such as *am.*

> A **regular verb** forms the simple past and past participle by adding *-ed* to the simple present, and it forms the present participle by adding *-ing* to the simple present.

I *play* today.	simple present
I *played* yesterday.	simple past
I have *played.*	past participle
I am *playing.*	present participle

> An **irregular verb** usually forms its simple past and past participle by changing a vowel of the simple present. The present participle of an irregular verb is formed in the same manner as a regular verb, by adding *-ing* to the simple present.

I *begin* today.	simple present
I *began* yesterday.	simple past
I have *begun.*	past participle
I am *beginning.*	present participle

If you are not sure you can correctly fill in the blanks of the model with the appropriate form of a verb, refer to the following partial list of irregular verbs or, preferably, to a dictionary.

Simple Present	Simple Past	Aux. + Past Participle	Aux. + Present Participle
am	was	been	being
begin	began	begun	beginning
bite	bit	bitten	biting
blow	blew	blown	blowing
break	broke	broken	breaking
bring	brought	brought	bringing
burst	burst	burst	bursting
choose	chose	chosen	choosing
come	came	come	coming
draw	drew	drawn	drawing
drink	drank	drunk	drinking
drive	drove	driven	driving
eat	ate	eaten	eating
fall	fell	fallen	falling
forsake	forsook	forsaken	forsaking
hear	heard	heard	hearing
lay	laid	laid	laying
lead	led	led	leading
lie	lay	lain	lying
ring	rang	rung	ringing
rise	rose	risen	rising
see	saw	seen	seeing
set	set	set	setting
show	showed	shown	showing
sit	sat	sat	sitting
slay	slew	slain	slaying
steal	stole	stolen	stealing
throw	threw	thrown	throwing
wake	woke (waked)	waked	waking
wear	wore	worn	wearing
write	wrote	written	writing

PRACTICE SENTENCES 2-6

In the following sentences underline the correct principal part of the verb.

Example: Juan (<u>did</u>, done) the project for his history class.

1. He (did, done) everything his teacher assigned.

2. By the middle of the week, he had (complete, completed) the research.

3. Then he (begin, began) to write.

4. He was not (use, used) to putting so much time into a project.

5. He even (drew, drawed) several maps.

6. The projects were (suppose, supposed) to be due Tuesday.

7. But Juan had (did, done) everything by Friday.

8. On Monday he (saw, seen) another student's project.

9. Juan knew he had (wrote, written) a better paper.

10. In fact, the teacher said Juan had (did, done) the best work of anyone in the class.

 Writer's Tip A common error in using principal parts is failing to put the final *-d* on a word. Though the final *-d* may not always be noticed in speech, its absence in writing is readily apparent.

Incorrect: I use to be a good speller.
Correct: I used to be a good speller.

Incorrect: I was suppose to finish my lab report.
Correct: I was supposed to finish my lab report.

Also, do not use the past participle as though it were the simple past: *I done the job* and *I seen that movie*. Though such sentences rarely cause confusion, they can be very distracting to your readers. Correcting such sentences is easy. Simply use the proper form of the verb:

I did the job.
I saw that movie.

EDITING PRACTICE 2-7

Correct the errors with principal parts in the following sentences by rewriting the sentences in the space provided.

Example: Jim done his science project on time.

Jim did his science project on time.

1. The newspaper boy throwed the paper in the bushes.

   _____

2. Valerie drunk a two-liter Coke with her pizza.

   _____

3. I have drove a hundred miles each week this quarter.

   _____

4. Jay blowed up more than 150 balloons for the dance.

   _____

5. Van had ate over thirty shrimps by 6:30.

   _____

6. Ruth brung three friends with her to the initiation ceremony.

   _____

7. By mid-morning Mrs. Covington had went to the grocery and the bank.

   _____

8. The child had stole three video games before being caught.

   _____

9. *Paradise Lost,* wrote by John Milton, is a great English epic.

   _____

10. The scientist throwed his notes to the floor in disgust.

    _____

Tense

The **tense** of a verb indicates time. There are only six basic tenses.

THE SIX VERB TENSES

present	present perfect
past	past perfect
future	future perfect

> The **present tense** indicates an action that is going on at the present time or that occurs habitually.

The man <u>looks</u> off into the distance.
> *Looks* reflects an action going on at the present time.

The seasons <u>change</u> four times a year.
> *Change* reflects an action that occurs habitually.

Sometimes the present tense indicates future action.

My plane <u>leaves</u> at 5:00 P.M.
> *Leaves* indicates an action that will occur in the future.

The present tense is also used to express general truths.

Water <u>freezes</u> at 32 degrees Fahrenheit.

> The **past tense** indicates an action completed at a specific time in the past.

Luis Astorga <u>broke</u> his arm last week.
> *Broke* indicates a completed past action.

> The **future tense** indicates an action that will take place in the future.

Ms. Jones <u>will repair</u> the television set tomorrow.
> *Will repair* indicates an action to be performed in the future.

The "perfect" tenses always contain a form of the verb *have (have, has, had)* and the past participle.

The **present perfect tense** is formed from the appropriate present tense form of the verb *have* (*has* or *have*) plus the past participle and indicates an action that is completed at the present time or that is continuing into the present.

John Grisham has completed the research for his new book.
Has completed indicates an action completed at the present time.

I have played golf for many years.
Have played indicates an action continuing into the present.

The **past perfect tense** is formed from the past tense form of the verb *have* (*had*) plus the past participle and indicates an action completed before a specific time in the past.

The girl had broken the vase before her mother could get there.
Had broken indicates an action completed before the mother's arrival.

The **future perfect tense** is formed from the future tense of the verb *have* (*will have* or *shall have*) plus the past participle and indicates an action that will be completed before a specific time in the future.

The teacher will have graded the papers before class tomorrow.
Will have graded indicates an action that will be completed before class time tomorrow.

PRACTICE SENTENCES 2-8

In the blanks provided, indicate the tenses of the italicized verbs.

Example: *Have* you ever *taken* a course with a lab?

<u>present perfect</u>

1. I once *took* a chemistry course.

_____

2. It *had been offered* before.

   _____

3. It *will be offered* again next spring.

   _____

4. I wish I *had* not *taken* it.

   _____

5. I *was* in lab two afternoons a week.

   _____

6. The course *is* interesting and worthwhile.

   _____

7. But afternoon labs *will* always *be* a problem for me.

   _____

8. My employer *expects* me at work every day at 2:00.

   _____

9. He *has made* it perfectly clear that I am to report for work.

   _____

10. Any more afternoon labs and I *will be* out of a job.

    _____

Writer's Tip Some writers unnecessarily shift from one tense to another. For example, in the sentence *During the meeting Mr. Oliver explained the need for a tax increase while Mr. Leer explains the disadvantages,* there is no reason to shift from the past tense used for Mr. Oliver to the present tense used for Mr. Leer. Such shifts are very distracting to readers and can greatly confuse them.

EDITING PRACTICE 2-9

Correct all needless shifts in tense in the following sentences by rewriting each sentence in the space provided.

Example: Jerry washes and waxed his car twice a year.

    Jerry washes and waxes his car twice a year.

1. He cleans the upholstery first and then did the dash.

   _____

   _____

2. When he finished this, he vacuums the carpets.

   _____

   _____

3. He then wet down the outside and washes it with soap.

   _____

   _____

4. Jerry then washed the tires and cleans them.

   _____

   _____

5. He took several soft rags and dries the car.

   _____

   _____

6. He applies wax to about one-fourth of the car at a time and rubbed it off.

   _____

   _____

7. This makes the car shine and looked good.

   _____

   _____

8. He worked for four hours and takes the pretty car to a dealer.

   _____

   _____

9. The dealer looks at the car and talked with the manager.

   _____

   _____

10. The dealer offers Jerry four hundred dollars and showed him a newer model.

    _____

    _____

Active Versus Passive Voice

Active voice and *passive voice* refer to the arrangement of the subject and verb. Each verb tense can be in either the active voice or the passive voice.

> In **active voice,** the subject usually comes before the verb. It is clear that the subject is doing the action.

Nelson played the game.
> The verb *played* is in the active voice because the subject *Nelson* is doing the action.
> *Who* or *what played?* Nelson

The passive voice is composed of a form of the auxiliary verb *be* (*am, are, is, was, were*) followed by a past participle.

> In **passive voice,** the object of the active sentence becomes the subject of the passive sentence.

The game was played by Nelson.
> The verb *was played* is in the passive voice because the subject *game* is the receiver of the action.
> *Who* or *what was played?* Game

The passive voice creates indirect and clunky sentences, which is why good writers consider the active voice stronger and therefore better than the passive voice. In most cases, try to keep your writing in the active voice. The active voice is much more direct since the subject clearly performs the action. However, you need to know both voices because sometimes passive voice works better. For instance, because the passive voice deemphasizes the doer of the action, it is often used to soften the effect of a complaint. In speaking to the letter carrier, you are much more polite when you say "My magazine was torn" than when you say "You tore my magazine." Also, there are times when the doer of the action is unknown, as in the sentence, *The letter was not signed.*

PRACTICE SENTENCES 2–10

In the blanks provided, indicate whether the verbs in the following sentences are in the active or passive voice.

Example: The little girl's dress was soiled by the ice cream cone.

_____passive_____

1. The bat was made by the Louisville Slugger Company.

_____

2. The girl outran the shortstop's throw.

_____

3. Michael Jordan played basketball for the Chicago Bulls.

_____

4. My mother works with an accounting firm in Atlanta.

   _____

5. The company car was sold by the business manager.

   _____

6. Andrew drove his mother's car into the driver's door of my car.

   _____

7. The bill was padded by the mechanic.

   _____

8. The batteries in the child's toy ran down in just one week.

   _____

9. The teacher talked to the student about his sloppy work.

   _____

10. The entire crew was blamed by the supervisor.

    _____

EDITING PRACTICE 2-11

In the space provided, rewrite the passive sentences to make them active and the active sentences to make them passive.

Example: The experiment was performed by Dr. Frankenstein.

   Dr. Frankenstein performed the experiment.

1. Phil poured the concrete for the museum steps.

   _____

   _____

2. The memo was prepared by the CEO.

3. The television show was censored by the network.

4. The amateur radio operator kept authorities abreast of local conditions.

5. The professor announced the date of the next test.

6. Margaret requested a twelve-month contract.

7. The roses were sprayed by the gardener.

8. Eudora Welty wrote the novel *Losing Battles*.

9. The problem was solved by the plumber.

_____

_____

10. The actress accepted the award.

_____

_____

Writer's Tip

Be sure to avoid needless shifts from active voice to passive voice and vice versa.

John <u>played</u> football for three years in high school, but the sport <u>was</u> not <u>enjoyed</u> by him.

There is a needless shift from the active voice to the passive voice. Rewrite the sentence to say: John *played* football for three years in high school, but he *did* not *enjoy* the sport.

EDITING PRACTICE 2-12

Correct all needless shifts in voice in the following sentences by rewriting each sentence in the space provided.

Example: Let's do well on this project, so honors will be won by all.

   Let's do well on this project, so we can

   all win honors.

1. I ordered my wife's Christmas gift in July, but it has not been received.

_____

_____

2. Danny dunked the basketball, but his finger was broken on the rim.

_____

_____

3. Greg prepared many different dishes, but only one was eaten by Maria.

_____

_____

4. The player declared his innocence, but a drug test was refused by him.

_____

_____

5. Heather said she really admired Jose, but his ring was refused by her.

_____

_____

6. The appraiser looked over the car carefully, and it was declared a total loss by him.

_____

_____

7. The Express Mail package was lost in Chicago, but the postman delivered it on time.

_____

_____

8. The ad campaign was rejected by the company, so Fred redesigned it.

_____

_____

9. The radio was dropped by Morris, and he repaired it.

_____

_____

10. The manager submitted the proper requisition form, but no action was taken by the boss.

_____

_____

Person and Number

> The **number** of a verb simply indicates whether the verb is singular or plural.

The boy <u>sings</u>. (singular)
The boys <u>sing</u>. (plural)

The -*s* on *sings* indicates that it is singular. Do not be confused. Most nouns form their plurals by adding an -*s*: *chair* becomes *chairs*. Verbs are just the opposite.

The singular and plural forms of the verb are often arranged by person.

> **Person** indicates the speaker, the person or thing spoken to, or the person or thing spoken about.

There are first person, second person, and third person. The *first person* indicates the person speaking:

Ⓘ will do the assignment.

The *second person* indicates the person or thing spoken to:

Ⓨⓞⓤ should repair the bicycle immediately.

Batteries, ⓨⓞⓤ had better not give out on me during a test.

The *third person* indicates the person or thing spoken about:

The ⓛⓐⓦⓝⓜⓞⓦⓔⓡ is ready now.

The first person singular pronouns are *I, my, mine,* and *me*. The first person plural pronouns are *we, our, ours, us*. The second person singular and plural pronouns are *you, your,* and *yours,* used when addressing both one individual and when addressing more than one individual. The third person singular pronouns are *he, him, his, she, her, hers, it,* and *its*. The third person plural pronouns are *they, them, their,* and *theirs*.

Pronouns

Person	Singular	Plural
First	I, me, my, mine	we, us, our, ours
Second	you, your, yours	you, your, yours
Third	he, him, his, she, her, hers, it, its, one	they, them, their, theirs

Agreement in Number

Person	Singular	Plural
First	I choose	we choose
Second	you choose	you choose
Third	he chooses	they choose

 As you can see the third person singular form of the present tense verb is the one that ends in *s*. In your writing, do not make needless shifts in person and in number.

> One expects praise when they succeed.
>> *One* is the third person singular *(he, she),* but *they* is the third person plural. There is a needless shift in number.

> A person should be modest when we are successful.
>> *A person* is the third person singular, but *we* is the first person plural. There is a needless shift in both person and number.

EDITING PRACTICE 2–13

Correct all needless shifts in number and person in the following sentences by rewriting each sentence in the space provided.

Example: An individual should try to get the best job they can.

> *An individual should try to get the best job*
>
> *he or she can.*

1. Several students forgot her books.

2. The hairdressers posted a list of her charges.

3. We should contribute all that he can.

   _____

4. Sue and Terry got her art supplies in the bookstore.

   _____

5. An individual should put a lot of thought into their major.

   _____

6. The students studied hard for her history test.

   _____

7. The women did all her laundry on Sunday afternoon.

   _____

8. The men cleaned his shotgun before the morning hunt.

   _____

9. If some individual wishes to join the group, you should sign up in A 216.

   _____

10. The rose died because they were diseased.

    _____

Adverbs

Like adjectives, **adverbs** are modifiers. Unlike adjectives, which modify nouns and pronouns, however, adverbs modify verbs, adjectives, and other adverbs. As we will see later, adverbs can also modify entire sentences. Adverbs answer the questions *How? Where? When? Why? To what extent?* and *On what condition?*

v.   adv.

Jackie Joyner-Kersee runs gracefully.

Gracefully is an adverb modifying the verb *runs*. It answers the question *How? Runs how?* Gracefully.

v.   adv.   adv.

Jackie Joyner-Kersee runs very gracefully.

Now *gracefully* still modifies the verb *runs* but is itself modified by the adverb *very*. *Very* also answers the question *How? How gracefully?* Very gracefully. *Very* modifying *gracefully* is an example of an adverb modifying another adverb.

Jackie Joyner-Kersee ran an extremely graceful race.

Extremely is an adverb modifying the adjective that modifies the noun *race. How graceful?* Extremely graceful.

Now you have examples of adverbs modifying verbs, other adverbs, and adjectives.

Many adverbs, like *extremely* and *gracefully,* end in -*ly.* But many adverbs do not.

adv.   adv.

Joan Caterman swims quite well.

Swims how? Well (*well* modifies the verb *swims*). *How well?* Quite well (*quite* modifies the adverb *well*).

There is the book.

There is an adverb telling where the book is.

Do the assignment now.

Now is an adverb telling when.

Henri will not lie.

Not is an adverb that modifies the verb *will lie* by restricting its meaning.

In a sentence with the word *cannot,* remember *can* is a verb (auxiliary), but *not* is an adverb.

v. adv.   v.

Tanya cannot swim.

With practice you will be able to identify adverbs easily.

PRACTICE SENTENCES 2-14

Underline all the adverbs in the following sentences.

Example: Cecilia <u>carelessly</u> took her health for granted.

1. She worked diligently at two jobs.

2. Plus, she dedicatedly worked on a college degree at the same time.

3. On top of this, she had two children she loved deeply.

4. She survived well under these conditions for over two years.

5. However, one day she collapsed completely.

6. She had a stroke that damaged her left arm and leg severely.

7. She was completely disoriented for months.

8. For some reason the doctors had difficulty diagnosing her problem correctly.

9. Nevertheless, she visited a physical therapist regularly.

10. In less than a year, Cecilia was nearly back to normal.

Prepositions

> **Prepositions** show the position (pre*position*) of one word in relation to another. They are usually short words such as *in, by,* and *to.*

Think of a chair, and then think of a preposition as a word that shows the position of various objects in relation to the chair:

The chair is <u>on</u> the carpet.
The chair is <u>in</u> the truck.
The chair is <u>by</u> the fireplace.
The chair is <u>behind</u> the sofa.
The chair is <u>beside</u> him.
The chair is <u>against</u> the wall.
The chair is <u>near</u> her.

The underlined words are all prepositions. Notice that *carpet, truck, fireplace, sofa, him, wall,* and *her* are all either nouns or pronouns.

> A **preposition,** then, shows the relationship between a noun or pronoun and some other word in the sentence. The noun or pronoun referred to is generally the one that follows the preposition and is called the **object of the preposition.**

                                          n.

That man with the hat always dresses well.

    With is a preposition that shows the relationship between the noun *hat* and the word *man. Hat* is the object of the preposition *with.*

                                          n.

The driver crashed through the guardrail.

    Through is a preposition that shows the relationship between the noun *guardrail* and the word *crashed. Guardrail* is the object of the preposition *through.*

                                  pro.

John gave the book to her.

    To is a preposition that shows the relationship between the pronoun *her* and the word *gave. Her* is the object of the preposition *to.*

Here is a list of words that are commonly used as prepositions:

PREPOSITIONS

*according to	after
about	against
above	along
across	among
around	*in spite of
at	*instead of
*because of	into
before	like
behind	of
below	off
beneath	on
beside	*on account of
besides	over
	(continued)

---

*Multiword prepositions are sometimes called phrasal or group prepositions.

between	past
beyond	till
**but (when it means *except*)	through
by	throughout
*by means of	to
despite	toward
down	under
during	underneath
except	until
for	up
from	upon
in	with
*in addition to	within
*in back of	without

---

*Multiword prepositions are sometimes called phrasal or group prepositions.

**See page 273.

PRACTICE SENTENCES 2–15

Underline the prepositions in the following sentences.

Example: Joan moved the computer *into* her office.

1. She put the monitor on her desk.

2. The keyboard is near her hands on the desk.

3. The computer itself is beside the desk.

4. The manual is on a shelf above the monitor.

5. Everything is conveniently located for her.

6. Currently she is working on a word-processing program.

7. She has a spreadsheet program on the same disk.

8. Joan works at the computer throughout the day.

9. She is pleased with the work she can accomplish with the machine.

10. But a few minutes ago, she accidentally erased a thirty-page report due in three hours.

PRACTICE SENTENCES 2-16

In the space provided, construct sentences of your own using the prepositions listed.

Example: for: Because he was not ready for the biology test, Bartoleme cut class that day.

1. after _____

_____

2. since _____

_____

3. without _____

_____

4. until _____

_____

5. before _____

_____

Conjunctions

Conjunctions are connecting words. They connect words and word groups.

Carol and Ted have an ideal relationship.
And connects the words *Carol* and *Ted*.

Either Renée or Barbara will be married by the end of the year.
Either . . . *or* connects the words *Renée* and *Barbara*.

Eddie will go to the game if it doesn't rain.
If connects *Eddie will go to the game* to *it doesn't rain.*

Conjunctions are classified as either coordinate or subordinate. **Coordinate conjunctions** connect words of equal grammatical units.

> Maples and oaks are good shade trees.
>> *And* connects the equal grammatical units *maples* and *oaks* (noun subjects).

> I drove through the city and into the desert.
>> *And* connects the equal grammatical units *through the city* and *into the desert* (prepositional phrases).

> Alfred loves his dog, Pug, but Pug bites him at every opportunity.
>> *But* connects the equal grammatical units *Alfred loves his dog, Pug* and *Pug bites him at every opportunity* (main clauses).

The coordinate conjunctions are:

COORDINATE CONJUNCTIONS

and	but	yet	so (some-
or	for	nor	times)

Correlative conjunctions are coordinate conjunctions that are used in pairs.

> My watch is either in the cabinet or on the table.
>> *Either . . . or* connects the equal grammatical units *in the cabinet* and *on the table*.

Common correlative conjunctions are:

CORRELATIVE CONJUNCTIONS

both . . . and
either . . . or
neither . . . nor
not only . . . but also

The other type of conjunction is subordinate. The **subordinate conjunction** connects unequal grammatical units (see Chapter 4).

> Although I studied diligently, I could not make an A on the test.
>> *Although* connects the unequal grammatical units *Although I studied diligently* and *I could not make an A on the test.*

Conjunctions will be explained in more detail in Chapter 4, on clauses. Nevertheless, you may find the following partial list of subordinate conjunctions helpful:

SUBORDINATE CONJUNCTIONS

after	as though	since	when
although	because	so that	whenever
as	before	than	where
as if	even though	though	wherever
as much as	if	unless	while
as long as	in order that	until	

Notice that some subordinate conjunctions can also be prepositions. If such a word introduces a group of related words that does not contain a subject and a verb, it is a preposition. If it introduces a group of related words that does contain a subject and a verb, the word is a subordinate conjunction:

After the dance everyone went home.

> *After* is a preposition introducing the group of related words not containing a subject and a verb: *After the dance.*

After the dance came to an end, everyone went home.

> *After* is a subordinate conjunction introducing the group of related words containing a subject and a verb: *After the dance came to an end.*

PRACTICE SENTENCES 2–17

Underline the coordinate conjunctions in the following sentences.

Example: Sherry <u>and</u> her family went camping over the weekend.

1. They had a nice time, but the weather was hot and humid.

2. They couldn't decide whether to concentrate on swimming or hiking.

3. Sherry and her son Jeff went swimming.

4. Her husband Chris and son Billy hit the hiking trails.

5. After two and a half hours Chris and Billy returned to the lake.

6. They were hot and tired so they hit the water ASAP.

7. After supper Jeff and Billy put the tent up.

8. They argued whether to put it in the shade or out in the open.

9. Jeff and Billy put the tent in a clear area near the lake.

10. Fortunately it rained and cooled things off, but unfortunately the tent leaked.

PRACTICE SENTENCES 2-18

Underline the subordinate conjunction in the following sentences.

Example: <u>Before</u> Pedro enrolled in the local community college, he checked out its academic reputation.

1. He talked to some of the instructors first because he wanted to determine their attitudes toward students.

2. After he talked to the instructors, he conversed with some of the students to get their opinions.

3. After he completed these discussions, he decided the school looked pretty good.

4. He signed up for the electronics program because he liked the job opportunities.

5. He felt that there would be many possible jobs in the local area.

6. Pedro found that the instructors and students were all willing to help.

7. Pedro, who had a knack for electronics, performed quite well in the pursuit of his degree.

8. When he graduated, Pedro had a GPA of 3.6.

9. He applied only at Universal Electronics when he sought a job.

10. After Pedro had worked at Universal for three years, the company thanked the college for preparing Pedro so well.

Interjections

Interjections are words or groups of words that express emotion.

Although they add little to the meaning of a sentence, they are considered a part of speech. Generally they come at the beginning of a sentence, but not always.

Heavens! How could you make such a mess?
Heavens is an interjection.

Gee whiz, that is a good paint job.
Gee whiz is an interjection.

Damn! That hammer didn't do my finger any good at all.
Damn is an interjection.

I'll do the best I can, by golly.
By golly is an interjection.

PRACTICE SENTENCES 2–19
Underline the interjections in the following sentences.

Example: Holy Toledo! That pan was hot!

1. Good heavens, Bob, let me help you with that.

2. Ouch! I dropped a hammer on my sore toe!

3. Good grief, Ed, why don't you just ask her if she will go out with you?

4. At least pick up a drill and look as if you're doing something, for heaven's sake!

5. Gee, after three days of rain I hope we can finally have our picnic.

Identifying Parts of Speech

You should realize that the part of speech of a word depends on how the word is used in a sentence. The same word can be one of several parts of speech, depending on its context or use in a particular sentence. The word *but*, for instance, is commonly used as a conjunction, as in the sentence *Mary went to the beach, but I stayed home.* On the other hand, the word *but* is a preposition in the sentence *Everyone went to the championship game but me.* Look at these different uses of the word *yellow:*

Yellow is my favorite color. (noun)
Mary has a yellow car. (adjective)
The shirt yellowed in the washing machine. (verb)

Do not be misled into thinking that what you call a preposition in one sentence will always be used as a preposition. When in doubt, consult a dictionary. A good dictionary will classify a word according to the various parts of speech it can be and give examples of usage.

Commonly Misused Words

English contains many words that sound alike but are spelled differently and/or have different meanings. Words like these are called homonyms. Here are some examples:

> *accept* (to receive or to not protest something), *except* (to leave something out)
> *affect* (v. to alter a situation, to pretend or create a certain appearance), *effect* (n. the actual change; can be used as a verb meaning to cause a change)
> *all ready* (set to go, prepared), *already* (has happened previously)
> *coarse* (adj. rough), *course* (n. class or pathway)
> *desert* (an arid land region), *dessert* (a course eaten after an entrée)
> *formally* (adv. with great ceremony), *formerly* (adv. before)
> *lead* (n. a metallic ore, v. present tense of to show the way, to be the head of), *led* (v. past tense of to lead)
> *loose* (adj. not tight), *lose* (v. to misplace something)
> *moral* (adj. ethical, a sense of right and wrong), *morale* (n. confidence)
> *passed* (v. went by), *past* (n. an earlier time period)
> *personal* (private, close to you), *personnel* (people who work for an organization)
> *rational* (adj. clear thinking), *rationale* (n. a reason or purpose for something)
> *than* (creates a comparison), *then* (time reference to clarify a sequence)
> *threw* (v. past tense of throw), *through* (prep. from one end to another)
> *weather* (climate conditions), *whether* (implies alternatives or possibilities)

Other homonyms exist. Write down more examples.

_____ _____ _____ _____

_____ _____ _____ _____

_____ _____ _____ _____

_____ _____ _____ _____

_____ _____ _____ _____

Other words having similar meanings often get used incorrectly. Here are some examples:

amount (refers to a bulk quantity), *number* (refers to separate parts counted together)

between (used for two items), *among* (used with three or more items)

convince (to change someone's belief or attitude), *persuade* (to encourage or move someone to action)

famous (well known), *notable* (important), *notorious* (well known for negative reasons)

mad (insane, informal for angry), *angry* (use in formal speech)

Many words are commonly misspelled or misused for a variety of reasons. Sometimes the wrong spelling is used in advertising (such as *lite* or *thru*). In other cases, the writer has guessed incorrectly (such as *alot, irregardless,* or *should of*).

Lite should *be light.*
Thru should be *through.*
Alot should be *a lot.*
Irregardless should be *regardless.*
Should of should be *should have.*
This also applies to *could of, would of, had of, might of,* etc.

Writer's Tip A computer program with a spelling checker won't catch correctly spelled wrong words. Always proofread after running a spelling checker.

Don't despair if you find yourself misusing words. Proper usage takes practice. Give yourself time, and write. Your spelling and diction will improve.

REVIEW EXERCISE 2-A IDENTIFYING PARTS OF SPEECH

In the blanks provided, indicate the part of speech of each word in the sentence (noun, pronoun, adjective, verb, adverb, preposition, conjunction, or interjection).

Example: Astronomy is a popular hobby.

Astronomy _____noun_____

After they discussed their feelings, Willie and Shehesia got married.

1. After _____

2. they _____

3. discussed _____

4. their _____

5. feelings _____

6. Willie _____

7. and _____

8. Shehesia _____

9. got _____

10. married _____

MASTERY TEST 2-A USING PARTS OF SPEECH

Compose a sentence that contains each of the following parts of speech. Underline the featured part of speech.

Example: an adjective

   Henry designed and made a leather belt.

1. coordinate conjunction

_____

_____

2. a possessive pronoun

_____

_____

3. an adverb

_____

_____

4. a preposition

_____

_____

5. a subordinate conjunction

_____

_____

6. an interjection

_____

_____

7. a pronoun

_____

_____

8. a preposition

_____

_____

9. a coordinate conjunction

_____

_____

10. a noun

_____

_____

EDITING TEST 2-A USING VERBS CORRECTLY

In the space provided, rewrite these sentences to correct any errors in tense, voice, person, or number.

Example: If he could dance, he will try out for the school play.

If he could dance, he would try out for the

school play.

1. The Belton County Historical Society has held its annual historical celebration last week.

   _____

   _____

2. Musicians and craftsmen was on hand for entertainment.

   _____

   _____

3. One folklorist sung several ballads.

   _____

   _____

4. Several of the needleworkers displayed her quilting techniques.

   _____

   _____

5. If you were at the celebration, you would have had a good time.

_____

_____

6. Some delicious food was served, and everyone enjoyed eating it.

_____

_____

7. One man travels three hundred miles to attend the event.

_____

_____

8. He was a flat-foot dancer, and a special routine had been worked out by him.

_____

_____

9. However, he wished he would not have eaten so much.

_____

_____

10. He had dance beautifully in the past, but his performance this year was awful.

_____

_____

Writing Assignments

Assignment 2-1 Write one paragraph (about half a page) about why pets (at least cats and dogs) are good for people in nursing homes. Do you think that each person in a nursing home should have his or her own pet (if he or she wants one) or that nursing homes should have several "group" pets that can visit with anyone? What is it about contact with animals that could be good for nursing-home clients?

Assignment 2-2 Write three paragraphs (about one and a half pages) about animal testing in laboratories. Is it OK to test certain animals (mice, rats, etc.) but not others (cats, dogs, monkeys, rabbits, etc.)? If you feel that it's OK to test some animals, what types of experiment do you feel should be allowed? Why?

Go Electronic!

For additional readings, exercises, and Internet activities, visit the Longman English pages at:

   http://longman.awl.com/englishpages

If you need a user name and password, please see your instructor.

More Practice with Your Writing and Grammar Skills

For additional practice with your writing and grammar skills, use the Writer's ToolKit CD-ROM included with this text. The ToolKit provides a wealth of computerized tutorials and practice activities.

chapter 3

Phrases

> A **phrase** is a group of related words that does not contain a subject and a verb.

Phrases also act as particular parts of speech. That is, the words that make up a phrase may act together as one part of speech. For example, in the sentence *Dave Kingman hit the ball over the fence*, the phrase *over the fence* functions as an adverb because it answers the question *Where?* The two main types of phrases are prepositional phrases and verbal phrases.

Prepositional Phrases

> A **prepositional phrase** begins with a preposition, ends with the noun or pronoun object, and contains all the modifiers in between, if any.

In the earlier phrase *over the fence, over* is the preposition, *fence* is the noun object, and *the* is the modifier. Prepositional phrases always function as either adjectives or adverbs.

The man in the wool suit is uncomfortable.
> *In the wool suit* modifies the noun *man* and is therefore an adjective phrase. Which man?

The cassette recorder <u>with a built-in radio</u> is expensive.
With a built-in radio modifies the noun *recorder* and is thus an adjective phrase. Which recorder?

The principal ran the banner <u>up the flagpole</u>.
Up the flagpole modifies the verb *ran* and is therefore an adverb phrase. Ran where? Up the flagpole.

There was no game <u>because of the rain</u>.
Because of the rain modifies the verb *was* and is thus an adverb phrase. Why was there no game? Because of the rain.

Clearly, then, prepositional phrases are groups of related words that do not contain subjects and verbs and that function as adjectives or adverbs.

PRACTICE SENTENCES 3-1

Underline the prepositional phrases in the following sentences.

Example: The game <u>for the championship</u> had the entire city excited.

1. The Cardinals from the east side had an outstanding center.

2. He stood six feet nine inches in his bare feet.

3. The Eagles from the south side had two outstanding guards.

4. The main problem for the Eagles was rebounding.

5. In the first half the Cardinals had a fifteen-point lead.

6. The Eagle coach came up with a plan.

7. He played a triangle and two, with his two biggest men on the Cardinal center.

8. With the Cardinal center pinned in, the Eagle guards scored easily.

9. The Eagles had pulled within one point.

10. However, the Cardinal center won the game with a sky hook.

Verbal Phrases

A **verbal** is a word that is derived from a verb but that functions as another part of speech. A **verbal phrase** consists of a verbal and all its modifiers and objects. There are three types of verbals: infinitives, participles, and gerunds.

Infinitives

> An **infinitive** begins with the word *to* and is followed by a verb form.

> To conserve energy is a wise policy.
>> *To conserve* is an infinitive. It begins with the word *to* and is followed by a verb form, *conserve*.

> John took his date to the movies.
>> *To the movies* is not an infinitive. Though the phrase begins with the word *to*, it is not followed by a verb form. *To the movies* is a prepositional phrase.

Like verbs, infinitives may have auxiliaries that indicate tense and voice: *to conserve, to have conserved, to be conserved, to have been conserved, to be conserving, to have been conserving.*

> The office building to have been auctioned burned last week.
>> *To have been auctioned* is the present perfect tense, passive voice form of the infinitive.

Infinitives also retain enough verb qualities to take objects and adverb modifiers.

> The group to present the play is well trained.
>> The infinitive is *to present*. To present what? Play. *Play* is the object of the infinitive.

> An **infinitive phrase** consists of the infinitive, its object if it has one, and its modifiers if it has any.

> To elect a qualified president is our goal.
>> *To elect* is the infinitive, *president* is the object of the infinitive, and *a* and *qualified* are modifiers.

One of the modifiers may be another phrase.

> To elect a qualified president for next year is our goal.
>> The prepositional phrase *for next year* is another modifier in the infinitive phrase. Thus, the infinitive phrase contains a prepositional phrase within it.

Infinitive phrases can function as either nouns, adjectives, or adverbs.

To run the mile under 3:50 is every miler's dream.
> *To run the mile under 3:50* is an infinitive phrase used as a noun since it is the subject of the sentence. It answers the question *Who?* or *What?* asked in front of the verb. *Who* or *what is?* to run the mile under 3:50.

Notice that the whole phrase functions as a one-word noun. If the sentence read *Speed is every miler's dream,* then the subject would be the one-word noun *speed* rather than the phrase *to run the mile under 3:50.*

As adjective phrases, infinitives follow the noun or pronoun they modify.

The obstacle to be overcome is nothing to a man of his ability.
> *To be overcome* is an infinitive phrase used as an adjective modifying the noun *obstacle.* Notice the phrase follows the word it modifies.

Finally, infinitives can function as adverbs.

Jack married the banker's daughter to get a job at the bank.
> *To get a job at the bank* is an infinitive phrase functioning as an adverb. The phrase modifies the verb *married* and answers the question *Why?*

Occasionally, infinitives come at the beginning of sentences and modify the whole sentence rather than any particular word in the sentence. Since the most important word in a sentence is generally the verb, however, such infinitive phrases are said to function as adverbs.

To be frank about it, I haven't had any luck with your TV set.
> *To be frank about it* modifies the whole sentence and is therefore considered an infinitive phrase functioning as an adverb.

 A CHECKLIST FOR INFINITIVES

An infinitive can:
1. Indicate tense and voice.
2. Take an object and its modifiers.
3. Function as a noun, an adjective, or an adverb.
4. Modify an entire sentence.

PRACTICE SENTENCES 3-2

In the blanks provided, indicate whether the italicized infinitive phrases function as adjectives, adverbs, or nouns.

Example: *To be elected* was the politician's goal.

_____noun_____

1. The teacher wanted *to make a point to his class.*

   _____

2. The student wanted a job *to pay off some of his bills.*

   _____

3. The monument *to be constructed* is still in the planning stage.

   _____

4. The car *to be sold at the auction* is a Studebaker Hawk.

   _____

5. *To be chosen a member of the school choir* was May's dream.

   _____

6. Bob wanted *to repair the car* before his trip to Denver.

   _____

7. Michael played well in the game *to impress Nancy.*

   _____

8. The package *to be mailed* is certified.

   _____

9. Dean wants *to complete the course on time.*

   _____

10. The grass *to be mowed* was over a foot tall.

    _____

Participles

Participles are two principal parts of the verb: either the past participle or the present participle.

> The **past participle** of the verb is the form that belongs in the blank: I have _____. If the verb is a regular verb, then the past participle will end in -*ed*.

I have <u>stopped</u>.
I have <u>looked</u>.
I have <u>intended</u>.

If the verb is an irregular verb, then the past participle will end in something other than -*ed*, the most common endings being -*en* or -*t*.

I have <u>chosen</u>.
I have <u>bitten</u>.
I have <u>slept</u>.
I have <u>bent</u>.

> The **present participle** of the verb is the form that belongs in the blank: I am _____ *ing*. The present participles of both regular and irregular verbs end in -*ing*.

I am <u>stopping</u>.
I am <u>looking</u>.
I am <u>intending</u>.
I am <u>choosing</u>.
I am <u>biting</u>.
I am <u>sleeping</u>.
I am <u>bending</u>.

Remember, the preceding examples are verbs, not verbals. In the sentences *I have done* and *I am stopping, have done* and *am stopping* are verbs; they express action. To be a verbal, a verb form must function as another part of speech. Participles as verbals must function as adjectives.

I am working.
  Am working is a verb.

John Draughn, working in his garden, spotted a rattlesnake.
  Working in his garden is not a verb. *Working* is a verbal functioning as an adjective modifying the noun *John Draughn. Working* is a participle.

In summary, the most common endings of participles are *-ed, -en, -t,* and *-ing.* But remember, any verb form that belongs in the blank *I have* _____ can be a participle; thus a few participles will end in something other than *-ed, -en, -t,* or *-ing.*

I have <u>blown</u>.
I have <u>done</u>.
I have <u>rung</u>.
I have <u>heard</u>.

Participles as verbals always function as adjectives. That is all they can ever be. Like infinitives, participles are derived from verbs and therefore can have objects and modifiers.

A **participial phrase** begins with a participle, ends with its object, and contains all the modifiers.

<u>Selecting Ann Abrams for the job</u>, the executive feels confident of his choice.
> *Selecting* is the participle, *Ann Abrams* is the object of the participle, and *for the job* is a modifying phrase. The whole participial phrase *selecting Ann Abrams for the job* is used as an adjective modifying the noun *executive.*

Since participles are derived from verbs, they can have different tense forms just as infinitives can.

<u>Having been elected to the board</u>, Carlos was elated.
> The entire participial phrase is underlined. The participle itself is *having been elected.* This is the perfect passive participle form. The whole phrase *having been elected to the board* functions as an adjective modifying the noun *Carlos.*

When a participial phrase comes at the beginning of a sentence, it should modify the first noun or pronoun that comes after it. A comma sets off the introductory participial phrase. In the last example, *having been elected to the board* modifies the noun *Carlos.* Participial phrases that do not modify the first noun or pronoun that follows them are said to be dangling.

<u>Blowing the litter everywhere</u>, the street was a mess because of the wind.
> *Blowing the litter everywhere* is a participial phrase, but it cannot modify the noun *street.* The street cannot blow the litter around. The sentence should be rewritten to eliminate the dangling participle: Blowing the litter everywhere, the wind made a mess of the street.

<u>Working with her hair for hours</u>, the dryer scorched Sharon's scalp.
> As written, the sentence says the dryer was working on Sharon's hair for hours, a truly talented dryer.

Can you rewrite the preceding sentence so that it no longer contains a dangling participle?

EDITING PRACTICE 3-3

Each of the ten sentences in this exercise contains a dangling participle. Rewrite each sentence so that the participle is not dangling.

Example: Cleaning the house thoroughly, the refrigerator gave Albert the most trouble.

<u>Cleaning the house thoroughly, Albert had the</u>

<u>most trouble with the refrigerator.</u>

1. Racing down the hill, a tree stopped the children's sled.

_____

_____

2. Having studied diligently for the test, a good grade was Craig's reward.

_____

_____

3. Sleeping outside on a cold January night, the new sleeping bag still wasn't enough to keep Angela warm.

_____

_____

4. Having purchased a new tennis racket, Jason's game showed no improvement.

_____

_____

5. Having been married for six years, the ring on Adrian's finger began to seem like a burden.

   _____

   _____

6. Finished with the test, the papers were turned in by the students.

   _____

   _____

7. Being scientists, the white mice were studied by the professors.

   _____

   _____

8. Repaired by the jeweler for forty-five dollars, Mary still could not get the watch to keep good time.

   _____

   _____

9. Determined to do a good job, the house was painted slowly by Paulette.

   _____

   _____

10. Spayed at the local animal clinic, Shannon now had a "safe" pet.

    _____

    _____

Participial phrases do not necessarily have to come at the beginning of sentences. When one does not, it will come immediately after the noun or pronoun it modifies.

The car <u>being repaired with body filler</u> is on the back lot.
Being repaired with body filler modifies the noun *car*.

Van Adler is the teller <u>making all the mistakes.</u>
Making all the mistakes is the participial phrase modifying the noun *teller*.

Occasionally, however, participial phrases are tacked on to the end of sentences, far removed from the words they modify. The sentence you just read is an example. *Far removed from the words they modify* is a participial phrase that modifies the noun *phrases*. Here is another example:

The old veteran can be seen every morning, shuffling his feet and hanging his head.
The two participial phrases *shuffling his feet* and *hanging his head* are tacked on to the end of the sentence and modify *veteran*.

Such sentences can be effective if used sparingly.

 A CHECKLIST FOR PARTICIPLES

A participle:
1. Always functions as an adjective.
2. Can have an object and modifiers.
3. Can have different tense forms.
4. Should come directly before or after the noun or pronoun it modifies.

PRACTICE SENTENCES 3–4

In the blanks provided, indicate the noun or pronoun that the italicized participial phrase modifies.

Example: Violetta, *selected for the job opening,* had just completed her college degree.

_____Violetta_____

1. *Studying the field of accounting for four years,* Violetta wasn't sure what area of accounting she wanted to go into.

_____

2. *Looking through many journals that advertised job openings,* she found many openings in auditing.

   _____

3. The journals *listing these job openings* indicated many cities where jobs were available.

   _____

4. *Selecting where she preferred to practice,* the new graduate was faced with numerous choices.

   _____

5. San Francisco, *being the site Violetta selected,* had thirty-three openings in auditing.

   _____

6. *Choosing among eighteen different companies,* she began to study the firms.

   _____

7. *Comparing salary and location,* she eliminated eleven of the firms quickly.

   _____

8. *Selecting the five firms with the finest reputations,* Violetta set up interviews with them.

   _____

9. Violetta, *having confidence in herself,* performed well at all of the interviews.

   _____

10. *Settling into her new job and new city,* she is now a happy, successful young *woman.*

   _____

Gerunds

The third type of verbal is called a gerund.

> **Gerunds** are present participles and thus always end in *-ing*. A gerund always functions as a noun.

Though both participles *and* gerunds can end in *-ing,* participles can function only as adjectives and gerunds can function only as nouns.

Like other nouns, gerunds are generally either subjects, direct objects, or objects of prepositions.

> Running is a good way to stay trim.
> > *Running* is the subject of the verb *is.*

> Maria enjoys running.
> > *Running* is the direct object of *enjoys.*

> Robert Hamstring stays in shape by running.
> > *Running* is the object of the preposition *by.*

Like participles and infinitives, gerunds can also take objects and modifiers. A gerund phrase consists of the gerund, its object if there is one, and any modifiers. In the gerund phrase *doing the laundry, doing* is the gerund, *laundry* is the object of the gerund, and *the* is the modifier.

Read the following sentence:

> Jogging five laps leisurely is good exercise.
> > *Jogging five laps leisurely* is the gerund phrase. *Jogging* is the gerund, *five* is an adjective modifying the noun *laps,* which is the object of the gerund, and *leisurely* is an adverb modifying the gerund *jogging,* telling how. But don't gerunds function as nouns? Yes, they do, and adverbs are not supposed to modify nouns. The reason the adverb *leisurely* can modify the gerund *jogging* is that gerunds are verbals. Since verbals are derived from verbs, a verbal used as a noun can retain enough qualities of a verb to be modified by an adverb. In a similar manner adverbs can modify infinitives used as nouns.

> To shoot accurately is every hunter's desire.
> > *Accurately* is an adverb modifying the infinitive *to shoot,* which is the subject of the verb *is.*

A CHECKLIST FOR GERUNDS

A gerund:

1. Always ends in -*ing*.
2. Functions as a noun.
3. Can be a subject, a direct object, or an object of a preposition.
4. Can take objects and modifiers.

PRACTICE SENTENCES 3–5

In the blanks provided, indicate whether the italicized gerund phrases function as subjects (subj.), direct objects (d.o.), or objects of prepositions (o.p.).

Example: Clara enjoys *getting up early*.

_____*d.o.*_____

1. The local civic groups helped the homeless by *sponsoring a charity bazaar.*

   _____

2. *Getting up early* is not part of my normal routine.

   _____

3. By *turning in early tonight*, I may be ready for the day's activities.

   _____

4. Some women prefer *working in mills to fast-food restaurants.*

   _____

5. *Selecting a good camera* can take some study.

   _____

6. The opponents won the election by *stuffing the ballot boxes.*

   _____

7. Upon *receiving a good credit rating*, Tom applied for six credit cards.

   _____

8. Emily likes *receiving praise and attention.*

   _____

9. *Driving at speeds over a hundred miles an hour* is a thrill and a challenge.

   _____

10. *Doing laundry and cleaning house* can ruin a weekend.

    _____

You should not have trouble with participles and gerunds if you remember that participles (which do not always end in *-ing*) are always used as adjectives and that gerunds are always nouns. Just because a verbal ends in *-ing*, do not immediately think "gerund." Remember, the *-ing* verbal could be either a participle or a gerund. Look to see if the verbal is used as an adjective or as a noun. If the verbal ending in *-ing* is not the subject, direct object, or object of a preposition (the most common functions of a noun), it is probably a participle. Also, if a gerund appears at the beginning of a sentence, it is usually the subject of a sentence.

> Getting the car ready for the race was an expensive project.
> *Getting the car ready for the race* is the subject of the verb *was.*

If a participle comes at the beginning of a sentence, it should modify the first noun or pronoun following it.

> Mowing the lawn every Saturday, John established a ritual for himself.
> *Mowing the lawn every Saturday* is a participial phrase modifying the noun *John. Participial* is the adjective form of the noun *participle,* and thus the term used to describe this type of phrase.

Notice that a participial phrase appearing at the beginning of a sentence is set off from the main clause with a comma. On the other hand, a gerund at the beginning of a sentence is not generally set off with a comma, because it is undesirable to separate the subject from the verb with a comma.

The main thing to remember, however, is that participles are always adjectives and gerunds are always nouns. Look to see whether the verbal names (gerund) or modifies (participle). In your own writing, participles and gerunds should be no problem. Use them in your writing. Though no technique should be used too often, verbal phrases—especially introductory participial phrases—can make your writing lively.

Without verbal phrase: Elaine is ready to serve the ball and sees her opponent is not in position for a backhand return.

With verbal phrase: Seeing her opponent is not in position for a backhand return, Elaine plans to put her serve in the corner.

Notice how the introductory participial phrase alters the subject-verb pattern and immediately gets the reader's attention with the action word *seeing*.

✔ **CHECKLIST: PARTICIPLES VS. GERUNDS**

Participles	Gerunds
1. Used as adjectives	1. Used as nouns
2. Set off by a comma	2. Go with the verb
3. Don't always end in *-ing*	3. Always end in *-ing*

PRACTICE SENTENCES 3-6

In the blanks provided, indicate whether the italicized phrase is a participle or a gerund.

Example: *Being on his own for the first time,* Ramon was lost.

_____participle_____

1. *Washing his own clothes* was a new experience for him.

_____

2. *Looking at all those knobs on the washer and dryer,* Ramon thought about doing his laundry in the sink.

_____

3. *Going to the grocery store* was also puzzling for him.

_____

4. Ramon, *standing in the store,* saw cleaning solutions for every item in his home.

   _____

5. *Confused by the unbelievable assortment of cleaners,* he just bought brand names he had heard of.

   _____

6. *Taking all the goodies home with him,* Ramon was ready to go to work.

   _____

7. *Deciding what part of the house he would clean first* was his first choice.

   _____

8. He started *cleaning the kitchen.*

   _____

9. The newly mopped kitchen floor, *being extremely sticky,* dampened his enthusiasm.

   _____

10. *Considering all the circumstances,* Ramon hired a cleaning service.

    _____

REVIEW EXERCISE 3-A IDENTIFYING TYPES OF PHRASES (I)

In the blanks provided, indicate whether the italicized phrase is a preposition, infinitive, participle, or gerund.

Example: AIDS is a disease *to be concerned about.*

<u>infinitive</u>

1. *Being an indiscriminate killer,* AIDS can kill anyone.

   _____

2. Homosexuals, *proven vulnerable to the disease,* are not the only victims.

   _____

3. Drug addicts *sharing the same needle* are also susceptible.

   _____

4. *Donating blood* has infected some people with the disease.

   _____

5. *Being careful of any exchange of bodily fluids,* medical personnel use special masks and gloves.

   _____

6. *Feeling safe from the disease at one time,* heterosexuals are now vulnerable.

   _____

7. Any partner can transmit the disease *to anyone else.*

   _____

8. *Relying on the results of one's HIV test* is no guarantee.

_____

9. The disease, *being undetected by testing,* can strike years after the initial exposure.

_____

10. AIDS may lead to a morality *based on fear.*

_____

REVIEW EXERCISE 3-B IDENTIFYING TYPES OF PHRASES (II)

In the blanks provided, indicate whether the italicized phrase is a preposition, an infinitive, a participle, or a gerund.

Example: *Getting ready every morning* takes Stephanie over an hour.

_____gerund_____

1. The chair *to be repaired* was badly broken.

_____

2. *Jogging three miles before breakfast* is part of Ben's daily routine.

_____

3. The teacher *selected for the award* was honored.

_____

4. Colin wanted *to receive the promotion.*

_____

5. *Working hard on the assignment,* Judy was proud of her paper.

_____

6. Larry practiced diligently *to qualify for the tournament.*

_____

7. *To be qualified as an instructor* requires many hours of classroom work.

_____

8. *Released from the hospital,* Nick headed for home.

    _____

9. Tony parked *near the emergency room.*

    _____

10. *Washing four neighborhood cars* earned Brook some spending money.

    _____

MASTERY TEST 3-A   USING PREPOSITIONAL AND VERBAL PHRASES

Write sentences that contain the phrases indicated.

Example: participial phrase at the beginning of a sentence

Having studied until 4:00 a.m. the night before,

Jenny was exhausted when she took the test.

1. gerund phrase used as a direct object

_____

_____

2. infinitive phrase in present perfect tense

_____

_____

3. participial phrase following the noun it modifies

_____

_____

4. infinitive phrase used as a direct object

_____

_____

5. gerund phrase used as a subject

_____

_____

6. prepositional phrase functioning as an adjective

_____

_____

7. infinitive phrase used as a subject

_____

_____

8. gerund phrase used as an object of a preposition

_____

_____

9. prepositional phrase functioning as an adverb

_____

_____

10. infinitive phrase functioning as an adjective

_____

_____

Writing Assignments

Assignment 3-1 Write one paragraph (about half a page) about how the food you eat can help or hurt your health. Why do you eat the foods you do? What foods are your favorites? Do you eat them for comfort? Energy? Other reasons?

Assignment 3-2 Write three paragraphs (about one and a half pages) about why you think many young men and women develop eating disorders (anorexia, bulimia). What kinds of stresses or pressures might cause someone to have an eating disorder?

Go Electronic!

For additional readings, exercises, and Internet activities, visit the Longman English pages at:

> http://longman.awl.com/englishpages

If you need a user name and password, please see your instructor.

More Practice with Your Writing and Grammar Skills

For additional practice with your writing and grammar skills, use the Writer's ToolKit CD–ROM included with this text. The ToolKit provides a wealth of computerized tutorials and practice activities.

Clauses

In Chapter 2 you learned that conjunctions are connecting words; they connect words and word groups. The two main word groups conjunctions connect are phrases and clauses. Remember that a phrase is a group of related words that does not contain a subject and a verb. *At the man's home* is a phrase, a prepositional phrase.

> A **clause** is a group of related words that does contain a subject and a verb.

Until the checkered flag was waved is a clause. The subject is *flag* and the verb is *was waved*.

> Phrases and clauses can be quite similar, the main difference being that a clause contains a subject and a verb whereas a phrase does not contain either a subject or a verb.

Look at the following examples:

Before the dance my date took me out to dinner.
Before the dance began, my date took me out to dinner.

In the first example, *before the dance* is a phrase; it does not contain a subject and a verb. In the second example, *before the dance began* is a clause; it contains the subject *dance* and the verb *began*. The two sentences are similar in meaning, but the structure of the word groups is quite different.

Main Clauses and Subordinate Clauses

There are two types of clauses: main clauses and subordinate clauses. Of course, because they are clauses, both types contain subjects and verbs.

A **main clause** expresses a complete thought.

I received an **A** on my theme.
> The sentence contains a subject and a verb and expresses a complete thought. The main clause *I received an A on my theme* can stand alone. It does not need anything else to complete its meaning.

Sometimes the subject of a main clause is a pronoun. Because the noun for which the pronoun stands will be clear in the context of the other sentences, such a main clause still expresses a complete thought. For example, in the sentence *She is perhaps the best American poet of the nineteenth century,* the pronoun *she* would be clearly understandable to a reader who has been reading about Emily Dickinson. In determining whether a clause expresses a complete thought, do not let pronouns confuse you.
> The other type of clause is a subordinate clause.

A **subordinate clause** does not express a complete thought. It depends on a main clause to complete its meaning.

If I were taller, I could play center on the basketball team.
> *If I were taller* is a subordinate clause. It does not express a complete thought; it cannot stand alone. It depends on the main clause *I could play center on the basketball team* to complete its meaning.

Coordinate conjunctions (*and, or, nor, but, for, yet, so*) can connect only words or word groups of equal rank. Therefore, they can connect two main clauses or two subordinate clauses. They cannot connect a main clause to a subordinate clause because main clauses and subordinate clauses are not of equal rank.

John hid the ring in the attic, but Maria found it.
> The conjunction *but* connects the main clauses *John hid the ring in the attic* and *Maria found it.*

Whoever is the most dependable and whoever finishes first will receive a bonus.
> The conjunction *and* connects the two subordinate clauses *whoever is the most dependable* and *whoever finishes first.*

Whoever finishes first and he will receive a bonus.
> Clearly the sentence is incorrect. A coordinate conjunction cannot connect a subordinate clause *(whoever finishes first)* and a main clause *(he will receive a bonus).*

PRACTICE SENTENCES 4–1

Underline the main clauses in the sentences below.

Example: I recently bought a computer because it could help me with my schoolwork.

1. Although there were many to choose from, I selected one in the eighteen-hundred-dollar price range.

2. Because I do a lot of typing, I was most interested in a good word processor.

3. Microsoft Word and Word Perfect were the programs that I had heard the most about.

4. I chose Microsoft Word for my system.

5. I had difficulty learning the program because I had originally learned on another word-processing program.

6. After I was able to operate Microsoft Word, I tackled Power Point.

7. The program was confusing because I didn't even know what it was supposed to do.

8. A friend suggested the Excel spreadsheet as my next task.

9. Although I am not fascinated by numbers, I found the program fun.

10. I may continue experimenting with the computer if I keep discovering so many new things.

> **Subordinate conjunctions** can connect only word groups of unequal rank. In other words, they connect main clauses to subordinate clauses.

Until the project is completed, Barbara will not leave the laboratory.
The word *until* subordinates the clause *until the project is completed* and connects it to the main clause *Barbara will not leave the laboratory. Until* is a subordinate conjunction.

Randy made a donation because he felt the money would help.
Because is a subordinate conjunction connecting the subordinate clause *because he felt the money would help* to the main clause *Randy made a donation.*

The following list of words often used as subordinating conjunctions may help you recognize both the conjunctions themselves and the subordinate clause they introduce:

SUBORDINATING CONJUNCTIONS

after	as though	since	until
although	because	so that	when
as	before	than	whenever
as if	if	though	whereas
as long as	in order that	unless	wherever
as much as			while

Writer's Tip Good writers often use subordinate clauses to include specific details that qualify or explain a main clause. The most important point is always stated in the main clause. It is sometimes difficult to tell what the writer's main point is when main clauses and subordinate clauses are used carelessly. Look at the following main clauses:

June wants a lucrative career.
June goes to law school.

If your main point is that June goes to law school, you might say:

Since June wants a lucrative career, she is going to law school.

On the other hand, if your main point is that June wants a lucrative career, you might say

June wants a lucrative career when she finishes law school.

Be aware that different subordinate conjunctions can serve different purposes. The subordinate conjunction *because* explains *why*.

Why?

Scott walked three miles in a blizzard *because his car broke down.*

The subordinate conjunctions *if* and *unless* answer the question: On what condition?

On what condition?

If you do your homework on Tuesday, you can go to the carnival Wednesday night.

On what condition?

You will not obtain your realtor's license *unless you study for the state licensing examination.*

Some subordinate conjunctions tell when an event will occur.

When?

The annual Snow Bowl will be held *when the first snowflakes fall.*

Clearly, subordinate clauses are useful tools for writers.

More About Subordinate Clauses

Subordinate clauses are sometimes introduced by relative pronouns rather than by subordinate conjunctions.

> A **relative pronoun** is a pronoun that can connect a subordinate clause to a main clause.

A few of the most common relative pronouns are:

COMMON RELATIVE PRONOUNS

who	whose	that
whom	which	

Relative pronouns serve much the same function in subordinate clauses as subordinate conjunctions; however, since pronouns can be subjects and objects of verbs whereas conjunctions cannot be, a distinction must be made between the two.

Do the job while you are feeling well.

> *While* is a subordinate conjunction connecting the subordinate clause *while you are feeling well* to the main clause *do the job*.

The man who will win the race must practice constantly.

> *Who* connects the subordinate clause *who will win the race* to the main clause *the man must practice constantly*. However, *who* cannot be considered a subordinate conjunction. A subordinate conjunction cannot be the subject of a verb, but *who* is the subject of the verb *will win*. Thus, *who* is given the special name *relative pronoun*. The word *who* is a pronoun taking the place of the noun *man*. The sentence literally means *The man (the man will win the race) must practice constantly*.

Relative pronouns eliminate repetition. Look at the following examples.

Without a relative pronoun: Ms. Carr works sixty hours a week. Ms. Carr wants a more responsible position with the company.

With a relative pronoun: Ms. Carr, *who* works sixty hours a week, wants a more responsible position with the company.

Notice that the sentence with the relative pronoun combines two sentences into one and names Ms. Carr only once. As we mentioned, relative pronouns connect subordinate clauses to main clauses. Here, *who works sixty hours a week* is a subordinate clause. Without the main clause, *Ms. Carr wants a more responsible position with the company*, the subordinate clause is incomplete.

PRACTICE SENTENCES 4–2
Underline the subordinate clauses in the following sentences.

Example: Molly was afraid to go home <u>because her husband was there</u>.

1. Although he has abused her for years, she has not told anyone.

2. He would get better if she didn't say anything.

3. Some of her friends suspected because they saw bruises on her face and arms.

4. Many battered women are hesitant to mention abuse because they are afraid.

5. Although it shouldn't be the case, some are ashamed to admit abuse.

6. Because his parents were alcoholics, her husband had been an abused child.

7. Although he had never harmed the children, she was afraid of that possibility.

8. Molly studied spouse abuse when she was in college.

9. She decided to talk to her professor when she recognized her situation.

10. Even though he sympathized with her, the professor told her to confront the problem in a clinical setting.

Adjective Clauses

Subordinate clauses are like phrases in that they function as either adjectives, adverbs, or nouns.

> **Adjective clauses** modify nouns or pronouns and always follow the words they modify. Adjective clauses are frequently introduced by relative pronouns.

Just like one-word adjectives, adjective clauses answer the questions *Which one? What kind? How many? and Whose?*

The man who repaired my car graduated from MIT.
> *Who repaired my car* is an adjective clause introduced by the relative pronoun *who,* modifying the noun *man,* and answering the question *Which man?*

Jackel and Swaim Company has an antique chest that I want.
> *That I want* is an adjective clause introduced by the relative pronoun *that,* modifying the noun *chest,* and answering the question *Which chest?*

It is not unusual, however, to find adjective clauses introduced by subordinate conjunctions.

Meet me at the bar where we first met.
> *Where we first met* is an adjective clause modifying the noun *bar,* introduced by the subordinate conjunction *where,* and answering the question *Which bar?*

Now is the time when a decision must be made.
> *When a decision must be made* is an adjective clause modifying the noun *time,* introduced by the subordinate conjunction *when,* and answering the question *Which time?*

PRACTICE SENTENCES 4–3

In the following sentences, underline the adjective clauses.

Example: The workout machine that I bought is versatile.

1. The bench, which is covered in leather, is five feet long.

2. All the attachment parts and accessories, which are high-quality steel, work together smoothly.

3. The base, which is solid and level, provides a good foundation for the entire machine.

4. The leg lift, which can handle four hundred pounds, is connected to the pile of weights at the front of the machine.

5. The lift bar, which can be set at three different positions, has comfortable hand grips.

6. The weights, which are made of shiny steel, range from twenty-five pounds to four hundred pounds.

7. I planned a daily schedule that I intended to follow every day.

8. After three weeks on the machine that I had bought, I could feel my body firming.

9. My body, which was firming up nicely, began to get lazy.

10. Now my fine machine, which has so many good features, rests undisturbed in the basement.

Adverb Clauses

> **Adverb clauses** modify adjectives, verbs, or other adverbs and are introduced by subordinate conjunctions such as *where, if, when, because, although,* and *before.* Like one-word adverbs, adverb clauses answer the questions *How? When? Where? Why? To what extent?* and *On what condition?*

If I clean the house today, I can play golf this weekend.
> *If I clean the house today* is an adverb clause introduced by the subordinate conjunction *if* and answering the question *On what condition?*

I could not work the problem <u>because my mind was on the game</u>.
> *Because my mind was on the game* is an adverb clause beginning with the subordinate conjunction *because* and answering the question *Why?*

Mow the lawn <u>after you go to the grocery store</u>.
> *After you go to the grocery store* is an adverb clause beginning with the subordinate conjunction *after* and answering the question *When?*

PRACTICE SENTENCES 4-4

Underline the adverb clauses in the following sentences.

Example: <u>If the garage isn't painted soon</u>, it may begin to rot.

1. We finally added a garage to the house twenty years after the home was constructed.

2. The garage protects us and the cars whenever the weather is bad.

3. The garage needed gutters, however, because the roof spilled over right at the entrance.

4. When we had enough money, the gutters were added.

5. If we had it to do over again, we would have the garage painted.

6. We thought we would paint the garage when the construction was finished.

7. Although we had good intentions, we did not finish the job.

8. Even though the flat ceiling is easy to paint with rollers, we didn't get it painted.

9. The peaks were not painted because we did not have a ladder.

10. Whenever our neighbors speak of community pride, we bow our heads in shame.

11. They may be glad if our garage rots and collapses.

PRACTICE SENTENCES 4-5

Underline the adverb clauses in the following sentences.

Example: Nathan bought a truck <u>because he hauled a lot of equipment to his land on the river</u>.

1. When the weather was nice, he carried a gas stove, an inflatable boat, inner tubes, and several friends.

2. Nathan and his friends usually stayed until it got dark.

3. The truck was easy to pack up since it didn't have a camper top.

4. Sometimes Nathan went camping by himself because he liked time alone by the river.

5. Once when he was there by himself, a violent thunderstorm came up.

6. Even though the road was muddy, the truck came through fine.

7. On another occasion, Nathan went to the river while there was snow on the ground.

8. Although snow was up to the axle, the truck kept going.

9. Nathan returned home because he got cold.

10. He got stuck in his driveway because he could not see the ice under the snow.

Remember that adjective clauses and adverb clauses are modifying clauses. That is, they add extra information to clarify something else. Sentences that contain adjective and adverb clauses must also contain main clauses. If they did not, the sentences would not express complete thoughts.

If I clean the house today is a subordinate clause; it does not express a complete thought. On the other hand, *The man graduated from MIT, Jackel and Swaim Company has an antique chest,* and *I can play golf this weekend* are all sentences, expressing complete thoughts. Notice that modifying clauses can be omitted from sentences and the sentences still express complete thoughts. Another thing to remember in studying subordinate clauses is that the whole clause works as one word.

The <u>black</u> car needs a good coating of wax.
Black is a one-word adjective describing *car.*

The car <u>that is painted black</u> needs a good coating of wax.
That is painted black is an adjective clause modifying the noun *car.*

In analyzing the subordinate clause, though, you cannot say *Which car? Black* car. You must say *Which car? The one that is painted black.* The words in a subordinate clause are a unit. You cannot separate the words and have the separated words modify the main clause. Again, you must consider the group of related words in the subordinate clause as one word.

Also, in studying clauses, do not be surprised to find phrases and clauses that seem to do the same thing.

The man <u>reading the road map</u> is lost.
The man <u>who is reading the road map</u> is lost.

The first sentence contains the participial phrase *reading the road map,* which modifies the noun *man.* The second sentence contains the adjective clause *who is reading the road map,* which modifies the noun *man.* Both the phrase and the clause do the same thing. The difference between them is grammatical. The phrase does not contain a subject and a verb, and the clause does. Sometimes different grammatical constructions can communicate the same meaning. This choice of different ways to say the same thing gives language flexibility and variety. If you have a good understanding of what phrases are and what clauses are, you will not have trouble distinguishing between them.

Noun Clauses

Noun clauses are usually introduced by relative pronouns.

John knows <u>who will win the race this year.</u>
> *Who will win the race this year* is a noun clause. It is the direct object of the verb *knows* and is introduced by the relative pronoun *who.*

Nouns, unlike adjectives and adverbs, are not modifiers. They are naming words. Nouns commonly function as subjects, direct objects, objects of prepositions, and predicate nominatives, though they can have other functions, too.

> The point that you must remember is that nouns are more important in sentences than adjectives and adverbs. If you take a noun clause out of a sentence, the sentence will no longer stand on its own.

<u>Whoever completes the assignment first</u> wins the cheesecake.
> *Whoever completes the assignment first* cannot be left out of the sentence without destruction of the meaning. *Wins the cheesecake* cannot stand on its own. It is not a main clause because it does not contain a subject and therefore cannot express a complete thought.

Adjectives and adverbs can be removed from a sentence just as your tonsils and your appendix can be removed from your body. Without adjectives and adverbs the sentence can still function, although the meaning of the sentence may be altered. For example, *The boys who wear white socks are spurned by the girls* implies a different meaning from *The boys are spurned by the girls. Who wear white socks* is an essential adjective clause because it is essential to the meaning of the sentence. The girls do not spurn all the boys, only those who wear white socks. The sentence without the adjective clause, however, indicates that the girls spurn all the boys. Nevertheless, whether the sentence contains the adjective clause or not, it still functions and still makes sense. On the other hand, if a noun clause is removed from a sentence, the sentence can no longer function, just as your car could no longer function if the engine were removed.

Remember the importance of a noun clause to a sentence, or you will not always be able to recognize a complex sentence. A complex sentence contains one main clause and at least one subordinate clause. (See Chapter 5 for more on complex sentences.) When the subordinate clause is an adjective clause, the main clause still makes sense without it:

> **Adjective:** Anna gave Phil, who is her neighbor's husband, a gold ring.
> With the adjective clause *who is her neighbor's husband* omitted, the main clause still expresses a complete thought, *Anna gave Phil a gold ring.*

When an adverb clause is omitted from a sentence, the main clause that is left can stand alone.

> **Adverb:** I would like to finish the novel before I mow the lawn.
> With *before I mow the lawn* omitted, the main clause still expresses a complete thought, *I would like to finish the novel.*

The sentences containing the adjective clause and the adverb clause are complex sentences. Each sentence contains one main clause and one subordinate clause.

The sentence you read earlier containing a noun clause is also a complex sentence.

> Whoever completes the assignment first wins the cheesecake.

In this sentence the subordinate clause is the noun clause *whoever completes the assignment first,* which functions as the subject. The main clause is the whole sentence. Thus the sentence is a complex sentence containing one main clause and one subordinate clause. When the subordinate clause is a noun clause, it is so important to the main clause that it is inherently part of the main clause itself. If you put the subordinate clause in brackets and underline the main clause, the sample sentence looks like this:

> [Whoever completes the assignment first] wins the cheesecake.

Notice what happens if the subordinate clause is a noun clause functioning as the object of a preposition.

> Give the lab report to [whoever is on duty.]

The main clause would be left hanging at the word *to* without an object for the preposition if the subordinate noun clause were omitted. Notice again that the subordinate clause is a group of related words functioning as one word. If the sentence had read, *Give the lab report to Dr. Smith,* then *Dr. Smith* would have been the object of the preposition *to.* Now, however, instead of just one person's name you have a clause *(whoever is on duty)* functioning as the object of the preposition. The principle is the same.

Since noun clauses function as subjects, direct objects, objects of prepositions, or predicate nominatives, you may find it helpful to study examples of each before you start identifying noun clauses in practice sentences:

Subject: Whoever shoots an arrow through the axe handles will win Penelope's hand.

Direct object: I think that Sam Brame is the best-dressed man in town.

Object of preposition: The boss is saving the gold drafting set for whoever produces the best design.

Predicate nominative: The job is what Greg needs.

PRACTICE SENTENCES 4-6

Underline the noun clauses in the following sentences, and in the blanks provided indicate whether each is used as a subject, a direct object, an object of a preposition, or a predicate nominative.

Example: Roy Lee knew that he wanted to meet the new girl at work.

<u>d.o.</u>

1. He felt that she was friendly and pretty.

_____

2. But he didn't know who she was.

_____

3. He wanted someone to introduce him to whoever this new girl in the neighborhood might be.

_____

4. Someone told him that her name was Tomasina.

_____

5. Roy Lee asked that she join him for a cup of coffee.

_____

6. Whatever restaurant they attended was fine with him.

   _____

7. He enjoyed her company and found out that her name *was* Tomasina.

   _____

8. Whatever her background might have been soon became unimportant.

   _____

9. He believed that the relationship could never work.

   _____

10. Tomasina would not go out with whoever smoked cigarettes.

    _____

Misplaced Subordinate Clauses

Effectively using subordinate clauses can improve your writing. But an improper use of subordinate clauses can confuse, if not amuse, your reader. You must make sure that adjective clauses are placed near the words they modify.

> The book belongs to the young student that contains three hundred pages of color reproductions.
>> As stated, the student contains three hundred pages of color reproductions.

The sentence should have been written so that the adjective clause *that contains three hundred pages of color reproductions* was placed nearer the word it modifies:

> The book that contains three hundred pages of color reproductions belongs to the young student.

> John Fergusson bought a tractor from a local farmer that runs on diesel fuel.

A sentence like this would amuse your reader—at your expense. The adjective clause should be placed nearer the word *tractor:*

> From a local farmer, John Fergusson bought a tractor that runs on diesel fuel.

Mixed Sentence Construction

In mixed sentence construction the subject and the predicate do not agree. Sometimes you end sentences differently than how you began them. Mixed sentence construction creates awkward, grammatically incorrect sentences that are unclear. There is no magic rule for avoiding this except to pay close attention to sentence structure when you revise and proofread.

Here is a common example of mixed sentence construction:

> The essay "How to Tame a Wild Tongue," the author describes the forms Spanish takes in border towns.

Here are two correct versions of the sentence:

> In the essay "How to Tame a Wild Tongue," the author describes the forms Spanish takes in border towns.

> The essay "How to Tame a Wild Tongue" is about the forms Spanish takes in border towns.

Another common example of mixed sentence construction is the following sentence:

> Because they were tired caused them to fall asleep during the movie.

Here are two correct versions of the sentence:

> Because they were tired, they fell asleep during the movie.

> They were tired, and they fell asleep during the movie.

Sentences that seem to have questions built into them also commonly lead to mixed sentence construction:

> She asked him did he drive or walk.

Often, writers sense that there is a question in a sentence like this, so they tack on a question mark, which isn't grammatically correct:

> She asked him did he drive or walk?

Here are two correct versions of the sentence:

> She asked him if he drove or walked.

> She asked him, "Did you drive or walk?"
> > In the second correct version, the question mark is appropriate because the question has been separated from the main clause as dialogue.

REVIEW EXERCISE 4–A   IDENTIFYING TYPES OF SUBORDINATE CLAUSES

In the blanks provided, indicate whether the clauses (in italics) are adjective (adj.), adverb (adv.), or noun (n.) clauses.

Example: *Whoever mows my lawn* will be paid twenty-five dollars.

_____ noun _____

1. *Although Calvin was in good physical shape,* he was lazy.

_____

2. He bought a new lawnmower from a friend *who owned a John Deere dealership.*

_____

3. The mower, *which operated perfectly,* usually remained parked in an outbuilding.

_____

4. He asked people *if they knew a teenager willing to mow his lawn.*

_____

5. He discovered *that his own neighbor would do the job.*

_____

6. It took four mowings *before the young man did the job correctly.*

_____

7. *Although he liked the fellow,* Calvin discovered damage to the new mower.

   _____

8. The blades were dull and pitted *even though the mower had been used only a month.*

   _____

9. Calvin's friend who owned the John Deere dealership said the damage amounted to over a hundred dollars.

   _____

10. *After he considered the situation,* Calvin decided to mow the lawn himself.

   _____

Name _____

Class _____

Section _____ Score:_____

EDITING TEST 4–A   CORRECTING MISPLACED SUBORDINATE CLAUSES

In the space provided, rewrite each of the following sentences by placing the modifying subordinate clauses nearer the words they modify.

Example: Mr. DeCinzio is the tall man using the snow shovel who is our mayor.

Mr. DeCinzio, who is our mayor, is the tall man

using the snow shovel.

1. Becky used her new blender to make a carrot cake for her friend that she got for Christmas.

   _____

   _____

2. Renata has a dead skunk in her driveway that needs to be removed.

   _____

   _____

3. Darren shot the deer with his rifle that was eating all his corn.

   _____

   _____

4. Because he was caught smoking in the men's room, the principal sent Roberto home.

   _____

   _____

5. The doctor gave Brian medicine for his sick stomach who had already missed four days of work.

_____

_____

6. Alice told her husband to be home promptly for dinner who had been arriving later and later.

_____

_____

7. The young man broke several pieces of equipment in the chemistry lab that was not doing well in the course.

_____

_____

8. The employees were ignored during the merger who had worked there for thirty years.

_____

_____

9. The piece of metal struck Herman in the head that had to be removed.

_____

_____

10. Ling dropped the iron on her foot, which was set for 130 degrees.

_____

_____

MASTERY TEST 4-A   USING SUBORDINATE CLAUSES

Write sentences containing the following specified clauses, and underline the clause.

Example: an adjective clause beginning with *that*

The tall brick building that is located on South

Campus is not adequately lighted at night.

1. an adjective clause beginning with *who*

   _____

   _____

2. a noun clause used as the object of a preposition

   _____

   _____

3. an adverb clause beginning with *since*

   _____

   _____

4. a noun clause used as a predicate nominative

   _____

   _____

5. an adverb clause beginning with *unless*

   _____

   _____

6. a noun clause used as a subject

_____

_____

7. an adverb clause beginning with *if*

_____

_____

8. a noun clause used as a direct object

_____

_____

9. an adjective clause beginning with *which*

_____

_____

10. an adverb clause beginning with *because*

_____

_____

Writing Assignments

Assignment 4-1 Write one paragraph (about half a page) about your most treasured physical possession. How does your enjoyment of it differ from the enjoyment you get in your most treasured relationship (best friend, parent, sibling, or other)? What can an object give you that a person can't? What can a person give you that an object can't?

Assignment 4-2 In three paragraphs (about one and a half pages), compare and contrast a local and national news program (pick one story from each broadcast). Is the local newscaster different from or similar in appearance to the national newscaster? Does each newscaster present his or her information differently? Which story (local or national) seems more important to you? Why?

Go Electronic!

For additional readings, exercises, and Internet activities, visit the Longman English pages at:

    http://longman.awl.com/englishpages

If you need a user name and password, please see your instructor.

More Practice with Your Writing and Grammar Skills

For additional practice with your writing and grammar skills, use the Writer's ToolKit CD–ROM included with this text. The ToolKit provides a wealth of computerized tutorials and practice activities.

Sentence Types, Sentence Variety, and Sentence Combining

In order to give your writing variety, you will need to use the four types of sentences: simple, compound, complex, and compound-complex.

Later in this chapter, you will learn how to use your knowledge of sentence types to write more effective sentences through the use of sentence variety, parallelism, and the control of excessive main clauses and subordination.

Sentence Types

Simple Sentences

> A **simple sentence** contains one main clause. That is, it contains one subject and one verb and expresses a complete thought.

s.   v.
Jake loves Ruth.

s.   v.
Anne has become a successful lawyer.

Both sentences are simple sentences. An imperative command can also be a simple sentence.

Stop!
Hush!

Stop! and *Hush!* are simple sentences. The subject *you* is understood, and the individual words express a complete thought. Simple sentences can also have compound subjects.

> John, Ted, Bob, Alice, and Sheila went to the country fair.
>> The subject is compounded five times. Grammatically, however, it still has only one subject and one verb and thus is a simple sentence. Similarly, the verb can be compounded.

> Shirley cleaned the house, washed her dress, and went to dinner at Delmonico's.
>> The verb is compounded three times, but the sentence is still a simple sentence. It contains several verbs, which all have the same subject.

And, of course, a simple sentence can contain a compound subject and a compound verb.

> John, Mary, Ted, Susan, Greg, and Peggy went to dinner, danced until 8:00, and saw a play at the local theater.
>> This sentence is still just a simple sentence. It contains only one verb and one subject. The same group of nouns is the subject of the same group of verbs.

Remember when studying sentence types that you are counting only clauses. All you have to do is learn the four types of sentences and then count the number of main and subordinate clauses in a sentence to see which type of sentence you have. But only clauses count.

> By hanging onto the window ledge, Barbara was able to escape the fire in her room.
>> *Hanging onto the window ledge* is a participial phrase and *to escape the fire in her room* is an infinitive phrase, but the sentence is a simple sentence because it contains only one verb, *was*, and one subject, *Barbara*. The whole sentence, of course, expresses a complete thought. Do not be misled by regarding verbal phrases as subordinate clauses. Remember, phrases do not contain subjects and verbs.

PRACTICE SENTENCES 5-1

Underline the subject(s) and circle the verb(s) in each of the following simple sentences.

Example: Angel (plays) in the sprinkler every afternoon.

1. She connects the hose by herself.

2. She attaches the sprinkler and turns the faucet.

3. In no time, she is soaking wet and having fun.

4. Sometimes her brother Julio joins her.

5. Angel and Julio turn the sprinkler on each other.

6. Usually one of them gets mad.

7. The last time, Julio squirted his sister good.

8. Angel ran to Mommy and told on him.

9. Mommy and Angel talked to Julio and warned him.

10. With Mommy back in the house, Julio gave Angel a face full of water.

Compound Sentences

> A **compound sentence** contains two or more main clauses and no subordinate clauses. You might think of a compound sentence as two or more simple sentences put into one sentence.

The main clauses of a compound sentence can be joined in two ways. They may be joined by a semicolon:

In some ways transformational grammar is easier than traditional grammar; transformational grammar uses fewer terms.

They may be joined by a comma and a coordinate conjunction *(and, or, nor, for, but, yet, so)*.

In some ways transformational grammar is easier than traditional grammar, but most students prefer the traditional approach.

Remember that a compound sentence can be composed of more than two main clauses. It can have as many main clauses as you can think up, as long as it contains no subordinate clauses.

In some ways transformational grammar is easier than traditional grammar, but most students prefer the traditional method; they are more comfortable with the vocabulary of traditional grammar, and they are hesitant to face a new way of studying the language.

That compound sentence contains four main clauses and no subordinate clauses.

First main clause:	In some ways transformational grammar is easier than traditional grammar,
Second main clause:	but most students prefer the traditional method;
Third main clause:	they are more comfortable with the vocabulary of traditional grammar,
Fourth main clause:	and they are hesitant to face a new way of studying the language.

The first and second main clauses are joined by a comma and the coordinate conjunction *but*. The second and third main clauses are joined by a semicolon. The third and fourth main clauses are joined by a comma and the coordinate conjunction *and*.

As you have seen, compound sentences connect main clauses. However, the main clauses they connect should relate to each other logically. For example, a sentence such as *James Comer is a strong Democrat, and Lassie has fleas* is ridiculous. Though grammatically correct, the sentence contains two main clauses that are not logically related.

PRACTICE SENTENCES 5–2

Indicate the break(s) between the main clauses in the following compound sentences by putting a circle at the break(s) between main clauses.

Example: William decided to get a dog, but he didn't know what kind.

1. He talked to some people, but everyone told him something different.

2. Some people prefer small dogs, yet many others like big dogs.

3. He looked through some books, but they didn't help him.

4. Finally, William went to a nearby pet store, and he looked at the varieties available.

5. He didn't like the thought of a dog in the house, and he preferred larger dogs anyway.

6. William got his girlfriend Jane to go with him to the pet store, but she was only going to provide advice.

7. At the store William fell in love with a beautiful Irish setter, and Jane liked the dog also.

8. William wanted to buy the dog, but the price was five hundred dollars.

9. He really wanted the dog, so he paid the price, and he and Jane took the dog to its new home.

10. The dog likes to get into other people's garbage and chase cars, but William has never regretted the five hundred dollars.

Complex Sentences

> A **complex sentence** has one main clause and one or more subordinate clauses.

[After I read the article], I disagreed with the author even more than before.

> *After I read the article* is an introductory adverb clause. *I disagreed with the author even more than before* is a main clause. The sentence is complex.

The man [who wins the most primaries] will receive the nomination in Philadelphia, [where the convention is to be held].

> The above sentence has one main clause (underlined) and two subordinate clauses (bracketed), so it is a complex sentence. (See pp. 278–279.)

Remember from the preceding chapter, however, that noun clauses are different from modifying clauses. With noun clauses the subordinate clause will be an integral part of the main clause.

[Whoever wins the primaries] will go to Philadelphia.

> *Whoever wins the primaries* is a noun clause, subject of the verb *will go*. The main clause is the whole sentence *W129hoever wins the primaries will go to Philadelphia.* You must consider the noun clause subject to be an integral part of the main clause; obviously *will go to Philadelphia* could not be a main clause since it neither contains a subject nor expresses a complete thought. The whole sentence is a complex sentence.

PRACTICE SENTENCES 5-3

In the following sentences, underline the main clauses and bracket the subordinate clauses.

Example: <u>Bella decided</u> [that she was going to take up gardening.]

1. The first thing that she did was till a spot of ground in her backyard.

2. After she finished with the tilling, she went to the local garden supply store and bought some seed.

3. She knew that she had to plant the seeds the proper depth and the proper distance apart.

4. She added some fertilizer to each hole that she dug.

5. Then Bella turned the sprinkler on the area that she had prepared.

6. After she had done all this, she waited for the plants to come up.

7. Three weeks later she saw that nothing was growing in the garden.

8. She decided that she needed some help.

9. A friend who had tended a garden for years came over to have a look.

10. Bella's friend told her that she had added too much fertilizer to each plant.

You should realize that some subordinate clauses functioning as adjectives and nouns may omit the relative pronouns ordinarily used to connect the subordinate clause to the main clause.

A 1956 Thunderbird is the car I want.
> *I want* is an adjective clause modifying the noun *car*. The sentence could be written with the relative pronoun included: A 1956 Thunderbird is the car *that I want.*

The same situation occurs with noun clauses.

The man at the nursery knows I want the pink azalea.
> *I want the pink azalea* is a noun clause that functions as the direct object of the verb *knows.*

The sentence could be written this way:

The man at the nursery knows *that I want the pink azalea.*

Both sentences are complex sentences whether the relative pronoun is present or not.

Remember, a clause is a group of related words that contains a subject and a verb. Every time you find a different verb that takes its own subject, you have another clause. In the sentence *The man at the nursery knows I want the pink azalea,* you should recognize that *man* is the subject of the verb *knows* and that *I* is the subject of the verb *want.*

Compound-Complex Sentences

> A **compound-complex** sentence contains two or more main clauses and one or more subordinate clauses.

I wanted to go to the outdoor concert, but I had to change my plans since my lab report is due by 5:00 P.M.
I wanted to go to the outdoor concert is a main clause; *but I had to change my plans* is a main clause; *since my lab report is due by 5:00 P.M.* is a subordinate adverb clause telling why or on what condition.

Here the main clauses are underlined and the subordinate clauses are in brackets:

I wanted to go to the outdoor concert, but I had to change my plans [since my lab report is due by 5:00 P.M.]

Look at the following sentence:

[When the plants started producing,] we noticed a problem [because many of the tomatoes had rotten spots on the bottom;] we called a botanist, and he told us the solution.

Notice that the sentence contains three main clauses and two subordinate clauses. The sentence is compound-complex.

Do not forget that some of your subordinate clauses in compound-complex sentences may be noun clauses.

noun clause
I know [what you want to hear,] so you are not going to be disappointed.

Also, you must remember that some of the relative pronouns may be omitted in compound-complex sentences just as they are in complex sentences.

Dr. Smith said [you performed well], but he told me [you had some trouble with a chapter] [you had worked on the week before].
You performed well is a noun clause direct object; the relative pronoun *that* is omitted. *You had some trouble with a chapter* is a noun clause direct object; again the relative pronoun *that* is omitted. *You worked on the week before* is a subordinate adjective clause modifying *chapter;* the relative pronoun *that* is omitted.

PRACTICE SENTENCES 5–4

Underline the main clauses in the following compound-complex sentences and bracket the subordinate clauses.

Example: <u>Ramona wants to get a job</u> [that will pay her well,] <u>but she doesn't have a college degree.</u>

1. Mort bought a new car, but he was dissatisfied with it since it could go only 120 miles an hour on a racetrack.

2. Sue got her pepperoni pizza, but she sent it back when she saw anchovies on it.

3. Because he was not a very good dancer, Alfred was uncomfortable at parties; in fact, he was even uncomfortable around girls.

4. Look before you leap, or you may regret your move for a long time.

5. The jury members entered the courtroom when the judge called them, but they still had not reached a decision.

6. The man said that he did not agree with the new law; furthermore, he intended to change it.

7. Arlene looked at houses for days, but she bought the one on Lowe Street because she liked the floor plan and the location.

8. William thought his watch was broken, but it only needed a battery.

9. Fred purchased a scientific calculator since he was not good in math, and his grades improved significantly.

10. Lamont saw the most beautiful girl he had ever seen, but she was just a picture in a magazine.

✔ **A CHECKLIST FOR SENTENCE TYPES**

Sentence Types	Main Clauses	Subordinate Clauses
Simple	1	0
Compound	2 or more	0
Complex	1	1 or more
Compound-Complex	2 or more	1 or more

Sentence Variety and Improvement

Sentence Variety

Good writing contains a variety of sentence structures and types. It has introductory phrases and clauses sometimes; short, simple sentences sometimes; and long, involved compound-complex sentences sometimes; occasionally, good writing has a compound sentence or two, though compound sentences are perhaps the least used of the four types.

> Denise wanted to buy a 1978 Volkswagen convertible. She knew it was a classic. She was not sure she could afford the price the owner asked. Seven thousand dollars seemed like too much. She considered offering $6,000. She really thought $5,000 or $5,500 was more reasonable. She knew the car had to be hers. She test-drove it and offered $5,300. There was some negotiating. Denise and the owner settled on a price of $6,000. The owner wanted more. Denise felt it was too much. But now Denise is the proud owner.

The paragraph is rather dull and choppy. It lacks variety and a smooth flow. Now read the revised version of the paragraph and see the difference:

> Although Denise knew the 1978 Volkswagen convertible was a classic, she was not sure she could afford the price asked by the owner. Thinking $7,000 was too much, she considered offering $6,000. In her mind she felt $5,000 or $5,500 was a more reasonable price, but in her heart she knew the car had to be hers. She test-drove it and offered $5,300. After some negotiation, Denise and the owner settled on a purchase price of $6,000. The owner felt she should have gotten more, and Denise felt she had paid too much. However, Denise is now the proud owner of a classic automobile.

The revised version has more complex sentences.

If used skillfully, complex sentences and compound-complex sentences can communicate more information in fewer sentences and with a smoother flow than simple sentences and compound sentences. If you are conscious of varying your sentence patterns when you write, you can greatly improve your writing. There are, however, other techniques besides varying sentence types:

1. Beginning sentences with participial phrases is an excellent way to alter the potentially monotonous subject-verb-object pattern.

> Bob loves Cheryl deeply, and he proposed to her last Friday night.

The sentence is grammatically correct. But look what happens when the sentence is rewritten with an introductory participial phrase:

> Loving Cheryl deeply, Bob proposed to her last Friday night.

The verbal quality of *loving* immediately gets the reader's attention. Also, the sentence has a little more suspense since the reader has to wait longer before coming to the main part of the sentence.

2. Another useful technique for getting variety in your sentence structures is to begin some sentences with introductory adverb clauses.

> The championship game was canceled because of rain. Everyone stayed in the dorm.

The two sentences do not even seem to belong together. But by use of an introductory adverb clause, the two sentences become one sentence.

> Since the championship game was canceled due to rain, everyone stayed in the dorm.

Sentence variety can be improved somewhat just by the use of an adverb or adverbs at the beginning of the sentence.

> Interestingly enough, everyone stayed in the dorm.

Interestingly enough is an adverbial expression. Since it does not modify any particular word in the sentence, it is known as an absolute construction. The expression just used is called an *adverb absolute*. Be sure not to overuse the adverb absolute construction; it is merely a technique for achieving variety and is not necessarily beneficial or detrimental. Some readers do not like adverb absolutes like *interestingly* and *hopefully*. Author and commentator Edwin Newman has a sign over his office door that reads, "Abandon *hopefully,* all ye that enter here."

EDITING PRACTICE 5–5

The following sentences begin with the subject; rewrite them using either introductory participial phrases, introductory adverb clauses, or adverb absolutes.

Example: Sonya worked all summer, and she earned the money for her college tuition.

> Working all summer, Sonya earned the money for her college tuition.

1. Susan's car was badly damaged in an accident, and she had to start taking a taxi to work.

2. Nicole was planning to get married, and she had a lawyer prepare a prenuptial agreement.

_____

_____

3. Lewis dropped his lunch tray in the cafeteria. He was extremely embarrassed.

_____

_____

4. Emilia already has plans for her tax refund. She wants a ten-speed bicycle, some six to seven ounces of leather for her projects, and a new SLR camera.

_____

_____

5. Sara finally got her car started and then went on to work.

_____

_____

6. Sheila gave a fine performance on opening night even though she had never acted before.

_____

_____

7. It is interesting that the town's new zoning limits do not include the mayor's house.

_____

_____

8. Lee wants to be a professional dancer, but his father says he can't make a living at dancing.

_____

_____

9. Libby, although she is only fifteen, is the soloist at her church.

_____

_____

10. Byron is depressed now, but he will feel better on payday.

_____

_____

Parallelism

Another way to improve your sentence structure is by the effective use of parallelism.

> **Parallelism** is the similarity of grammatical form between two or more elements that serve the same function. The underlying principle of parallelism is that in a series nouns should be balanced with nouns, verbs with verbs, adjectives with adjectives, infinitive phrases with infinitive phrases, etc.

In the sentence _I have an apple, an orange, and a tomato,_ the words _an_ before _apple, an_ before _orange,_ and _a_ before _tomato_ illustrate the correct parallel use of words. The sentence _I bought an apple, orange, and a tomato_ is not parallel. The word _an_ appears before the word _apple_ and _a_ appears before _tomato,_ but since there is no adjective before the word _orange,_ the series is not parallel. Errors of this kind are known as _faulty parallelism._ Such errors can be distracting to readers. Notice the faulty parallelism in the following sentence: _This summer I want to get plenty of rest, to attend summer school, and play golf._ As is often the case, the faulty parallelism can be corrected in more than one way. The sign of the infinitive _(to)_ can be added before _play golf: This summer I want to get plenty of rest, to attend summer school, and to play golf._ Or the sign of the infinitive may be given just once, so that the other two phrases are parallel to the word _to: This summer I want to get plenty of rest, attend summer school, and play golf._ The second way is preferable because fewer words are used to achieve equal clarity.

Phrases are parallel when infinitives are paired with infinitives and gerunds are paired with gerunds.

Parallel: Jack wants to be elected chairman and to set up a new finance committee.
The infinitive phrases *to be elected chairman* and *to set up a new finance committee* are parallel.

Parallel: Dawn likes riding horses and playing tennis.
The two gerund phrases *riding horses* and *playing tennis* are parallel.

Faulty parallelism arises when phrases are not in the same grammatical form.

Not parallel: Dawn likes riding horses and to play tennis.
The gerund phrase *riding horses* is not grammatically equal to the infinitive phrase *to play tennis*.

Parallel subordinate clauses repeat the relative pronouns that introduce them.

Parallel: Kurt knows that he will get the job and that he will be good at it.
The subordinate clauses *that he will get the job* and *that he will be good at it* are parallel because both are introduced by the relative pronoun *that* and both are objects of the verb *knows*.

When one of the relative pronouns is omitted, the sentence is confusing.

Not parallel: Kurt knows that he will get the job and he will be good at it.

Sometimes entire sentences are parallel (or balanced).

Parallel: The country will move ahead with the administration's new programs. The citizens will move ahead with the country.

Writer's Tip Parallel sentences are often used in speeches because they are dramatic and effective. However, too many parallel sentences in writing may seem repetitious. In your writing be sure the elements you connect are parallel.

Not parallel: Joan runs to lose weight, for exercise, and because she enjoys running.
The sentence connects an infinitive phrase *(to lose weight)*, a prepositional phrase *(for exercise)*, and an adverb clause *(because she enjoys running)*. The sentence can be made parallel if all the elements are made grammatically equal.

Parallel: Joan runs because she loses weight, gets exercise, and enjoys running.

Not parallel: We can improve ourselves by setting goals and determination.

Parallel: We can improve ourselves by setting goals and having determination.

Not parallel: Whether in a crowd or when he was alone, Conrad was always the same.

Parallel: Whether alone or in a crowd, Conrad was always the same.

> **Not parallel:** Irving Smith is a man with a muscular build and who attends a health spa every week.
>
> **Parallel:** Irving Smith is a man who has a muscular build and (*who*) attends a health spa every week.

Sentence Combining

Sentence combining contributes to a smooth flow of sentences. If your writing sounds like a machine gun, most likely you have a string of main clauses. They can be a series of simple sentences, but they can also be poorly written compound sentences. A variety of sentence patterns can help you avoid such choppiness.

Too many main clauses in a row result in choppy and distracting writing. The Tom, Dick, and Jane books students once learned to read in elementary school are an example of how too many simple sentences cause choppiness:

> Tom has a sister. His sister is Jane. Tom and Jane have a neighbor. The neighbor is Dick. Dick has a dog. The dog is Spot.

If it were not for the excitement of learning to read, children would have a difficult time enduring many such sentences. By looking at *which* ideas relate to each other, you can begin thinking about *how* you might connect them. For instance, the passage about Tom, Jane, Dick, and Spot is both dull and choppy. Clearly something needs to be done. The first two sentences relate closely to one another, so they can be rewritten as *Tom has a sister, Jane.* Instead of stating that Tom and Jane have a neighbor, you can imply this by writing *Their neighbor Dick . . . .* The last four sentences are closely related, so they can be combined: *Their neighbor Dick has a dog named Spot.* This is only one way to rewrite the sentences, but it shows how the flow can be improved.

Compound sentences can be equally choppy when you merely string together a lot of main clauses in one sentence:

> I really like to go bowling on Friday nights, and I am pretty good, and I might make the all-star team, but I don't know many people at the bowling lanes, and I need to know the judges selecting the all-stars.

You can avoid such strung-out compound sentences by subordinating some of the clauses, by using compound verbs, by using phrases, and by rewriting the one sentence into two or more sentences.

> I enjoy my Friday night bowling and bowl pretty well. By getting to know more people at the bowling lanes, I would have a good chance of making the all-star team. A prospect must know the judges.

The long, stringy sentence has now become three sentences. There is greater variety, the paragraph is easier to read, and the essential information is not altered.

One of the main reasons for sentence combining is showing respect for your reader. Variety and smooth flow don't change your meaning, but they make your ideas more interesting and easier to follow.

EDITING PRACTICE 5-6

Here are some choppy sentences. Combine them to make them flow more smoothly.

Example: Donna likes to read books. She would rather read a novel than a textbook. Her English literature textbook is more interesting than her economics textbook. Donna hopes to become a book editor or an author.

> *A person who enjoys reading and someday hopes to be*
>
> *an editor or author, Donna would rather sit down with*
>
> *a novel than either her English literature or (especially)*
>
> *her economics textbook.*

1. Renee wants to be a doctor. She is taking Anatomy I and Biology I. The work is hard. She has to memorize many terms. She gets bored. She is determined.

---

2. Teresa is a first-year business major, and Matt is a second-year business major, and both like business, but Teresa likes advertising, and Matt likes retail.

---

3. Trevor draws well. His work is in demand. He has designed three posters. The posters are for different events. One is for a swim meet. One is for a book sale. One is for a Lauryn Hill concert.

_____

_____

_____

4. My dog Max loves pizza. He eats pepperoni pizza. He eats mushroom pizza. He eats cheese pizza. He likes all kinds of pizza.

_____

_____

_____

5. Blue roses are rare, but they exist, but they're hard to find, and they're also hard to grow, but you can grow them if you live in the right climate, but most people don't.

_____

_____

_____

6. Gabe likes soccer. He also likes baseball. He plays basketball, too. He likes all of these sports. He's good at all of them. He's best at baseball.

_____

_____

_____

7. Raelene wants to be a stockbroker. She keeps up with the stock market. She usually guesses right. Raelene will probably be a successful stockbroker.

_____

_____

_____

8. I like hip hop, but I also like the Beatles, and I like some of the blues, too, and I listen to all kinds of music, and the musical styles overlap sometimes, and I like to figure out what style is influencing another style.

_____

_____

_____

9. Maria does well in both math and English, but she likes math better, and she thinks math is easier, and she wants to do some kind of work that uses math a lot, but she isn't sure what jobs she would like, so she has to do some career research.

_____

_____

_____

10. Steffen prefers cats to dogs. He likes both animals. Cats are his favorite, though. Some people give him a hard time. They think guys should like dogs better. He just ignores them. He has six cats.

_____

_____

_____

Avoiding Excessive Subordination

 Mark Twain once wrote a story about an old man who tries to tell a story about a ram. Unfortunately, the narrator gets so bogged down in details that the story never gets told. Whenever the narrator thinks of another character, he gives so much of the character's genealogy that he forgets the character's significance to the story. The reader never does learn anything about the ram; the narrator goes to sleep before completing his tale. Your writing can get bogged down in details, too, if you subordinate excessively.

Look at the following sentence:

> The man who is now my next-door neighbor recently bought himself a new car that is so big it won't fit into his garage, which was built by the previous owner of the house, who owned a Volkswagen.

The sentence is grammatically correct, but it sounds as though it is continually running downhill. The only cure for a sentence like this is to rewrite it, rearranging the details and perhaps leaving some of them out.

> The garage, having been built for the previous owner's Volkswagen, could not accommodate my neighbor's new car.

The sentence is even more effective if shorter still.

> The garage built for the previous owner's Volkswagen could not accommodate my neighbor's new car.

REVIEW EXERCISE 5-A   IDENTIFYING SENTENCE TYPES

In the blanks provided, indicate whether the sentences are simple, compound, complex, or compound-complex.

Example: Smoking is under attack nationwide.

_____simple_____

1. Everyone knows that smoking is a bad habit.

   _____

2. Smoking puts foreign substances in your body and in the air.

   _____

3. It is true that smokers are not always considerate of those around them.

   _____

4. Nonsmokers think that they should not be exposed to secondary smoke, but others claim that nonsmokers are not the ones leading the charge to restrict smokers.

   _____

5. Many smokers feel it is the government that is trying to curtail smoking.

   _____

6. The Surgeon-General's office produces research saying that secondary smoke is harmful.

   _____

7. Many people simply do not believe that the tests are scientific or accurate; they feel that the tests are run to support a predetermined outcome.

_____

8. The tobacco companies, of course, object to the results of the tests.

_____

9. They claim that the test results are invalid.

_____

10. Whom should we believe, and how do we protect the rights of smokers and nonsmokers?

_____

EDITING TEST 5-A   CORRECTING FAULTY PARALLELISM

Each of the following sentences contains errors in parallel structure. Rewrite each sentence and correct the faulty parallelism.

Example: The typewriter needs repairing and to be cleaned.

The typewriter needs repairing and cleaning.

1. Swanson doesn't know whether he is to load the computer or if Jim will.

   _____

   _____

2. Sylvia enjoys working with trainees and likes to encourage them.

   _____

   _____

3. Lisa was instructed to deliver the package to maintenance and then she was to report to her supervisor.

   _____

   _____

4. Jerome likes to exercise, to read, and rest.

   _____

   _____

5. Whether Vincent wears dress clothes or if he is wearing casual clothes, he always looks neat and clean.

   _____

   _____

6. Participants in the event could use shovels, picks, or they could use post-hole diggers.

_____

_____

7. I would like to have a house, a farm, and barn.

_____

_____

8. Raymond enjoys reading and to watch television.

_____

_____

9. Whether Amanda weighs 120 pounds or if she weighs 170 pounds, she always feels overweight.

_____

_____

10. The computer came with a CPU, a monitor, and printer.

_____

_____

Name _____

Class _____

Section _____ Score: _____

MASTERY TEST 5-A   SENTENCE COMBINING (I)

The following sentences are short and choppy. Using introductory elements such as participial phrases and adverb clauses, combine the following choppy sentences into a smoothly flowing paragraph. Be sure not to add or delete significant words in your combination.

Example: Napoleon was famous.
            He was a general.
            He lost a big battle.
            The battle was Waterloo.
            The opponent was England.
            England was led by Wellington.
            Wellington was a duke.
            Wellington won the battle.

Although Napoleon was a famous general, he

lost the big battle of Waterloo. His opponent was

an Englishman, the Duke of Wellington.

            The snows have stopped.
            The sun has come out.
            It is spring.
            The grass is green.
            The flowers are blooming.
            The insects are coming to life.
            Moths are flying.
            They gather.
            They gather around every light.
            They get in.
            It is your house they enter.
            They are annoying.
            They don't bother anything.

_____

_____

MASTERY TEST 5-B   SENTENCE COMBINING (II)
(Same directions as Mastery Test 5-A)

1. Emil lives in a rural area.

2. It is a rural area.

3. There are few stores.

4. He cannot purchase much locally.

5. The only stores are basic.

6. There is a grocery store.

7. Emil likes merchandise.

8. He likes merchandise not available locally.

9. He orders from catalogs.

10. The catalogs come in the mail.

11. He has ordered fancy tents.

12. He has ordered a telescope.

13. He has ordered musical instruments.

14. One instrument is an accordion.

15. One is a concertina.

16. One is a fife.

17. Emil owns many things.

18. He owns a credit card.

19. He now owes five thousand dollars on the card.

MASTERY TEST 5-C SENTENCE COMBINING (III)
(Same directions as Mastery Test 5-A)

1. Collette is a student.

2. She is a student at SMU.

3. She is a good student.

4. She likes her field of study.

5. It is law.

6. She has a reason.

7. The reason is capital punishment.

8. She is against it.

9. To her it is wrong.

10. It is not moral.

11. It is cruel and inhumane punishment.

12. As a lawyer she has a voice.

13. She can be heard.

14. She has an audience.

15. The audience is for her views.

16. She likes the study of law.

17. She looks forward to graduation.

18. She looks forward to starting her own practice.

_____

_____

_____

MASTERY TEST 5-D SENTENCE COMBINING (IV)
(Same directions as Mastery Test 5-A)

1. Lucian has an interest.

2. The interest is in the environment.

3. He looked around him.

4. He didn't like what he saw.

5. He saw polluted creeks.

6. He saw polluted rivers.

7. He saw trash along the highways.

8. He saw trash in the cities.

9. He wanted to act.

10. He wanted to do something.

11. He wanted to clean up the environment.

12. He wanted to get people interested.

13. He wanted them interested in cleaning things up.

14. The public had to give support.

15. No one could do much alone.

_____

_____

_____

_____

_____

Writing Assignments

Assignment 5-1 Choose one of the following statements, and in one paragraph (about half a page), describe how it relates to your personality and life experience. Does it represent your values in some way? Does it demonstrate the kind of person you would like to be? Does it express a way you have of dealing with challenging, pleasant, personal, work, or other experiences?

All work and no play makes Jack/Jill a dull boy/girl.
Sometimes it's OK to tell a little white lie.
A bird in the hand is worth two in the bush.
People are more important than possessions.
Possessions are more satisfying than people.

Assignment 5-2 Study a fashion advertisement in a magazine. In three paragraphs (about one and a half pages), discuss what message the advertisement gives about being a man or a woman. Does it demonstrate a certain way to be handsome or pretty? Does it ignore truths about normal human bodies? Is the advertisement helpful to the human self-image? Harmful? Both? Use and analyze specific examples from the advertisement to support your ideas.

Go Electronic!

For additional readings, exercises, and Internet activities, visit the Longman English pages at:

http://longman.awl.com/englishpages

If you need a user name and password, please see your instructor.

More Practice with Your Writing and Grammar Skills

For additional practice with your writing and grammar skills, use the Writer's ToolKit CD-ROM included with this text. The ToolKit provides a wealth of computerized tutorials and practice activities.

chapter 6

Agreement

Subject–Verb Agreement

> The main thing to remember about **subject-verb agreement** is that the subject must agree with the verb in number. If the subject is singular, the verb should be singular; if the subject is plural, the verb should be plural.

Errors in agreement are easy to correct. By careful proofreading, you could probably identify all such errors. Nevertheless, it is not surprising that many people make careless slips. Children just learning the language know that the plural of *boy* is formed by adding an *-s.* They consider it only logical that the verb should also have an *-s,* so they say *The boys shows their rocks.* Unfortunately, the English language is not so conveniently logical.

> In English most nouns form their plurals by adding an *-s.*

Singular	add -s	Plural
house		houses
chair		chairs
desk		desks
car		cars
book		books
sofa		sofas
phone		phones
girl		girls

But verbs do not form their plurals in the same way. Look at the following conjugation:

Singular	Plural
I look	we look
you look	you look
he, she, it looks	they look

Notice that the form of the verb that ends in -s is singular, not plural. It is the third person singular form of the verb that ends in -s.

Singular remove -s	Plural
comes	come
runs	run
sees	see
throws	throw
jumps	jump

Notice, also, that only the present tense presents a problem. If a verb is in the past tense, for example, there is no -s form.

I looked	we looked
you looked	you looked
he, she, it looked	they looked

Remember the basic rule of subject-verb agreement: the subject must agree with the verb in number.

The boy looks.
> The word *boy* is a singular noun, so it takes the singular form of the verb *(looks)*.

The boys look.
> The word *boys* is plural, so the verb *(look)* is plural.

PRACTICE SENTENCES 6-1

In each of the following sentences, underline the correct verb choice.

Example: The crackers (is, <u>are</u>) in the box.

1. The computers for the office (is, are) to arrive this afternoon.

2. The plants (is, are) guaranteed for one year.

3. The snow blower (runs, run) smoothly.

4. The rare coins (costs, cost) over seven thousand dollars.

5. Clarissa (practices, practice) the piano three hours each day.

6. The chain saws in the local hardware store (comes, come) with many accessories.

7. My cat (eats, eat) as if there will be no tomorrow.

8. The list of volunteers for the tornado relief (is, are) growing daily.

9. The maintenance staff (puts, put) in long hours.

10. The books on the shelf (is, are) in bad condition.

Writer's Tip Beware of the following situations concerning subject-verb agreement, so you can avoid awkward choices in your writing.

> **1.** Words having an *s* in the last syllable can be misleading.

The scientist studies the problem every day.
> *Scientist* is singular because it does not end in -*s*. The verb correctly takes the singular form. If you are not careful, however, you will hear the *s* in *scientist* and consider it plural and commit the following error:

The scientist study the problem every day.
> *Scientist* is singular, but the verb *study* is plural; the subject and verb do not agree in number.

The verb can also have an *s* sound.

Quarterbacks risk their careers every time they are tackled.
> *Risk* is a verb with an *s* sound. You must realize that the verb is plural as it is and thus is correctly used with the plural *quarterbacks*. The following error is easy to make.

The quarterback risk his career every time he is tackled.
> The verb *risk* has an *s* sound, and it almost sounds correctly used. However, the third person *quarterback* is a singular noun and should have a third person singular verb, which is the verb form ending in *-s*.

The quarterback risks his career every time he is tackled.

Sometimes both the subject and the verb end in *s* sounds.

The scientist exists to work and to learn.
> Both the subject *scientist* and the verb *exists* end in *-s* sounds. But since the subject is singular and does not end in *-s* and since the verb is singular and does end in *-s*, the subject and verb agree in number. Avoid the following error:

The scientist exist to work and to learn.
> The subject is singular, but the verb is plural; thus the sentence contains an agreement error.

---

2. Some people tend to reverse the basic rule that subject and verb should agree in number.

Nonstandard: Bob do very well when given enough time.
Standard: Bob does very well when given enough time.

In the first sentence *Bob* is the singular subject, but the verb is the plural *do;* the subject and verb do not agree in number.

In the second sentence *Bob* is the singular subject and *does* is the singular verb; the subject and verb agree in number. Try to avoid writing sentences like the first example.

Nonstandard: The girls goes to a square dance every Saturday night.
Standard: The girls go to a square dance every Saturday night.

The subject and verb do not agree in the first sentence because the subject *girls* is plural but the verb *goes* is singular.

There is agreement between the subject and the verb of the second example, however. The subject *girls* and the verb *go* are both plural.

PRACTICE SENTENCES 6-2

Underline the correct verb in each of the following sentences.

Example: Elise (study, <u>studies</u>) her course notes every evening.

1. Cass (appraise, appraises) diamonds for his father's jewelry store.

2. Psychologists (say, says) everyone has some mental hangups.

3. Mrs. Williams (celebrate, celebrates) the anniversary of her gall bladder surgery every year.

4. Statisticians (say, says) Americans are getting taller.

5. Iris (go, goes) to her aerobics class every Tuesday.

6. Scientists (tell, tells) us not to smoke.

7. Criminologists (attend, attends) all the meetings they can.

8. Bernice (see, sees) her father at least once a week.

9. Mr. and Mrs. Stevens (send, sends) their daughter off to school each morning.

10. Ernest (play, plays) the title role in *The Importance of Being Earnest.*

---

3. Words and phrases coming between the subject and the verb can be misleading.

The statues in the park on Main Street are beautiful.
> *Statues* is the subject, and since it is plural, it takes the plural form of the verb *are*. *Park* and *Street* are singular, but they are objects of prepositions, not part of the subject.

John, as well as several other men, loves Mary.
> Even though the word *men* comes between the subject *John* and the verb *loves*, the sentence still must have a singular verb agreeing with the singular subject.

Similarly, if the subject were plural, the verb would be plural:

Several men, including John, love Mary.
> The plural subject *men* is not affected by the expression *including John* and therefore the verb is correctly plural, *love*.

PRACTICE SENTENCES 6-3

Underline the correct verb in each of the following sentences.

Example: The bridge with all the wire supports (<u>is</u>, are) an engineering miracle.

1. The man with the three Honda motorcycles (has, have) a broken leg.

2. The boss, as well as his employees, (expresses, express) concern for the future of the company.

3. John's collection of records, tapes, and CDs (is, are) well known by the local radio stations.

4. Many homes in this country (has, have) more than one television set.

5. Becky, along with her children, Jason and Nikki, (wax, waxes) the cars every summer.

6. The three telephones in the house (is, are) all on the same line.

7. Many NASCAR fans, including Tonya, (follows, follow) every race.

8. All of the flowers in the garden (was, were) beautiful this year.

9. The runner with the expensive shoes, warm-up suit, and athletic bag (finishes, finish) last in every race.

10. The girls with a good attitude and a desire to learn (makes, make) the best grades in the class.

---

4. Subjects connected by *and* are generally plural. That two subjects joined by *and* are plural should be obvious: one plus one equals two.

Bud and Roscoe are fine men.

> *Bud* is singular; *Roscoe* is singular—but together they are two men, and thus the subject is plural and needs a plural verb, *are*.

Of course, there may be more than two singular subjects joined by *and*:

Mark Twain, Henry James, Nathaniel Hawthorne, Herman Melville, and William Faulkner are just a few of America's well-known authors.

> Though each author is an individual, together the five authors make up a plural subject that needs the plural verb *are*.

Sometimes the two "subjects" joined by *and* relate to the same person.

My best friend and adviser is my wife.
Friend and *adviser* both mean the same person, and thus the verb is singular, *is*. Such sentences do not cause much confusion because the meaning is normally clear.

Ham and eggs is a good dish.
Though there are two separate nouns joined by *and,* the verb is singular *(is)* because *ham and eggs* refers to one particular dish.

PRACTICE SENTENCES 6–4
Underline the correct verb in each of the following sentences.

Example: The students and the faculty really (enjoys, enjoy) the first Student Appreciation Day.

1. The star guard and star center (averages, average) over eighteen points per game.

2. My roommate and I (spends, spend) much time together.

3. William Wordsworth's best friend and companion (was, were) his sister.

4. Bob, Ted, Carol, and Alice (participates, participate) in many community activities.

5. Both television sets in the house (needs, need) repairing.

6. The public and the law (is, are) beginning to crack down on drunk drivers.

7. Rupert's guns and knives (was, were) highly valued by an appraiser.

8. Lena's three cars all (needs, need) new paint jobs.

9. All types of handheld tape recorders (has, have) come down in price.

10. Mr. and Mrs. Orion (wants, want) to visit Hawaii.

---

5. Indefinite pronouns are sometimes treated as singular and sometimes as plural.

Indefinite pronouns such as *another, anyone, anybody, anything, each, either, everyone, everybody, everything, neither, no one, nobody, nothing, one, someone, somebody,* and *something* are grammatically considered singular in formal English.

Everyone on the team performs well.
> Though the word *everyone* seems to indicate more than one person the word is an indefinite pronoun that is considered to be grammatically singular, and thus *everyone* takes the singular form of the verb, *performs.*

Remember, grammar organizes the way language is used; grammar is not necessarily logical because language is not necessarily logical. You say, "The trousers are hanging on the line," even though the noun *trousers* indicates only one (singular) garment.

Each of the women puts in as much time as she can on the project.
> *Each* is an indefinite pronoun considered to be singular, so it takes the singular verb, *puts.*

Indefinite pronouns such as *several, both,* and *many* are plural when used as subjects.

Both of the men are in the race.
> *Both* is clearly plural, and therefore the verb is plural.

Several of the runners have as many as five pairs of track shoes.
> *Several* is plural and takes the plural verb *have.*

Indefinite pronouns such as *none* and *some* can be either singular or plural depending on meaning.

Some of the gold was pure.
> The word *some* is used in a singular sense to indicate one particular portion and takes the singular verb.

Some of the men were exhausted after the workday ended.
> *Some* is used as an indefinite pronoun like *several, both,* and *many.* It clearly means more than one of the men and therefore takes the plural verb.

None of that money is mine.

None of the applicants were hired.

PRACTICE SENTENCES 6-5

Underline the correct verb in the following sentences.

Example: Someone (<u>is</u>, are) going to have to take responsibility.

1. Both of the men (does, do) well when the pressure is on.

2. Somebody on the staff (wants, want) a new editor.

3. Everyone (is, are) convinced that an annual competition is worthwhile.

4. Some of the women (goes, go) to the track every morning.

5. Anything (goes, go) in the sport of rugby.

6. No one (likes, like) the aluminum bats used in college baseball.

7. Anyone who knows the rules (thinks, think) chess is a challenging game.

8. Some of the stolen bonds (was, were) recovered.

9. The coach said that anyone who hustles (makes, make) the team.

10. No one (wants, want) to do well more than Harvey.

> **6.** Singular subjects connected by *or, nor, either . . . or,* or *neither . . . nor* need a singular verb because either choice would be singular.

For example,

> Either Blanca or Larry is going to be appointed to the position.
> > If Blanca is chosen, the subject is singular. If Larry is chosen, the subject is singular. Therefore, the verb in either case would be singular, *is going.*

The same situation would exist with *neither . . . nor:*

> Neither Blanca nor Larry is going to be appointed to the position.

Be careful, however, when one of the subjects is singular and one is plural. The verb must agree with the subject nearer the verb.

> Neither the employees nor the owner has control over the strike.
> > The singular subject *owner* is nearer the verb, and thus the singular form of the verb *(has)* is used.

> Neither the owner nor the employees have control over the strike.
> > Now the plural subject *employees* is nearer the verb, so the correct verb form is the plural *have.*

PRACTICE SENTENCES 6-6

Underline the correct verb in the following sentences.

Example: Neither Paul nor Jean (<u>wants</u>, want) to work on the assignment.

1. Either the managers or the employees (is, are) to receive pay increases.

2. Neither the gym nor the library (is, are) to be opened this year.

3. Neither the students nor the instructor (is, are) about to be satisfied with the grades on the last test.

4. Neither the city manager nor the board members (plans, plan) to vote for the proposal.

5. Either the players or the coaches (is, are) planning to demand newer equipment.

6. Either the dean or the nursing instructors (is, are) to redesign the program for next fall.

7. Either Janis or Sue (is, are) qualified for the position.

8. Neither the workers nor the managers (likes, like) the new government regulations.

9. Neither Cara nor her sisters (is, are) ready for the tournament.

10. Neither Leroy nor Michael (enjoys, enjoy) the competition between them.

---

7. Sentences that have the verb preceding the subject require special attention. Many sentences beginning with prepositional phrases can be confusing.

Off the northwest coast of Scotland are the Western Isles.
> The subject is the plural *Western Isles*. Don't let the singular *coast* or the singular *Scotland* confuse you; both are objects of prepositions. Since the subject is the plural *Western Isles*, the verb is the plural *are*.

Sentences beginning with *there is* or *there are* alter the ordinary subject-verb order.

There is only one man working on the pump.
> The subject is *man*, and that is why the verb is singular.

There are three hundred men working on the reactor.
>This time the subject is the plural *men,* so the verb is the plural *are.*

In speech, especially, you have to be careful with *there is* or *there are* sentences since you have to choose your verb before you state your subject. In writing, you should avoid sentences beginning with *there is* and *there are.*

PRACTICE SENTENCES 6–7
Underline the correct verb in the following sentences.

Example: There (is, are) three ground hogs standing up in the field.

1. On the fence in the backyard (is, are) a tall stand of grass.

2. On the power lines over the driveway (is, are) more than a dozen birds.

3. There (is, are) a big mess in the kitchen.

4. In the park near the pond (stands, stand) a statue of Thomas Jefferson.

5. Behind the mirror on the wall (is, are) the looking-glass world.

6. There (is, are) three men and two women applying for the position.

7. There (is, are) a bat flying around the basement.

8. Under the bridge on Mockingbird Lane (is, are) seven or eight ducks.

9. There (is, are) a scar on the back of my right arm.

10. At the entrance into the park (stands, stand) a memorial to veterans.

> **8.** Nouns such as *family, jury, council, group, committee, board,* and *faculty* may be considered either singular or plural depending on meaning.

A word such as *family* is known as a collective noun. It can represent either one collective unit or the plural components of the unit.

A family is not as close a social unit as it used to be.
>The noun *family* refers to a collective unit (one group), and therefore the singular verb *is* must be used with the singular subject.

The family have to plan their activities for the week.
>In this sentence *family* is a plural word because it refers to the members of the group as several individuals, thus the plural verb, *have.*

The jury is returning to the courtroom.
The subject *jury* is a collective unit and therefore singular.

The jury are arguing among themselves.
The word *jury* is referring to twelve people as individuals and is therefore plural.

In general usage *the number* (meaning one particular number) is considered singular whereas *a number* (meaning some) is considered plural. The difference between *a number* and *the number* stems from the difference between the general article *a* and the definite article *the,* a difference most people never notice. If you say *a monkey,* you are referring to any monkey; whereas if you say *the monkey,* you are referring to a particular one.

The number of Phi Beta Kappa students is small.
A number of students are going to the game.
The number of select grapes is increasing every year.
A number of grapes are needed to make one bottle of wine.

PRACTICE SENTENCES 6-8

Underline the correct verb in the following sentences.

Example: A number of people (is, <u>are</u>) expected to be absent.

1. The class (is, are) deciding on its senior gift to the school.

2. The faculty (is, are) concerned about the shortage of time in its new exam schedule.

3. The number of freshmen elected at the last induction ceremony (is, are) small.

4. The board (has, have) to complete its budget by next Thursday.

5. The family always (studies, study) its vacation plans carefully.

6. A number of athletes on the team (was, were) suspended because of the drug test results.

7. The committee (is, are) thinking about reconsidering its findings.

8. The number of applicants for the scholarship (was, were) small.

9. The jury (orders, order) its meals at the same time each day.

10. The number of Hispanics attending medical school in Florida (increases, increase) each year.

> **9.** A relative pronoun used as a subject may take either a singular verb or a plural verb depending on the pronoun's antecedent. (Relative pronouns are words such as *who, whom, whose, which,* and *that* that serve as both pronouns and subordinators—as in the sentence *The man who receives the trophy must win the race by at least one lap.*)

Remember that an antecedent is the noun a pronoun takes the place of. If the antecedent of a relative pronoun is singular, the pronoun must take a singular verb.

        sing.   sing.

One problem ←(that)→ arises in nuclear reactors is excessive heat.
> *That* is a relative pronoun; its antecedent is the singular noun *problem.* Therefore, the verb *arises* must be singular to agree with its singular subject *that.*

        pl.   pl.

The problems ←(that)→ arise in nuclear reactors are many and complex.
> The plural word *problems* is the antecedent of the relative pronoun *that,* making the word *that* plural. Thus, the plural form of the verb *(arise)* must be used to agree with its relative pronoun subject.

   pl.   pl.

People ←(who)→ go down into the mines have courage.
> *People* is plural, so *who* is plural; the verb *go* must be plural to agree with the word *who.*

   sing.   sing.

A dog ←(that)→ is constantly scratching probably has fleas.
> *That* must be singular since its antecedent *dog* is singular. The verb *is* must then be singular to agree with its subject *that.*

He is one of those workers who want the best possible product.
> In this sentence the antecedent of *who* is the plural noun *workers;* thus the plural form of the verb *(want)* is used.

PRACTICE SENTENCES 6-9

Underline the correct verb in the following sentences.

Example: The firewood that (<u>was</u>, were) delivered yesterday was rotten.

1. The students usually prefer the professors who (prepares, prepare) their lectures thoroughly.

2. Most people trust whoever (inspires, inspire) them the most.

3. He is the man who (defines, define) *positive* as "mistaken at the top of one's lungs."

4. The equipment that (was, were) purchased for the camping trip never arrived.

5. The students who (contributes, contribute) the most to the paper this year will receive the best staff positions next year.

6. The clothes on display at the yard sale are not the ones that (is, are) for sale.

7. The animal that wins the prizes at the dog shows is not necessarily the one that (makes, make) the best pet.

8. An electrical appliance that (has, have) a damaged cord should be repaired.

9. Putting a lot of money into a lawn that is not properly maintained (makes, make) little sense.

10. The conference recognizes the athletes who (does, do) the most for their schools.

---

10. Gerund subjects take singular verbs. A gerund is a verbal that ends in *-ing* and functions as a noun. When the subject of a sentence is a gerund, use a singular verb.

Seeing all of Shakespeare's history plays performed was his goal.
   Seeing is the gerund subject, so the singular form of the verb *(was)* is used.

Playing tennis once a week is a good way to get the exercise your body needs.
   Playing is the singular gerund subject of the singular verb *is*.

PRACTICE SENTENCES 6–10

Underline the correct verb in the following sentences.

Example: Getting exercise thirty minutes a day (<u>is</u>, are) my goal.

1. Practicing with a slingshot (relaxes, relax) me.

2. Watching too much television (becomes, become) a habit after a while.

3. Playing a musical instrument (requires, require) much time, patience, and practice.

4. Riding a motorcycle alone in the woods (is, are) not a good idea.

5. Practicing the Morse code (is, are) relaxing to some people.

```
11.  Some nouns are grammatically singular though they end in -s.
```

Quite a few nouns are plural in form (end in -s) but singular in meaning. Words such as *news, physics, economics, aeronautics, athletics, aesthetics,* and *measles* are all singular nouns. These nouns should cause you little if any confusion because you never hear them in any other form.

sing. sing.
The news is all bad this evening.

sing. sing.
Measles is a disease potentially dangerous to some people.

sing. sing.
Aesthetics is very difficult to teach.

Many book, magazine, and newspaper titles end in -s but take singular verbs. Such a title is singular because it indicates the name of only one book, magazine, or newspaper.

The Complete Grimm's Fairy Tales is a fascinating collection of stories for young and old.
  Though the last word in the title is a noun ending in -s *(Tales)*, the verb must be singular *(is)*. After all, *The Complete Grimm's Fairy Tales* is only one title of one book.

sing. sing.
The New York Times has many readers every day.

sing. sing.
Changing Times comes out every month.

PRACTICE SENTENCES 6-11

Underline the correct verb in the following sentences.

Example: Physics (<u>is</u>, are) not an easy major.

1. The news (does, do) not come on until 6:30.

2. Measles (is, are) nothing to take lightly.

3. *The Life and Times of Judge Roy Bean* (is, are) interesting reading.

4. At higher levels economics (gets, get) very mathematical.

5. Athletics (is, are) a lucrative business these days.

6. *U.S. News & World Report* (is, are) a good source of information.

7. Aeronautics (is, are) an area of study for car designers.

8. *Gulliver's Travels* (is, are) Swift's best-known work.

9. Ham and eggs (is, are) a popular breakfast dish.

10. *The Chicago Sun-Times* (is, are) a famous newspaper.

Pronoun–Antecedent Agreement

> Pronouns and their antecedents must agree in number just as subjects and verbs do.

Many of the same principles apply because the situations are similar. When an antecedent is singular, the pronoun referring to it should be singular; when an antecedent is plural, the pronoun referring to it should be plural.

> **1.** A singular pronoun is used to refer to such words as *another, anyone, anybody, each, either, everyone, everybody, kind, man, woman, neither, no one, nobody, one, person, someone, somebody, sort,* and *type.*

A person must do her work on time.

> *Person* is the singular antecedent of the singular pronoun *her.* The pronoun and its antecedent are both singular and therefore agree in number.

The woman worked all Friday night preparing for the yard sale she was to have on Saturday.
> *Woman* is the singular antecedent of the singular pronoun *she.* The pronoun and its antecedent are in agreement.

Anyone can learn English grammar if he studies hard enough.
> *Anyone* is an indefinite pronoun considered to be singular. The singular pronoun *he* refers to the singular *anyone,* so pronouns and antecedent agree.

 Writer's Tip Even though many television commercials say things like "Everyone in today's chaotic world feels free to do their own thing," traditional usage requires a singular pronoun in place of the plural *their.* When the gender is in doubt, some writers prefer to use the *he or she* form:

> Any student may do the extra credit project if he or she feels it will be beneficial.

Since it is distracting to have a proliferation of *he or she* in a paper (as in the sentence *Every man or woman should do his or her own thing as he or she sees fit*), the problem can be avoided by use of a plural subject and the pronoun *their:*

> Today's students feel free to pursue their own interests.

Words such as *kind, type,* and *sort* require special attention when they are used with the adjectival pronouns *this* and *these, that* and *those.*

> These kind are generally preferred.
> > *These* is plural, and *kind* is singular. The sentence should read:

> This kind is generally preferred, **or** These kinds are generally preferred.

> Those type of inventions never work efficiently.
> > *Those* is plural, and *type* is singular. The sentence should read:

> This type of invention never works efficiently, **or** Those types of inventions never work efficiently.

PRACTICE SENTENCES 6-12
Underline the correct pronoun in the following sentences.

> **Example:** Anyone can do that trick if (he/she practices, they practice).

1. (That, Those) types of tomatoes are the best.

2. Each man is expected to keep up with (his, their) own equipment.

3. Everyone can keep (his/her, their) weight down if necessary.

4. The article said (this, those) aluminum baseball bats hit the ball fifteen to twenty feet farther than the wooden ones.

5. Each of the women had (her, their) own views about marriage.

6. Someone forgot to turn off (his/her, their) bath water.

7. Each person contributed what (he/she, they) could afford.

8. (These, This) kind of rose produces a small flower.

9. Every member of the faculty expressed (his/her, their) opinion concerning the new attendance policy.

10. It should be easy for either of the two women to prove (her, their) qualifications for the job.

---

2. Two or more antecedents joined by *and* are referred to by a plural pronoun.

Hugh and Jimmy do all they can to maintain the building.
> *Hugh* and *Jimmy* become plural by being connected with the conjunction *and;* therefore, the plural *they* is needed so the antecedents and pronoun will agree.

The buildings to be destroyed were the Kingsmore Building, the Avondale Tower, and the Madison Mart; they are all important buildings in the city's history.
> *They* is a plural pronoun referring to the antecedents *Kingsmore Building, Avondale Tower,* and *Madison Mart*—which are plural because they are connected by *and.*

PRACTICE SENTENCES 6-13

Underline the correct pronoun in the following sentences.

Example: Manuel and Francisco visited a lawyer to arrange a contract in (his, <u>their</u>) best interests.

1. Monica and her parents were not able to agree on where to spend (her, their) vacation.

2. Corey and Kathleen are both having trouble in (her, their) math course.

3. The administrators from the vocational area and the deans from the technical area are discussing contract provisions for (his, their) areas.

4. Eva and Marlena are glad to speak out about (her, their) views on the topic of abortion.

5. The lawyers for the defense team and the prosecutors were unable to decide on how to handle (his, their) cases.

---

3. Two or more singular antecedents joined by *or* or *nor* are referred to by a singular pronoun.

Either Jack or Tom will be ready when he is called.
>   No matter which of the two antecedents *(Jack, Tom)* is selected, the result will be a singular masculine antecedent; the pronoun *be* is singular and agrees with the antecedent in number.

Neither Sue nor Marie has advanced in the firm as rapidly as she expected.
>   *She* is the correct singular pronoun choice because the two singular antecedents joined by *nor* are both female.

When one of the choices is singular and the other is plural, however, the pronoun should agree with the nearer antecedent. This situation, of course, is similar to that of singular subjects joined by *or* or *nor*, which we discussed under Subject-Verb Agreement.

Neither the doctor nor the nurses will be well received when they announce the decision.
>   *Doctor* is singular, and *nurses* is plural; since the plural *nurses* is nearer the pronoun, the plural pronoun *they* is the correct choice.

PRACTICE SENTENCES 6-14

Under line the correct pronoun in the following sentences.

Example: Neither Tommy nor his teachers can understand the nature of (his, their) problem.

1. Either Aluna or Idi will attend the conference if (she, they) gets elected.

2. Neither the managers nor the employees would speak up for (his/her, their) suggested salary raises.

3. Either the astronauts or the NASA manager will get (his/her, their) way.

4. Neither the bank manager nor the bank customers understand (his/her, their) view about the new manager.

5. Either Robert or Juan will win the contract for the plans that (he, they) proposed.

6. Neither the show's star nor its producers cared for the script that (he/she, they) were given.

7. Neither the students nor the student government were pleased with the new regulations that (they, it) received.

8. Neither the shipmates nor the captain could confirm (his/her, their) reservations on the boat.

9. Either the golfers or the club professional will determine the rules for the tournament (he/she, they) want to arrange.

10. Either Gabriella or Maria will attend the meeting if (she, they) can.

> **4.** Collective nouns will be referred to by either singular or plural pronouns depending on meaning.

The team follows its coach's orders.
The team discuss their differences at every meeting.

Both sentences are correct. In the first, *team* is considered a unit (singular) and is referred to by the singular pronoun *its*. Pronoun and antecedent agree in number. In the second sentence, *team* is considered separate individual members (plural) and is referred to by the plural pronoun *their*. Pronoun and antecedent agree. Notice in both cases that because of the verb only one pronoun can be correct. As soon as you say *The team follows,* the *-s* on the verb makes *team* singular. To say *The team follows their coach's orders* would be inconsistent and therefore incorrect. Similarly, when you say *The team discuss* you have made the collective noun plural, and it requires a plural pronoun.

PRACTICE SENTENCES 6–15
Underline the correct pronoun in the following sentences.

Example: The jury are arguing about what (its, <u>their</u>) verdict will be.

1. The Board of Trustees is considering what (its, their) new drug policy will include.

2. The class of '98 is pleased with the gift (it, they) will make to the school.

3. The General Assembly are debating (its, their) own salary increase.

4. The committee feels it must make a decision soon if (its, their) credibility is to be maintained.

5. The team supports (its, their) coach.

6. The group are not in agreement on many of the issues (it, they) discuss.

7. The Arts Council is a tax-deductible contribution for (its, their) supporters.

8. The jury is not sure (it, they) can reach a decision today.

9. The Academic Council is considering adding a policy on academic probation to the student handbook (it, they) publishes.

10. The herd is resting peacefully in (its, their) pen.

---

5. The pronoun *who* is usually used in referring to people; the pronoun *which* in referring to animals and things, and the pronoun *that* in referring to either persons, places, animals, or things.

Person: There is the contestant (who) is most likely to win the pageant.

Animal: The dog (that) steals Mr. Brown's newspaper is an Irish setter.

Thing: My aunt's hand-carved bed, (which) she bought last year, is a beautiful piece of furniture.

Place: It is New York (that) I like most of all.

PRACTICE SENTENCES 6–16

Underline the correct pronoun in the following sentences.

Example: Trigger was the horse (<u>that</u>, who) Roy Rogers rode.

1. Anyone (who, which) wants to succeed should learn self-discipline.

2. The animal (who, which) was injured was taken to the veterinarian.

3. The man (that, which) won the car race used illegal equipment.

4. She loaned her horse to a boy (who, which) had never ridden before.

5. The businessman (who, which) lost the contract also lost his job.

Sexist Language

Since over 50 percent of the world's human population is female, it is important that your language reflect both genders. Sexist language occurs when only one gender (male or female) is used to refer to both genders. Here are some examples of sexist language:

> *Man* has come a long way in the sciences.
> A nurse goes through much clinical training before *she* gets licensed.
>> (It's also sexist to write "male nurse" because this, too, implies that nurses are female.)
> No one should let failure keep *him* from trying again.

One of the problems you run into when you're trying to write in nonsexist ways is the awkwardness that can result from various strategies. For instance, using *his or her, he or she, his/her,* or *her/his* works fine once or twice; however, repeating this kind of construction too frequently can ruin a sentence's flow. Here's an example:

> A horse trainer usually starts his or her day early. By 5:00 A.M., he or she is usually in the stalls, feeding, mucking out, and tending to any emergencies. Then he or she must work with his or her horses, after which he or she must groom the animals . . . .

You can see how awkward that example is. One way to avoid this problem is to use the plural case:

> Horse trainers usually start their days early. By 5:00 A.M., they are usually in the stalls, feeding, mucking out, and tending to any emergencies. Then they must work with their horses, after which they must groom the animals . . . .

The paragraph flows much more smoothly now, and neither gender is left out.

Note: *Their* used with a singular referent (for example, *A person needs to take their vitamins in the morning.*) is not grammatically correct. *Their* is plural, and the word it refers to must be plural, too.

Another way to avoid sexist constructions is to switch back and forth between genders, but this can seem awkward to a lot of readers. Here is an example:

> A successful guitar player spends much of her time, at least six hours a day, practicing. He must do this for at least ten to twelve years before being considered even a beginning expert.

When referring to professions, use terms that are gender neutral:

postal worker or *mail carrier* instead of *postman*
police officer instead of *policeman*
nurse instead of *male nurse*
chairperson or *chair* instead of *chairman*

These are only a few examples of gender-neutral professional titles. Space is provided for you to list other nonsexist professional titles.

_____ _____ _____ _____

_____ _____ _____ _____

_____ _____ _____ _____

_____ _____ _____ _____

REVIEW EXERCISE 6-A   MAKING SUBJECTS AND VERBS AGREE (I)

Underline the correct verb in the following sentences.

Example: The notice on the bulletin board (<u>lists</u>, list) those who passed the course.

1. Both Eugenia and Liz (enjoys, enjoy) many of the same things.

2. Rick's records and accounts (is, are) difficult to verify.

3. Either the sheriff or the prisoners (is, are) going to have problems at the trial.

4. The book club (is, are) going to have their last meeting next Tuesday.

5. Toshio, as well as eight of his employees, (wants, want) to get to the source of the company's problem.

6. The camping trip planned for the boys (is, are) scheduled for next weekend.

7. Both Booker and Chin (succeeds, succeed) in the local rodeo every year.

8. Christian (is, are) a character in *Cyrano de Bergerac*.

9. Neither the catcher nor the other players on the team (likes, like) the new coach.

10. The list of nominations (was, were) much longer than anyone expected.

Name _____

Class _____

Section _____ Score:_____

REVIEW EXERCISE 6-B   MAKING SUBJECTS AND VERBS AGREE (II)

Underline the correct verb in the following sentences.

Example: In the creek behind the house (stands, <u>stand</u>) three blue herons.

1. There (is, are) nine members of the Eureka Community College Drama Club.

2. Dwight, Bubba, and Lynn (works, work) as stagehands.

3. Either Nell or Juanita (plays, play) the female lead.

4. Tony and Rojas usually (performs, perform) the leading male roles.

5. There (is, are) one member of the club that prefers the comic roles.

6. If there is any humor in a character's part, Woodrow (wants, want) to play him.

7. Teresa is shy and (takes, take) any role assigned.

8. In a locked room behind the stage (is, are) all of the club's costumes.

9. *Macbeth* and *She Stoops to Conquer* (was, were) performed last year.

10. There (was, were) no costumes for *Macbeth* because no one could find the key to the locked room.

REVIEW EXERCISE 6-C   MAKING PRONOUNS AND ANTECEDENTS AGREE

Underline the correct pronoun in the following sentences.

Example: Betty and Regina decided to take (her, <u>their</u>) vacation together.

1. Josi and Katherine decided to open (her, their) own suntan parlor.

2. The equipment was more expensive than anticipated, and (it, they) arrived late.

3. Neither of the women knew what (she, they) was in for.

4. All of the customers insisted that (his, their) tanning booths were too hot.

5. Sure enough, the electrician had not done (his, their) job correctly.

6. The booths were set entirely too high for any customer to remain in for the full thirty minutes (she, they) paid for.

7. The thermostats were set to burn the customers, not to tan (him, them).

8. Josi and Katherine corrected all of the booths in (her, their) parlor.

9. Eventually the customers started coming back to improve (his, their) tans.

10. Josi and Katherine are building (her, their) bank accounts on the vanity of others.

EDITING TEST 6-A   CORRECTING AGREEMENT ERRORS
Correct the agreement errors in the following sentences.

                        work
Example: The men ~~works~~ hard laying the track every day.

1. A careful evaluation of the specifications are necessary.

2. The musician at the church play both the organ and the piano.

3. *The Canterbury Tales* are Chaucer's best-known work.

4. Becky, as well as Jason and Nikki, are planning a surprise party for Nanny.

5. Judd does not want to work for the Three Mile Island Company, but his bosses pays him too much to quit.

6. Ham and eggs are Colleen's favorite breakfast dish.

7. Guns and knives is both dangerous weapons.

8. Far back in the jungle lives Tarzan and Jane.

9. Mary Beth don't want to get married, but her friends says she should.

10. All previous editions of the book is outdated.

Name _____

Class _____

Section _____ Score:_____

EDITING TEST 6-B CORRECTING PRONOUN–ANTECEDENT AGREEMENT ERRORS

In the following sentences correct all the errors in pronoun-antecedent agreement.

Example: Either Vincent or Alfred will deliver ~~their~~ *his* acceptance speech Tuesday night.

1. I don't enjoy these kind of paintings.

2. Each of the men wanted to look their best for the photographs.

3. If a person scores high enough on the placement test, they can place out of the entry-level course.

4. Mumps are a disease that parents sometimes underestimate.

5. Neither the actors nor the director are always right.

6. All qualified employees are welcome to apply for the position if he or she is interested.

7. The team is convinced that the coach exploited them.

8. Cora and Gilda feel she is being misled.

9. Either the owner or the drivers is going to have the upper hand in negotiations.

10. A couple of the students acted as if she disagreed.

MASTERY TEST 6-A   CHANGING THE NUMBER

The following paragraph is written in the plural number (men are). Rewrite the paragraph in the singular number (man is).

Example: The men are anxious to go.

_____The man is anxious to go._____

1. The men got together and decided to go on a hunting trip. 2. Being all city dwellers, they didn't know much about hunting. 3. None of them even owned a gun. 4. They had no tents, lanterns, or stoves. 5. They went to Wal-Mart and got all their supplies. 6. They decided where they would hunt. 7. They planned their trip carefully. 8. Unfortunately, they forgot one detail. 9. They did not obtain hunting licenses. 10. They were all caught by the same game warden.

Writing Assignments

Assignment 6-1 In one paragraph (about half a page), explain what your favorite piece of furniture is and why. Is it a piece in your room? House? Workplace? What about it do you like? What do you use it for? Is there something about the location of this piece that makes it special, too?

Assignment 6-2 A denotation is the dictionary definition of a word, and a connotation is the emotional significance you attach to a word. For example, you may know that acorn squash is a tasty vegetable, but you may emotionally associate it with being sick to your stomach because you ate too much of it one time. Choose one of the following terms and in two to three paragraphs (about one to one and a half pages), explain its denotation(s) and connotation(s):

> feminism
> welfare
> apple pie
> computers

Go Electronic!

For additional readings, exercises, and Internet activities, visit the Longman English pages at:

   http://longman.awl.com/englishpages

If you need a user name and password, please see your instructor.

More Practice with Your Writing and Grammar Skills

For additional practice with your writing and grammar skills, use the Writer's ToolKit CD–ROM included with this text. The ToolKit provides a wealth of computerized tutorials and practice activities.

Identifying and Correcting Sentence Fragments

A sentence fragment is part of a sentence. But what is a sentence? Some people consider a sentence a word or group of words that expresses a complete thought. This definition, however, brings up another question: "What is a complete thought?" Just as the part of speech of a word in a particular sentence can be determined only by how the word is used in context, what may be considered a complete thought in one context may not make sense in another. For example, if someone you did not know and had not spoken with came up to you and said, "Flying," you might think the person was crazy. On the other hand, if you asked someone, "Are you flying or driving to the conference in Chicago?" the one-word answer *flying* would express a complete thought. Similarly, if you ask someone, "Will you go to the dance with me Saturday night?" the one-word answer *yes* or *no* is a complete thought. Clearly, whether an expression is considered a complete thought or not depends on the context.

Some writers, however, unintentionally treat incomplete thoughts as correct sentences. Such "sentences" can be very distracting to readers. Therefore you should learn what a grammatically complete sentence is in order to avoid unintentional fragments.

> A **grammatically complete sentence** is a word or group of words that contains a subject and verb (either stated or implied) and expresses a complete thought.

John Victor owns over a thousand books.

The sentence contains the verb *owns* and the subject *John Victor,* and the statement is a complete thought.

Jump!

The sentence contains the verb *jump,* and it has the implied subject *you.* The sentence is grammatically complete and expresses a complete thought.

> A **sentence fragment** is a word or group of words that is not grammatically complete or that does not express a complete thought yet begins with a capital letter and ends with a period, exclamation point, or question mark.

And was rowing hard to reach the lighthouse.

The group of words is a fragment. It does not contain a subject, and it does not express a complete thought.

Writer's Tip

You should strive to make your sentences grammatically complete. Although some writers occasionally construct intentional fragments, papers that are written primarily to inform the reader should avoid fragments. In informative writing, your main goal is clarity. Fragments do not help you attain this goal. Most sentence fragments are unintentional and are usually a result of rapid writing and poor proofreading. The first part of this chapter will help you learn to identify sentence fragments; the second part will give you guidance on how to eliminate fragments in your writing.

Types of Sentence Fragments

Knowing the most common types of sentence fragments can help you avoid using them. In general, four types of word groups are mistaken for sentences:

> **WORD GROUPS COMMONLY MISTAKEN FOR SENTENCES**
> 1. Phrases
> 2. Subordinate clauses
> 3. Nouns followed by modifiers
> 4. Sentences beginning with *and* or *but*

Phrases as Fragments

> One of the most common sentence fragment errors is mistaking phrases for grammatically complete sentences.

Remember, a **phrase** is a group of related words that does not contain a subject and verb. Since a phrase contains no subject and verb, it cannot be a grammatically complete sentence. Also, a phrase does not express a complete thought. Even if a prepositional, infinitive, participial, or gerund phrase begins with a capital letter and ends with a period, it is still a fragment.

> In that gigantic swamp in Harlow County.
> The two prepositional phrases constitute a fragment.

> To do the job adequately and proficiently.
> The infinitive phrase is a fragment.

> Having eaten thirteen bowls of oyster soup.
> The participial phrase is a fragment.

> Generating fifty kilowatts per day.
> The verbal phrase (potentially either participle or gerund) is a fragment.

Proofread your writing to see that you have not carelessly treated a phrase as a complete sentence.

PRACTICE SENTENCES 7–1

In the blanks provided, indicate whether the following word groups are complete sentences or phrases.

Example: Lacking privacy in their private lives.

_____ Phrase _____

1. Does the press have the right to investigate the private lives of public figures?

_____

2. Seeking out any information available.

_____

3. Printing rumors as readily as facts.

   _____

4. Many members of the general public resent such invasion of privacy.

   _____

5. On the other hand some people hang on every word.

   _____

6. All citizens reacting in an individual way.

   _____

7. The problem can become serious.

   _____

8. Some people around the world blaming the press for the death of Princess Di.

   _____

9. Some limits must be set.

   _____

10. But being qualified to set the new procedures.

    _____

Subordinate Clauses as Fragments

Another type of sentence fragment error is mistaking subordinate clauses for complete sentences.

Remember, a **subordinate clause** is a group of related words that contains a subject and a verb but that does not express a complete thought.

Note: A group of related words that contains a subject and a verb is not necessarily a grammatically complete sentence.

Since a subordinate clause depends on the main clause to complete its meaning, it cannot stand alone as a sentence.

Until the stadium is cleaned of all debris.
Whoever is elected to the student government association.
Which is a fine stream for trout fishing.

All these word groups are fragments. You must be careful in your writing to avoid such fragments.

PRACTICE SENTENCES 7-2

In the blanks provided, indicate which of the following word groups are complete sentences and which are subordinate clauses.

Example: Because Scott had been working on his car for over three years.

_____subordinate clause_____

1. He was excited about the upcoming car show.

   _____

2. Which was to be held in May at the fairgrounds.

   _____

3. He had built the car from the chassis up.

   _____

4. Although a few finishing touches were needed on the bodywork.

   _____

5. The car was just about ready to be shown.

   _____

Noun Followed by Modifier as Fragment

> Though phrases and subordinate clauses mistakenly treated as complete sentences are the main causes of fragments, there are others. Often a noun will be followed by an adjective clause that modifies it.

The pilot who shot down the Red Baron in World War I.

Who shot down the Red Baron in World War I is an adjective clause modifying the noun *pilot*. The entire group of words beginning with *the* and ending with the period is a fragment because it does not express a complete thought. The noun *pilot* appears to be a subject, but there is no verb for it to be the subject of. The fragment can be made into a complete sentence with a verb:

The pilot who shot down the Red Baron in World War I was not Eddie Rickenbacker.

Now the noun *pilot* is the subject of the verb *was* and the group of words is a complete sentence.

Fragments Caused by Beginning Sentences with *And* or *But*

> Another way writers mistakenly create fragments is by beginning sentences with *and* or *but*.

And was forced to find an alternative procedure.

The group of words is a fragment because there is no subject for the verb *was forced*. Because the mistake with *and* is so easy to commit, many teachers tell students not to begin sentences with the word *and* or *but*.

Actually, there is nothing grammatically wrong with beginning a sentence with the words *and* and *but* as long as what follows is a grammatically complete sentence. If the preceding sentence had been written *And the astronaut was forced to find an alternative procedure*, the sentence would have been grammatically complete. In fact, words like *and* and *but* can sometimes be effective in making sentences flow together smoothly.

Bob wants to ask Carol Downs to the class picnic. But he is afraid to ask her.

By setting the second sentence off with a period and a capital letter, the writer has emphasized Bob's lack of courage. Of course, such sentences beginning with coordinate conjunctions are generally used for either transition or emphasis; therefore, as like most effective writing techniques, they should be used sparingly. It is important to be sure that sentences beginning with coordinate conjunctions are grammatically complete.

Correcting Sentence Fragments

 Now that you have an understanding of sentence fragments, you should be able to proofread your own papers and remove any fragments you may have accidentally written. The two main things to check for in proofreading are:

1. That each group of words treated as a sentence must contain a subject and a verb.
2. That each group of words treated as a sentence containing a subject and a verb does not begin with either a subordinate conjunction or a relative pronoun.

If the group of words does not contain a subject and a verb, it is probably a phrase. If the word group contains a subject and a verb but is introduced by a relative pronoun or a subordinate conjunction, it is probably a subordinate clause.

In the event your proofreading does turn up a sentence fragment, you should not have much trouble correcting the error. If you can detect that a group of words is a fragment, you should have a good enough understanding of fragments and sentences by now to repair the fragment yourself.

> Fragments can be corrected in several ways. One of the easiest ways is to attach the fragment to another sentence.

Fragment: I really like to go swimming. In the pond near Ms. Johnson's apiary.

Correct the fragment by attaching it to the complete sentence:

Full Sentence: I really like to go swimming in the pond near Ms. Johnson's apiary.

Fragment: After I finished the novel. I went to bed.

Correct the fragment by attaching it to the complete sentence:

Full Sentence: After I finished the novel, I went to bed.

> Fragments can also be corrected by insertion of the missing subjects or verbs.

Fragment: The antique that I purchased in Williamsburg, Virginia.

Correct the fragment by providing the noun *antique* with a verb:

Full Sentence: The antique that I purchased in Williamsburg, Virginia, disintegrated.

Now *antique* is the subject of the verb *disintegrated* and the sentence is complete.

Fragment: But was not completed by the July 15 deadline.

Correct the fragment by providing the verb *was completed* with a subject:

Full Sentence: But the project was not completed by the July 15 deadline.

Now *project* is the subject of the verb *was completed* and the sentence is complete.

> Occasionally a fragment is so fragmentary or so confused that it must be completely rewritten.

Fragment: The botanical gardens in Chapel Hill, North Carolina, being the place.

The group of words should be completely rewritten:

Full Sentence: Only plants native to North Carolina can be found in the botanical gardens in Chapel Hill, North Carolina.

Be sure not to confuse verbals and verbs. The *-ing* form of a verb cannot be a main verb without an auxiliary.

Fragment: The bridge being over two thousand feet long.

Being is a verbal, not a verb. The verbal should be converted into a main verb.

Full Sentence: The bridge *is* over two thousand feet long.

EDITING PRACTICE 7-3

In the space provided, rewrite each fragment so that it becomes a complete sentence.

Example: The Turner landscape being sold for $350,000.

The Turner landscape was sold for $350,000

1. Amy's husband being fond of beer and peanuts.

_____

_____

2. The woman with the big red hat in front of me at church.

_____

_____

3. In the middle of downtown traffic at 5:00 P.M.

_____

_____

4. Having become more of a recluse since he lost his job.

_____

_____

5. Colette, having left her pocketbook in the classroom.

_____

_____

6. A beautiful white cat with warmth, charm, and fleas.

_____

_____

7. Successfully parallel parking in a very small space.

   _____

   _____

8. Falling off the boat when it hit the dock.

   _____

   _____

9. Sitting on the dock of the bay with a picnic basket.

   _____

   _____

10. And hit the ball over the left-field fence.

   _____

   _____

REVIEW EXERCISE 7-A IDENTIFYING SENTENCE FRAGMENTS

In the blanks provided, indicate whether the following word groups are complete sentences or fragments.

Example: Mariana purchased a new telescope.

complete sentence

1. Although she had been reading about telescopes for months.

2. She wasn't sure of the size or type she wanted to buy.

3. Having looked in several stores for what she wanted.

4. She even searched through half a dozen catalogs.

5. Finally, deciding what she wanted to buy.

6. She went to a local store and purchased one.

7. It was a ten-inch reflector.

8. In order to get above the nearby trees and lights.

_____

9. She built an observation deck over her carport.

_____

10. Learning a great deal from her platform and enjoying herself immensely.

_____

EDITING TEST 7-A CORRECTING SENTENCE FRAGMENTS (I)

In the following paragraphs, circle the number of every word group that is a fragment. Correct all sentence fragments.

Example: ① Being successful as an architect, 2. Carla is happy with her new life.

1. Although they were college students. 2. They decided to celebrate Halloween. 3. They found an old wooden house. 4. And fixed it up. 5. Each room had a sound system and special lighting effects. 6. One room had three chainsaws in it. 7. Because the sight and sound of chain saws frighten everyone.

8. The night before Halloween the guys invited some sorority girls over for a dress rehearsal. 9. Although they were frightened. 10. They had a great time. 11. To get in on the act. 12. They invited everyone they could. 13. All went well. 14. Until one of the candles was knocked over and started a fire. 15. Thanks to fast work. 16. The house was saved. 17. Although the haunted house ended with a flicker.

EDITING TEST 7-B   CORRECTING SENTENCE FRAGMENTS (II)

In the following paragraphs, circle the number of every word group that is a fragment. Correct all sentence fragments.

Example: 1. Greg enjoys watching westerns on television. 2. ᵇBecause he grew up with them.

1. Greg's favorite TV western was *Gunsmoke.* 2. Starring Matt, Kitty, Festus, and Doc. 3. As well as having good solid characters. 4. *Gunsmoke* usually had good plots. 5. Then there was *Bonanza.* 6. With Ben, Adam, Hoss, and Little Joe Cartwright. 7. Being more of a family show. 8. There was often more humor on *Bonanza.* 9. Greg's son Morris does not like westerns. 10. Since they were not part of his heritage. 11. He is more interested in science fiction and high-technology shows. 12. Even though he does condescendingly watch westerns with his father occasionally.

Writing Assignments

Assignment 7-1 Write one paragraph (about half a page) on the following: If you were to have either a soft drink or snack food named after you, what would it be? You can choose a drink/food that already exists or make up one of your own. How would its characteristics (e.g., flavor, appearance, consistency) reflect your character and personality? Would it be bubbly? Spicy? Unusual? Bizarre? What else?

Assignment 7-2 In three paragraphs (about one and a half pages), apply the above soft drink/snack food description to the United States. How does this drink/food reflect this country? Does it have a variety of flavors? Is it easy or difficult to eat? What else?

Go Electronic!

For additional readings, exercises, and Internet activities, visit the Longman English pages at:

http://longman.awl.com/englishpages

If you need a user name and password, please see your instructor.

More Practice with Your Writing and Grammar Skills

For additional practice with your writing and grammar skills, use the Writer's ToolKit CD-ROM included with this text. The ToolKit provides a wealth of computerized tutorials and practice activities.

Identifying and Correcting Fused Sentences and Comma Splices

When studying comma splices and fused sentences, you are learning as much about punctuation as you are about grammar. In this chapter, you will first learn to recognize these types of sentence errors; then you will see the four ways in which fused or comma-spliced sentences can be corrected.

Fused Sentences

> A **fused sentence** is the result of combining main clauses without putting any punctuation between them.

Last night I saw a production of *Macbeth* the local theater group gave a fine performance.

The break between main clauses is between the words *Macbeth* and *the*. Because no punctuation is present, the sentence is fused.

Last night I saw a production of *Macbeth* the local theater group gave a fine performance next month they are going to do *Julius Caesar*.

Now the sentence is fused in two places: between *Macbeth* and *the* and between *performance* and *next*.

PRACTICE SENTENCES 8-1

Circle the break between main clauses in each of the following fused sentences.

Example: Maude wanted to open her own photography studio she didn't know where to begin.

1. She talked with the owner of a studio in a nearby town he gave her some advice.

2. He suggested she purchase a good 35-mm Nikon camera it is good for most general-use purposes.

3. He further recommended she purchase a Rolleflex this camera is better for for more specific purposes.

4. He told her she would need some studio lighting he suggested several kinds of lights.

5. He reminded her of the importance of backdrops she would need at least three.

6. He recommended that she keep plenty of film for best results it should be kept in the refrigerator.

7. She couldn't afford to purchase all this equipment at one time she decided to open her studio with what she had.

8. She made her own backdrops they were more imaginative than ones in the supply stores.

9. Her customers came slowly at first her reputation spread, however.

10. Now her studio is making a profit she is happy and independent.

There are two correct ways to join the main clauses of a compound sentence:

TO JOIN THE MAIN CLAUSES OF A COMPOUND SENTENCE:

1. Use a semicolon.
2. Use a comma and one of the coordinate conjunctions (*and, or, nor, but, yet, so, for*).

John Davis spent over thirty hours preparing the report for his boss; it was never read.

> The sentence is correct because a semicolon joins the break between the main clauses.

John Davis spent over thirty hours preparing the report for his boss, but it was never read.

> The sentence is correct because the comma and the coordinate conjunction *but* join the break between main clauses.

Writer's Tip Notice that the sentence with the semicolon packs a punch. It is more direct and forceful. Although the sentence with the comma and the coordinating conjunction gives the same information, the fact that John Davis' report was not read has been de-emphasized by the inclusion of the comma and the coordinating conjunction. Thus, in your writing, the punctuation you use can determine the emphasis you wish to place on an idea. Naturally the main clauses being joined must be logically related.

I bought a Panasonic radio, and *Ulysses* was banned in this country until 1933.

Though the sentence is correctly punctuated, it is an extremely bad sentence. No amount of punctuation can improve such an illogical sentence.

EDITING PRACTICE 8-2

Correct each of the following fused sentences by putting a semicolon where it is needed.

Example: Jeannie has had trouble with her knee; doctors have been unable to help her.

1. She originally had trouble with cartilage damage this problem resulted in arthritis in her knee.

2. Her doctor performed arthroscopic surgery unfortunately, the surgery did not solve her problem.

3. The arthritis continued to get worse Jeannie was no better off.

4. She consulted three other orthopedic surgeons each agreed to try to help her.

5. One of the surgeons operated on her knee he removed as much of the affected area as possible.

6. He explained the procedure to her he indicated he would remove all damaged or diseased portions he saw.

7. But he informed her of a potential problem sometimes it takes many surgeries to remedy the problem.

8. Sometimes the problem is never corrected it is only alleviated temporarily.

9. Jeannie was feeling down in fact, she was getting downright depressed.

10. Now, after seven knee operations, she does not like the situation with her knee she is, however, glad that she can walk unassisted.

EDITING PRACTICE 8-3

Correct each of the following sentences by providing an appropriate coordinate conjunction to accompany the comma.

Example: Ghost stories and legends abound in North Carolina, *and* many books relating these stories have been written.

1. Many of the stories are said to be based on fact, there are people who have witnessed the events.

2. The Devil's Tramping Ground is a huge, bare circle in which no vegetation will grow, it is located in the central part of the state.

3. In the legend of the Devil's Tramping Ground, it is said the Devil removes any objects placed in the bare spot, no one has ever proved that it is actually the Devil who removes them.

4. Another story, the legend of the Brown Mountain Light, has many explanations, each one differs in its interpretation of the meaning of the mysterious light.

5. In the mountains of North Carolina, a mysterious light appears, there is no apparent reason for the light.

6. Some people say an old slave has come back from his grave carrying a lantern and looking for his master, a song called "The Brown Mountain Light" relates that version, although that is not the most popular explanation.

7. Another popular legend is of a young girl who hitches a ride with strangers and disappears from their car, she always appears on dark, foggy nights and wears a white gown.

8. Apparently, a young girl was killed on a bridge near Chapel Hill many years ago, ever since that foggy night, she has been trying to get someone to take her home.

9. Many people say they have stopped to pick her up and take her home, she always disappears without a trace before they reach her home.

10. You should never tell a North Carolinian that these stories are not true, you may be speaking to someone who has witnessed one of these mysteries.

Comma Splices

Now that you know how the main clauses of a sentence can be correctly joined by a comma, look at how they are often incorrectly joined by a comma.

> The **comma splice** error is the result of combining main clauses with a comma where the comma is insufficient punctuation.

Mary is a dedicated homemaker on the weekends, she vacuums the floors and puts everything in its proper place.

The break between main clauses occurs between *weekends* and *she*. The sentence is comma-spliced since a comma is not sufficient punctuation to join the main clauses.

Mary is a dedicated homemaker on the weekends, she vacuums the floors and puts everything in its proper place, then on Monday she ignores the house, she will not perform any domestic chores until Friday.

Now the sentence is comma-spliced three times: between *weekends* and *she,* between *place* and *then,* and between *house* and *she.* Remember, a sentence that is comma-spliced always contains a comma.

PRACTICE SENTENCES 8-4

Circle the comma-spliced breaks between the main clauses in the following sentences.

Example: Chilo thought he had gotten a good deal in the car he bought, he paid only twelve hundred dollars for it.

1. The body seemed to be in good shape, there were no bad dents anywhere.

2. He took it for a test run, everything seemed to work well.

3. The interior had a few rough areas, he thought he could repair them.

4. Then one day a fleck of paint fell off, under the paint there was nothing but rust.

5. On a trip to the repair shop the engine quit running, Chilo was stranded.

6. The mechanic told Chilo that the engine had frozen up, it couldn't be repaired.

7. Rebuilding the engine would not help, the block was cracked.

8. The mechanic gave him bad news, it would cost three thousand dollars to repair.

9. Chilo was quite angry, he consulted a lawyer.

10. The lawyer told Chilo there was little that could be done, the term he used was *caveat emptor.*

PRACTICE SENTENCES 8-5

Circle the comma-spliced breaks between main clauses in the following sentences.

Example: Christine likes to watch old movies, she and her dad often discuss them.

1. Some of the movies were made in the 1930s, 1940s, and 1950s, Christine was not born until 1971.

2. One of her favorites is *The African Queen,* it stars Humphrey Bogart and Katharine Hepburn.

3. Her father told her about the movie before they watched it, he thought she would enjoy it.

4. It is about a man and a woman on a dangerous boating excursion, the man and woman have very different personalities.

5. The woman is quite religious and conservative, the man is a gin-drinking capitalist with few convictions.

6. She convinces him to support Britain's war effort, he agrees just to humor her.

7. The woman demonstrates that she has courage and determination, she surprises her male companion.

8. As the movie progresses, a mutual admiration develops between the two, they fall in love.

9. In the end the two are willing to give their lives for each other, they wish to be married first.

10. Christine's father asked if she thought such romances actually existed in real life, she said she certainly hoped so.

Conjunctive Adverbs and Transitional Phrases

Words such as *however* and expressions such as *on the other hand* often occur at the break between main clauses. Such words and expressions are modifiers that are used to connect clauses. The individual words are called **conjunctive adverbs;** the multiword expressions are called **transitional phrases.**

> Conjunctive adverbs and transitional phrases are not coordinate conjunctions and cannot connect main clauses with just a comma.

My professor likes the novelist John Gardner, however, she believes John Updike is a better craftsman.
> The sentence is comma-spliced between *Gardner* and *however.* To keep the sentence compound, you would need to use a semicolon.

My professor likes the novelist John Gardner; however, she believes John Updike is a better craftsman.

Many of the following words and phrases appear at the break between main clauses:

Conjunctive Adverbs	Transitional Phrases
accordingly	as a result
additionally	at the same time
also	for example
besides	for instance
consequently	in addition
furthermore	in comparison

Conjunctive Adverbs	Transitional Phrases
hence	in contrast
henceforth	in fact
however	in other words
indeed	on the contrary
likewise	on the other hand
meanwhile	that is
moreover	
nevertheless	
nonetheless	
otherwise	
primarily	
still	
then	
therefore	
thus	

It may be easier for you to understand the difference between pure coordinate conjunctions and the words and phrases in the box if you realize that conjunctions are used to connect, whereas the listed words and phrases just help the sentence flow smoothly.

In the following sentence, *but* can be only where it is; it does not fit or make sense in any other position:

Aaron Davis, a most unlikely candidate, was nominated by his party, but because of previous obligations, he was unable to accept.

Correct: Ralph likes his secretary a great deal, but he likes his wife even more.

Incorrect: Ralph likes his secretary a great deal; he but likes his wife even more.

Incorrect: Ralph likes his secretary a great deal; he likes his wife even more but.

Notice that versions 2 and 3 are awkward and nonsensical. The reason is that *but* is a pure conjunction and can be used only to connect.

On the other hand, a word such as *however* can fit in several positions in the sentence and still make sense:

Ralph likes his secretary a great deal; however, he likes his wife even more.

1. Ralph likes his secretary a great deal; he likes his wife, however, even more.

2. Ralph likes his secretary a great deal; he likes his wife even more, however.

The word *however* (and the other words and phrases listed on the box) can be moved around in the sentence because it is not a pure connector.

Remember, only coordinate conjunctions can connect main clauses with just a comma before them; the other words and phrases cannot. Avoid sentences such as the following:

Jane thought she wanted to go to dental school she decided, however, to major in drama instead.

Though the sentence contains the word *however* with a comma before it, the sentence is fused between *school* and *she* and not comma-spliced, since *however* is not at the break between clauses.

Most important, you should remember that a sentence can be neither comma-spliced nor fused if it does not contain at least two main clauses.

Short Fiction of the Masters is a good anthology.

The sentence is just a simple sentence containing one main clause.

✔ **CHECKLIST: COORDINATE CONJUNCTIONS VS. CONJUNCTIVE ADVERBS/TRANSITIONAL PHRASES**

Coordinate Conjunctions:	Conjunctive Adverbs/ Transitional Phrases:
1. Used to connect clauses.	1. Help sentences to flow smoothly.
2. Make sense in only one position.	2. Make sense in several positions.
3. Need only a comma to connect.	3. Need additional punctuation to connect.

Ways to Correct Comma Splices and Fused Sentences

There are four ways to correct comma splices and fused sentences.

> **Fused:** Jane thought she wanted to go to dental school she decided to major in drama instead.

> **Comma splice:** Jane thought she wanted to go to dental school, she decided to major in drama instead.

1. The main clauses can be rewritten as separate sentences:

> Jane thought she wanted to go to dental school. She decided to major in drama instead.

2. One of the main clauses can be rewritten as a subordinate clause:

> Although Jane thought she wanted to go to dental school, she decided to major in drama instead.

3. A semicolon can be put between the main clauses:

> Jane thought she wanted to go to dental school; she decided to major in drama instead.

4. A comma and a coordinate conjunction can be put at the break between clauses:

> Jane thought she wanted to go to dental school, but she decided to major in drama instead.

The way you choose to correct a comma splice will depend on your personal preferences and on the meaning you wish to convey. For example, the coordinate conjunction *and* balances two main clauses, whereas the coordinate conjunctions *but* and *yet* contrast them.

> **Balancing:** Robert wanted to buy Janice an expensive winter coat, <u>and</u> he went to the nicest store in town to find one.

> Robert wanted to buy Janice an expensive winter coat, <u>but</u> he could not afford to get the one he really liked.

Subordinating one of the clauses de-emphasizes it.

> **De-emphasizing:** Although Robert wanted to buy Janice an expensive winter coat, he couldn't afford to get the one he really liked.

> Combining two main clauses in one sentence with a semicolon between them gives each clause equal emphasis and indicates the close relationship in meaning between the two.

Equalizing: Robert wanted to buy Janice an expensive winter coat; he went to the nicest store in town to find one.

Putting the main clauses in two separate sentences emphasizes each one more.

Emphasizing: Robert wanted to buy Janice an expensive winter coat. He could not afford to get the one he really liked.

No one method of correcting comma splices and fused sentences is more correct than another. Just strive for variety in your writing and avoid overworking any one technique.

EDITING TEST 8-A   CORRECTING FUSED SENTENCES AND COMMA SPLICES

In the spaces provided, rewrite the following comma splices and fused sentences, correcting the sentence faults by one of the four methods explained in this chapter.

Example: Blair has an appointment to get a permanent this afternoon she hopes the chemicals don't have a strong odor.

　　Blair has an appointment to get a permanent this afternoon,

　　but she hopes the chemicals don't have a strong odor.

1. Corbin prefers pizza with nothing on it but cheese and tomato sauce however, he will eat a pizza with all the toppings if someone else is buying.

　　_____

　　_____

2. Josh bought a boat for $250 he fixed it up by himself and was offered $3,000 for it.

　　_____

　　_____

3. Melanie plays the banjo very well she has won several contests.

　　_____

　　_____

4. James finally agreed to paint his grandmother's house as she wanted it, her house is the only purple one with maroon trim in the neighborhood.

　　_____

　　_____

5. Stephanie had an accident on her four-wheeler, she broke her arm in two places.

_____

_____

6. Dr. Gorriaran burned his tie in lab last week he got it too close to a Bunsen burner.

_____

_____

7. Rebecca dropped her English class after having missed several sessions in a row the class interfered with her job.

_____

_____

8. Juanita had no difficulty in her Spanish class it came to her naturally.

_____

_____

9. Ginger is a professional photographer who enjoys her work, she especially likes doing portraits of children.

_____

_____

10. Darryl's mother refuses to let him watch any R-rated movies he told her that all the best movies were R-rated.

_____

_____

MASTERY TEST 8-A IDENTIFYING FUSED SENTENCES AND COMMA SPLICES (I)

In the blanks provided, indicate whether the following sentences are correct, comma-spliced, or fused.

Example: Antwan and Anna decided to attend college together they signed up for a class in English composition.

<u>   Fused   </u>

1. Although the first day was quite confusing, they were still excited.

   _____

2. They liked their teacher; he was young and humorous.

   _____

3. He handed out a syllabus on the first day it seemed tough but fair.

   _____

4. They were required to write seven themes, four of them required research.

   _____

5. They wondered, however, if their teacher was a history buff.

   _____

6. Three of the themes that required research were on American history topics, the first one, for instance, was on whether Truman made the right decision when he had the atomic bomb dropped on Hiroshima.

   _____

7. The second topic related to the Civil War it dealt with whether or not U. S. Grant was a great general.

   _____

8. The third topic went back to the beginnings of American history, it asked if George Washington was a great president.

   _____

9. Antwan and Anna enjoyed researching these historical topics, but they wondered why they were studying them in an English class.

   _____

10. When the course was over, however, Antwan and Anna felt they had learned a lot of English and history.

   _____

Name _____

Class _____

Section _____ Score:_____

MASTERY TEST 8-B   IDENTIFYING FUSED SENTENCES AND COMMA SPLICES (II)

In the blanks provided, indicate whether the following sentences are correct, comma-spliced, or fused.

Example: Telephones have come a long way, they used to be only for the rich and only for short distances.

<u>comma-spliced</u>

1. Then the cost of telephone service came down nearly every home had one.

_____

2. Eventually lines were laid, and people could talk to each other around the world.

_____

3. Some people consider the telephone a business tool, others consider it more of a social necessity.

_____

4. Phones have changed shapes over the years they are now lighter in weight and more colorful.

_____

5. The princess phone proved very popular it was small and easy to carry in one hand.

_____

6. The princess model was a hit with women and teenagers; men were not as fond of it.

_____

7. Telephones used to be limited in their portability, they couldn't be used beyond the length of the cord.

_____

8. Now there is the cordless telephone the user does not have a cord to get in the way.

_____

9. In recent years the cellular phone was introduced, it can be installed in your car or even put in a pack you carry everywhere you go.

_____

10. In spite of all the changes, some people still consider the phone primarily a business tool, and others consider it essentially a social tool.

_____

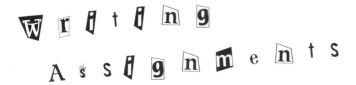

Writing Assignments

Assignment 8-1 Write one paragraph (about half a page) on the following: Imagine that your mind is a filing cabinet. How would it be organized? Would you have files for different people, thoughts, feelings, experiences, etc.? Would files be grouped in different drawers? Would the filing cabinet be comfortably organized or comfortably messy?

Assignment 8-2 Watch a cartoon and write three paragraphs (about one and a half pages) about what it says about U.S. values. Do you agree or disagree with the cartoon's message(s)? Why? Is there something you would prefer to see the cartoon do? Is there something that the cartoon does that you like? Dislike? What do you like or dislike about the character(s)?

Go Electronic!

For additional readings, exercises, and Internet activities, visit the Longman English pages at:

http://longman.awl.com/englishpages

If you need a user name and password, please see your instructor.

More Practice with Your Writing and Grammar Skills

For additional practice with your writing and grammar skills, use the Writer's ToolKit CD-ROM included with this text. The ToolKit provides a wealth of computerized tutorials and practice activities.

chapter 9

Pronoun Case and Reference

Case

> **Pronouns** are naming words that are used to take the place of nouns. Just like nouns, pronouns usually function as subjects, direct objects, indirect objects, objects of prepositions, and predicate nominatives. The **case of a pronoun** shows its function in a sentence. There are three cases in English: **nominative, objective,** and **possessive.**

Here is a list of pronouns classified by case:

Nominative	Objective	Possessive
I	me	my (mine)
you	you	your (yours)
it	it	its
we	us	our (ours)
he, she	him, her	his, her (hers)
they	them	their (theirs)
who	whom	whose
whoever	whomever	

Nominative Case

---
1. Pronouns used as subjects require the nominative case.

I am going to get a loan today.
> *I* is in the nominative case because it is the subject of the verb *am going.*

They will complete the float in time for the parade.
> *They* is in the nominative case because it is the subject of the verb *will complete.*

---
2. Pronouns used as predicate nominatives require the nominative case.

The winner was he who spoke first.
> *He* is in the nominative case because it is a predicate nominative.

It is I.
> *I* functions as a predicate nominative and is therefore in the nominative case.

---
3. An **appositive** is a noun or pronoun that renames or explains another noun or pronoun. When an appositive renames a word in the nominative case, it, too, is in the nominative case.

Two men, John and Bob, attended the special dinner.
> *Men* is the subject of the verb *attended* and is therefore in the nominative case. The words *John* and *Bob* rename the noun *men* and are therefore appositives.

Two men, Bob and I, attended the special dinner.
> Now *I* is a pronoun in the nominative case. It is in apposition with the subject *men,* which is a noun in the nominative case.

The girls, Judy and she, built a model of the Globe Theatre.
> *She* is in the nominative case because it is in apposition with a word in the nominative case, the subject *girls.*

PRACTICE SENTENCES 9-1

Underline the pronouns in the nominative case.

Example: <u>She</u> is an outstanding athlete.

1. She has an innate talent.

2. Nevertheless, she practices rigorously every day.

3. She feels that a great athlete is made as well as born.

4. Because she is as dedicated as she is, her coach doesn't push her.

5. Her coach knows she is an athlete who will do her best.

Objective Case

> **1.** Pronouns used as objects require the objective case. The most common types of objects are direct objects, indirect objects, and objects of prepositions.

Do you really love her?
> *Her* is the objective case because it is the direct object of the verb *do love.*

Judy gave him a sweater for his birthday.
> *Him* is in the objective case because it is the indirect object of the verb *gave.*

Give the free pass to me.
> *Me* is in the objective case because it is the object of the preposition *to.*

> **2.** The objective case is also used for a pronoun that functions as the object of a verbal.

To arrest him is the FBI's goal.
> *Him* is in the objective case because it is the object of the infinitive *to arrest.*

Getting him to the podium at last, Judy sat down.
> *Him* is in the objective case because it is the object of the participle *getting.*

---

3. Finally, a pronoun in apposition with a word in the objective case goes in the objective case.

The committee elected two representatives: Susan and me.
> *Me* is in the objective case because it is in apposition with the direct object *representatives*.

Save the biggest applause for the finalists: the Cardinals and us.
> *Us* is in apposition with the word *finalists*, which is the object of the preposition *for*.

Remember that a pronoun appositive can be in either the objective or the nominative case, depending on the case of the word the pronoun is in apposition with. You should also realize that the pronoun itself may take an appositive.

We runners were breathing hard during the race.
> *Runners* is in apposition with the pronoun *we*. *We* is used correctly in the nominative case because it is the subject of the verb *were breathing*.

The coach gave the trophy to us winners.
> *Us* is used correctly in the objective case because it is the object of the preposition *to*. *Winners* is an appositive and does not affect the pronoun choice.

PRACTICE SENTENCES 9-2

Underline the pronouns in the objective case.

Example: Mary gave <u>him</u> a brass spittoon.

1. The vice president promoted her to the position of sales manager.

2. The coach told us to hustle.

3. Mother told us girls to get quiet.

4. The man whom he most admired died in an accident.

5. Mrs. Terrill gave me a nice Christmas bonus.

Who/Whom

You need to be careful when *who* and *whom* appear in subordinate clauses.

> *Who* and *whoever* are nominative case forms that ordinarily function as subjects. But *who* and *whoever* are also often the subjects of the subordinate clauses in which they appear, not necessarily the subject of the whole sentence.

Who will win the British Open this year?
> In this sentence *who* is the subject of the whole sentence since *will win* is the only verb.

Whoever picks the most cucumbers will win a bushel of corn.
> In this sentence *whoever* is the subject of the verb *picks*, but the whole noun clause *whoever picks the most cucumbers* is the subject of the whole sentence. *Whoever* is just the subject of the verb in its clause.

John likes whoever travels to the games with him.
> *Whoever* is the subject of the verb *travels*. The whole noun clause *whoever travels to the games with him* is the direct object of the verb *likes*.

A subordinate *who/whom* clause may function as an object of a preposition.

He worked with whoever needed him most.
> *Whoever needed him most* is the object of the preposition *with*. *Whoever* is the subject of the verb *needed* in the subordinate clause.

The subordinate *who/whom* clauses may have other functions.

Knowing (who, whom) would win the election, the mayor withdrew from the race.
> *Who* is the subject of the verb *would win*. The whole noun clause *who would win the election* is the object of the participle *knowing*.

Give (whoever, whomever) eats the most an Alka-Seltzer tablet.
> *Whoever* is the subject of the verb *eats*. The whole noun clause *whoever eats the most* is an indirect object of the verb *give*.

Arthur Hall is a man (who, whom) greatly admires the films of W. C. Fields.
> This time the subordinate clause is an adjective clause. *Who greatly admires the films of W. C. Fields* modifies the noun *man*. *Who* is the correct choice because it is the subject of the verb *admires*.

> When the verb in a subordinate *who/whom* clause already has a subject, the correct choice is *whom*, functioning as a direct object of the verb in the subordinate clause.

Whomever she prefers will be appointed.

Whomever she prefers is the noun clause subject of the verb *will be appointed*. Within the noun clause *she* is the subject of the verb *prefers: She prefers whom?* The answer is *whomever*. Once you realize that the verb *prefers* already has a subject, you should realize that *whomever* is the direct object.

The woman (who, whom) John loves is a truck driver.

Whom is the correct choice because it is the direct object of the verb *loves* in the subordinate clause.

You should be careful with *who/whom* clauses in sentences that contain expressions such as *I think, I feel, I believe,* and *you may recall*. Such expressions are merely parenthetical interrupters that are not grammatically relevant. The expressions have to be mentally ignored.

Janet is the girl who I think deserves the award.

Janet is the subject of the verb *is*, and *who* is the subject of the verb *deserves*.

If you are careful in your writing to make sure each verb has a subject, you will avoid sentences such as *Janet is the girl whom I think deserves the award*. If *whom* were considered the object of the verb *think*, the verb *deserves* would not have a subject.

EDITING PRACTICE 9-3

Identify the correct sentences by placing a C *by the number; correct the errors in all others.*

Example: The senator was a man ~~whom~~ who was respected by all.

1. He was a high school student who accumulated an impressive record.

2. All of his former teachers feel he is a man whom can be trusted.

3. In college he began building a base for his political career by getting to know people who could be of help to him in the future.

4. He offered his assistance to those whom he thought could be of help to him.

5. He married a woman whom could help him with his goals.

6. He accepted a job with a lawyer who was well known within the party.

7. He learned from this man, who was influential in the party, that the right way was not always the profitable way.

8. But when he began to see that some attorneys whom he knew were getting in trouble with the courts, he decided to put ethics above ambition.

9. People soon began to realize that he was a man who could be trusted.

10. He is serving his fourth term in the Senate, and many constituents feel he is the man whom should be nominated for the presidency in the next election.

Pronouns in Comparison

> Pronouns are sometimes used following such words as *than* and *as*. Often such uses only imply a subject and/or verb. You must recognize what is omitted.

Fred likes Kathy better than I.
Fred likes Kathy better than me.

Both sentences are correct, but they mean quite different things. The first sentence has an implied verb:

Fred likes Kathy better than I [do].
I is the subject of the understood verb *do* (or *like*).

The second has an implied subject and verb.

Fred likes Kathy better than [he likes] me.
Me is the object of the understood expression *he likes*.

 In your own writing you want to communicate the right message to the reader. The sentence ending with *I* means something very different indeed from the one ending with *me*. As Mark Twain said, "The difference between the right word and the almost right word is the difference between lightning and the lightning bug."

Possessive Case

> The possessive case is used before a gerund.

Mr. Jones does not like Susan's staying out past midnight.
The proper noun *Susan* is possessive because it precedes the gerund *staying*.

His practicing four hours each day won him the prize.

> *His* is in the possessive case. It precedes the gerund *practicing,* which is the subject of the verb *won.*

He soon tired of our complaining.

> *Our* is in the possessive case because it precedes the gerund *complaining,* the object of the preposition *of.*

EDITING PRACTICE 9-4

Identify the correct sentences by placing a C by the number; correct the errors in all others.

Example: ~~Him~~ *His* getting up before noon surprised everyone.

1. My expecting a $75,000-per-year salary apparently startled my prospective employers.

2. I appreciated you helping me with the project.

3. Him raking the lawn was a nice contribution to the wedding.

4. Her running the third leg of the relay made the difference.

5. Me arguing with the police officer did not help my case.

 ### A CHECKLIST FOR PRONOUN CASE

The nominative case is required for pronouns used as:

1. Subjects
2. Predicate nominatives
3. Appositives in the subject

The objective case is required for pronouns used as:

1. Direct objects
2. Indirect objects
3. Objects of prepositions
4. Objects of verbals
5. Appositives in the object

The possessive case is required for pronouns used:

1. Before a gerund

Reference

As a writer you need to be certain your pronouns are in the right case. You must also be sure the noun the pronoun stands for (the antecedent) is obvious to the reader.

> When the reader cannot tell what noun the pronoun refers to, the writer has put up a barrier to communication known as **faulty pronoun reference.**

There is more than one type of faulty pronoun reference to avoid:

> **1.** Avoid sentences that have two possible antecedents for a pronoun.

Incorrect: Susan told Jane that she had an attractive coiffure.

The pronoun is *she,* but is the antecedent *Susan* or *Jane?*

Correct: Susan told Jane, "You have an attractive coiffure."

Now the reader knows that Jane has the attractive coiffure.

Incorrect: Bob told Ralph that he had stolen three dollars.

Is the antecedent of *he* supposed to be *Bob* or *Ralph?*

Correct: Bob confessed to Ralph that he had stolen three dollars.

Now the reader knows that the antecedent of *he* is *Bob.*

EDITING PRACTICE 9-5

In the space provided, rewrite the following sentences by eliminating the faulty pronoun reference.

Example: The golf pro told Bob his clubs were too short.

The golf pro said, "Bob, your clubs are too short."

1. Sara, the store owner, told Sue she had expensive tastes.

_____

_____

2. Mr. Adams informed Mr. Joyce that his stress level was too high.

_____

_____

3. Sally's mother told her she needed to go to the store.

_____

_____

4. The teacher told the student that she was too tired to perform at her best.

_____

_____

5. The gardener told his boss that he needed more money for the landscape to be developed as originally drawn.

_____

_____

2. Avoid sentences that have antecedents remote from the pronoun. An antecedent is said to be *remote* if it is too far from the pronoun.

The noise was disturbing to everyone in the class. The teacher felt the rusty machine was to blame. It reached a level of 180 decibels.

Does *it* refer to *noise* or *machine?*

The noise, which reached a level of 180 decibels, was disturbing to everyone in the class. The teacher felt the rusty machine was to blame.

Now there is no remote pronoun reference. The unclear *it* has been removed.

The amateur radio operators installed their equipment in the shopping center. The shoppers were very interested. They stayed through the lunch hour.

Does the *they* mean the operators or the shoppers?

The amateur radio operators installed their equipment in the shopping center; they stayed through the lunch hour. The shoppers were very interested.

Since the pronoun *they* comes in the same sentence as its antecedent *operators* and before the word *shoppers,* the reference is no longer remote.

A special type of obscure reference occurs when the antecedent is in the possessive case.

While John's car was being repaired, he played nine holes of golf.

The antecedent of *he* is *John's.* Good writers avoid placing the antecedent in the possessive case. One reason is *John's* is an adjective modifying *car,* telling which car. The antecedent of a pronoun should not be an adjective.

While John was having his car repaired, he played nine holes of golf.

Now the antecedent of both *his* and *he* is the nonpossessive word *John.*

EDITING PRACTICE 9–6

In the space provided, revise each of the following sentences so that the remote reference is eliminated.

Example: The rain dampened our mood and soaked our picnic lunch; it was not the same even after the sun came out.

The rain, which dampened our mood and our lunch,

ruined our picnic even though the sun came out.

1. The employees' cars have broken windshields and dented fenders; they were beaten with the club of a vandal.

   _____

   _____

2. Denise put a sash on her new dress; it was very attractive.

   _____

   _____

3. When Mary's idea was enthusiastically applauded, she was very happy.

   _____

   _____

4. The children all brought their radios to the birthday party; they played noisily all afternoon.

_____

_____

5. The apartment on the second floor has a window with a bright red shade; it is quite attractive.

_____

_____

---

3. Avoid sentences that have *this, that,* or *which* referring to the general idea of a preceding clause or sentence. Though some writers allow *this, that,* or *which* to refer to general ideas, more precise writers use a particular word as the antecedent of *this, that,* or *which.*

Careless: Democrats should support the party's candidates. This is what party members are told.

Precise: Party members are told to support the Democratic candidates.

Careless: Everyone wanted the man to stand up for his rights. That is what they came to see.
What is the antecedent of *that?*

Precise: Everyone came to see the man stand up for his rights.

EDITING PRACTICE 9-7

In the space provided, revise each of the following sentences so that the vague references caused by this, that, *and* which *are eliminated.*

Example: The Ronald Haney Company did not give any Christmas bonuses last year. That is unusual.

It was unusual for the Ronald Haney Company not to give

any Christmas bonuses last year.

1. John's becoming an engineer, which was a surprise to those familiar with his weakness in mathematics, is proving to be profitable for him.

   _____

   _____

2. Alice stayed up all night studying for the CPA examination. That is why she is so sleepy today.

   _____

   _____

3. The fine professor, who never published any articles, did not receive tenure, which is exactly what the students had predicted.

   _____

   _____

4. Keith cooked a nice Chinese dinner for Sue. That is unusual for him.

   _____

   _____

5. The car ran perfectly for Joe Wood during the test drive but then broke down on the way home, which is his usual bad luck.

   _____

   _____

---

4. Avoid implied antecedents. Antecedents should be stated rather than merely implied.

Implied: Although the test was easy, they had a lot of trouble.
Stated: Although the test was easy, the students had a lot of trouble.

Implied: Joseph Gluck delivered a good sermon. They told him so as they left the church.
Stated: Joseph Gluck delivered a good sermon. The members of the congregation told him so as they left the church.

EDITING PRACTICE 9-8

In the space provided, revise the following sentences so that the pronouns have stated antecedents.

Example: The man ate so voraciously he finished it in five minutes.

> *The man ate so voraciously he finished the steak in*
>
> *five minutes*

1. My father put a heavy chain on the dog's collar; he cannot escape.

   _____

   _____

2. We went outside; it did not need work.

   _____

   _____

3. After you finish sanding, I will take it to Ms. Jones.

   _____

   _____

4. When he photocopied the last page, he took it to be bound.

   _____

   _____

5. Because she had been writing all day, it was not a task she wanted to start again.

   _____

   _____

---

5. Avoid awkward use of the indefinite *it, you,* or *they*. The awkwardness results from the pronoun's lack of a specific antecedent.

Awkward: It says to jog three miles every day.
Improved: The article says to jog three miles every day.

Awkward: Many states require you to burn the headlight day or night when riding a motorcycle.
Improved: Many states require motorcyclists to burn the headlight day or night.

Awkward: At one revival they said watching television was a sin.
Improved: At one revival the preacher said watching television was a sin.

EDITING PRACTICE 9–9

In the space provided, revise the following sentences to eliminate the indefinite use of it, you, *and* they.

Example: Most of the summer jobs have been filled; they have hired only college graduates so far.

Most of the summer jobs have been filled; the employers

have hired only college graduates so far.

1. Diane recently read a book in which it tells the importance of physical fitness.

   _____

   _____

2. Mark, they say, has a lot of little eccentricities.

   _____

   _____

3. They say you should never swim after eating, but it has never bothered me.

   _____

   _____

4. It says the speed limit is 55 m.p.h.

   _____

   _____

5. They say money can't buy happiness, but I wonder if it is true.

_____

_____

---

6. Avoid using both the definite and the indefinite _it_ in a sentence.

Awkward: Although it is a good day to clean the pool, it is not extremely dirty.
The first _it_ is indefinite; the second _it_ refers to the noun _pool._
Improved: Although it is a good day for cleaning, the pool is not extremely dirty.

Awkward: We intended to plant a peach tree this fall. It is too late to plant it now.
The first _it_ is indefinite; the second _it_ refers to the noun _tree._
Improved: We intended to plant a peach tree this fall. It is too late now.

EDITING PRACTICE 9–10

In the space provided, revise each of the following sentences so that neither the definite nor the indefinite it _is present._

Example: Since it is my desire to teach, I hope I will be able to do it well.

Since I want to teach, I hope I will be a good teacher.

1. Although it is a good topic for a research paper, it cannot have so controversial a thesis.

_____

_____

2. It is a good time to wax the floor since the children are not at home to mar it.

_____

_____

3. It is a good time for playing tennis on the school court since it will not be in use.

   _____

   _____

4. Even though it rained on the day of our picnic, it was a great success.

   _____

   _____

5. Shirley passed the test even though it was hard. It is good she did.

   _____

   _____

Name _____

Class _____

Section _____ Score:_____

REVIEW EXERCISE 9–A USING PRONOUN CASE CORRECTLY

In the following sentences, underline the correct choice.

Example: The woman (who, <u>whom</u>) Alithea selects will probably get the condo.

1. (Whoever, Whomever) performs best at the tryouts will have the best chance to get on <u>Jeopardy</u>.

2. (We, Us) girls do not want to be accused of collusion.

3. It was (she, her) that paid the check.

4. (His, Him) applying for the newly available membership got him excited.

5. Moriano asked Andrea to go to the conference with (he, him).

6. Present the award to (whoever, whomever) has the best putting average.

7. (Whoever, Whomever) has the best Morse code speed will be the club president.

8. The young employee was not satisfied with the position (he, him) was offered.

9. (Him, His) having been trained in computers gave him an advantage.

10. Do you know (who, whom) will receive the scholarship?

EDITING TEST 9-A   USING PRONOUN CASE CORRECTLY
Correct the case errors in the following sentences.

                                                 me

Example: The assignment fell to Betty and ~~I~~.

1. Whom has applied for the job?

2. Me working hard on the paper paid off.

3. Us participants in the project were well rewarded for our efforts.

4. It could have been her that made the suggestion.

5. Mary does not like him borrowing her CDs and not returning them.

6. Whom do you believe is the most qualified candidate?

7. Ariel usually makes better grades than him.

8. Edna and her volunteered to join the school's planning committee.

9. She giving her dolls to her daughter was an enjoyable sacrifice.

10. Everyone but I enjoyed the movie.

Name _____

Class _____

Section _____ Score: _____

EDITING TEST 9–B   CORRECTING FAULTY PRONOUN REFERENCE (I)

In the space provided, revise each of the following sentences to eliminate faulty pronoun reference.

Example: They say never to volunteer for anything.

  Army veterans say never to volunteer for anything.

1. Bob told Herbert he should be going.

   _____

   _____

2. Gary's attending a university is expensive for his parents; he is being supported totally by them.

   _____

   _____

3. They say one should never swim alone.

   _____

   _____

4. Children should unquestionably obey all adults. This is what some children are taught.

   _____

   _____

5. Although it is not always necessary to have a physical exam, it could save some people a lot of suffering.

_____

_____

6. The ceiling with a hole in it presents a problem when it is full of people.

_____

_____

7. Although it was bad weather for a wedding, it went smoothly.

_____

_____

8. Jane told Ruth her hair needed trimming.

_____

_____

9. The store manager put an antique doll on the marble pedestal; a stranger wrote a bad check and took it.

_____

_____

10. They say Mr. Kelly is losing his mind.

_____

_____

EDITING TEST 9-C CORRECTING FAULTY PRONOUN REFERENCE (II)

In the space provided, revise each of the following sentences to eliminate faulty pronoun reference.

Example: The wardens patrol the river, which discourages illegal fishing.

The wardens' patrolling the river prevents illegal fishing.

1. After assigning the homework, Mr. Jones told them it was not necessary to turn it in.

   _____

   _____

2. They tell me that dependability in an employee is a desirable trait.

   _____

   _____

3. My high school English teacher taught grammar well. That is one thing I will never forget.

   _____

   _____

4. On a crisp and windy day, it is nice to feel it blowing through your hair.

   _____

   _____

5. Mr. Waters told Mr. Williams he would not be attending the convention.

    _____

    _____

6. It is one thing to be rich, but it is quite another to flaunt it.

    _____

    _____

7. They say a penny saved is a penny earned.

    _____

    _____

8. The textbook had a mistake in it, which confused the students.

    _____

    _____

9. The smell of smoke from burning wood in a fireplace gives me a feeling of security. This is one of my favorite memories.

    _____

    _____

10. When children trick-or-treat Ms. Lawson at Halloween, she always gives cookies and kisses them good-bye.

    _____

    _____

Writing Assignments

Assignment 9-1 In one paragraph (about half a page), describe the perfect bumper sticker for you. What would it say? Would you put it on your car, bicycle, backpack, or somewhere else where other people could see it? Would you keep it in a private place?

Assignment 9-2 Write three paragraphs (about one and a half pages) on the following: You are on a jury and are certain the defendant is guilty; however, there isn't enough evidence to convict him or her, so you have to decide in favor of "not guilty." Why is the presumption of innocence an important aspect of our justice system? Who is it protecting? Why? Do you think the requirements for finding someone guilty should change in some way? Why or why not?

Go Electronic!

For additional readings, exercises, and Internet activities, visit the Longman English pages at:

> http://longman.awl.com/englishpages

If you need a user name and password, please see your instructor.

More Practice with Your Writing and Grammar Skills

For additional practice with your writing and grammar skills, use the Writer's ToolKit CD–ROM included with this text. The ToolKit provides a wealth of computerized tutorials and practice activities.

chapter 10

Adjectives and Adverbs

Adjectives and adverbs are modifiers.

> **Adjectives** modify nouns and pronouns, and they answer
> the questions *Which one? What kind?* and *How many?*
> **Adverbs** modify verbs, adjectives, and other adverbs, and
> they answer the questions *How? When? Why? Where? To
> what extent?* and *On what condition?*

Forming Adjectives and Adverbs

Some adjectives are formed by addition of the endings *-al, -able,
-ful, -ish, -ive, -less,* and *-y* to the noun or verb form.

Noun or Verb	Adjective
mayor	mayoral
credit	creditable
fruit	fruitful
self	selfish
progress	progressive
use	useless
sleep	sleepy

Many adverbs are formed by addition of the ending *-ly* to adjectives.

Adjective	Adverb
brave	bravely
courageous	courageously
careful	carefully
religious	religiously

However, not all words ending in *-ly* are adverbs. The adjective *lonely* is a good example. Furthermore, not all adverbs end in *-ly;* for instance, *very, soon, now,* and *not* are all frequently used adverbs. Though most words ending in *-ly* function as adverbs, the only sure way to tell is to see how the word is used in the sentence.

> If the word modifies a noun or a pronoun, it is an adjective. If the word modifies a verb, an adjective, or another adverb, it is an adverb.

Using Adjectives and Adverbs Correctly

 Some writers use adjectives where they should use adverbs and vice versa. Though such usage is not often a serious barrier to communication, it can distract the reader. A useful rule to remember is that adverbs generally follow action verbs and adjectives generally follow linking verbs.

J. P. Wright dances gracefully to any kind of music.
> The action verb *dances* takes the adverb *gracefully. Gracefully* modifies the verb *dances* and answers the question *Dances how?*

Mario Andretti drives all racing cars expertly.
> *Expertly* is an adverb modifying the verb *drives* and answers the question *Drives how?*

The coffee tastes bitter.
> The adjective *bitter* follows the linking verb *tastes.*

The flowers smell sweet.
> The adjective *sweet* follows the linking verb *smell.*

PRACTICE SENTENCES 10-1

In the following sentences, underline the adverb that modifies the action verb.

    Example: Alicia studies <u>diligently</u> each day.

1. Hwan drove carelessly into the tree on the side of the road.

2. Mary uses her fax machine frequently.

3. The FBI agents opened the package carefully.

4. Bruce Lee handled his martial arts weapons flawlessly.

5. Ambrose combed his hair frequently.

6. Antonio's tape recorder did not work properly.

7. The astronomer studied his charts closely.

8. The teacher graded the term papers quickly.

9. Jasper used his credit card a little too frequently.

10. Tammy's stomach pained her terribly.

    Linking verbs, which generally take adjectives, do not express any action; they express a state of existence, being, or emotion. The adjective following a linking verb usually modifies the subject.

    Pat Johnson is lazy.
        Lazy is an adjective modifying the subject *Pat Johnson.*
        Lazy is a predicate adjective.

A list of commonly used linking verbs includes:

LINKING VERBS

is		appear
am		become
was		seem
were	forms of the	taste
been	verb *to be*	feel
being		smell
		look
		sound

PRACTICE SENTENCES 10-2

In the following sentences, underline the adjectives that follow the linking verbs.

Example: The golf course is <u>beautiful</u> this time of the year.

1. Grady's electric sander was expensive.

2. Ralph's dog is ready for the dog show this weekend.

3. The coffee in the cafeteria was bitter this morning.

4. Geraldo's hair looks nice.

5. Beatrice appeared confident after her interview.

6. The project has been ready for nearly two weeks.

7. Benny's new woodcarving was different.

8. The flowers on the table smelled fresh.

9. Sidney seems happy at this college.

10. Mia became enthusiastic about her new job after the first paycheck.

 In your writing, you must be aware of whether the verb is an action verb or a linking verb. Some of the linking verbs in our list can also be action verbs, depending on how they are used in the sentence:

> The bottle selling for $1,250 looks fragile.
>> *Looks* is a linking verb. The bottle has no eyes with which to look; it is not looking. Therefore, the adjective *fragile* is used to modify the subject *bottle*.

> Dick Allen looks carefully at every item on sale.
>> In this sentence *looks* is an action verb. Dick Allen has eyes, and he is looking. Therefore, the adverb *carefully* is used to modify the verb *looks*.

Look at these two sentences:

> The unblended Scotch tastes bitter.
> The man tastes the rare Scotch admiringly.

In the first sentence, the Scotch has no tongue with which to taste, so *tastes* is a linking verb. The subject *Scotch* is modified by the predicate adjective *bitter*. In the second sentence, the man can taste and is doing so. Therefore, the adverb *admiringly* modifies the action verb *tastes*. Do not carelessly use an adjective where an adverb should be used.

Faulty: Sing the song forceful.
Correct: Sing the song forcefully.
   Forcefully is an adverb modifying the action verb *sing*.

Faulty: The carpenter is a real fine man.
Correct: The carpenter is a really fine man.
   Really is an adverb modifying the adjective *fine*.

Faulty: Jane sure won that event.
Correct: Jane surely won that event.
   Surely is an adverb modifying the verb *won*.

Faulty: John plays his position good.
Correct: John plays his position well.
   Well is an adverb modifying the verb *plays*.

PRACTICE SENTENCES 10-3

In the following sentences, underline the correct word.

   Example: The cat studied the mouse (careful, <u>carefully</u>).

   1. The old coffee tastes (bitter, bitterly).

   2. Rick, not feeling well, ran the race (slow, slowly).

   3. Corey did not perform (good, well) on the test.

   4. The golfer studied the putt (careful, carefully).

   5. Donna's hair looks (good, well) today.

   6. Colin stroked the ball (smooth, smoothly).

   7. Lenny looks (careful, carefully) at wood before he buys it.

   8. Darrell talked (rapid, rapidly) during his job interview.

   9. Phil responded (angry, angrily) to his friend's insult.

   10. The violinist performed (admirable, admirably) at the concert.

Degrees of Adjectives and Adverbs

Adjectives and adverbs are said to have degrees.

> The **positive degree** does not compare; the **comparative degree** compares two persons or things; and the **superlative degree** compares three or more persons or things.

Positive degree: Inez is tall.
Comparative degree: Sharon is taller than Carletta.
Superlative degree: Mary is the tallest girl in the dorm.

Look at the following chart:

Number of Syllables in Word	Positive Degree	Comparative Degree	Superlative Degree
1	rich	richer	richest
1	brave	braver	bravest
2	fancy	fancier	fanciest
2	handsome	more handsome	most handsome
3	beautiful	more beautiful	most beautiful
4	mysterious	more mysterious	most mysterious

Notice that adjectives of one syllable form the comparative degree by adding -*er* to the positive degree and form the superlative degree by adding -*est* to the positive degree. (*Brave, braver, bravest* is an exception only because the *e* is already on the word.) Notice that adjectives of three syllables or more form the comparative degree by adding the word *more* before the positive degree and form the superlative degree by adding the word *most*. The words *more* and *most* in the comparative and superlative degrees indicate an ascending comparison.

Bob is more intelligent than Ralph.
Albert is the most intelligent of all.

To indicate a descending comparison, use the words *less* and *least*:

Bob is less intelligent than Ralph.
Albert is the least intelligent of all.

The chart indicates that words of two syllables may use either the -*er*, -*est* forms or the *more, most* forms. The main thing to remember, however, is that the two different forms should never be mixed. If you use -*er*, do not use *more*. It is poor usage to say *Bob is more richer than Ralph*.

Some comparative forms are irregular. These irregular forms must be memorized.

Positive	Comparative	Superlative
bad, badly	worse	worst
far	farther, further	farthest, furthest
good, well	better	best
little	less	least
many, much, several, some	more	most

Make sure your comparisons are logical. Some words are absolute in meaning and cannot be compared. *Unique, empty, dead, perfect, entirely,* and *round* are all absolutes. If a snowflake is unique, it is unique. It makes no sense to say one snowflake is more unique than another. The word *unique* means *one of a kind*, and thus by definition the word allows no comparison.

PRACTICE SENTENCES 10-4

In the following sentences, underline the correct word.

Example: Roberto is the (better, <u>best</u>) tennis player at the school.

1. He has the (harder, hardest) serve of all the players on the team.

2. He is also the (more accurate, most accurate) server.

3. However, his teammate Raul is the (better, best) at hitting volleys.

4. Roberto, though, has the (better, best) baseline game in the conference.

5. He is also the (better, best) at hitting lob shots.

6. Roberto and his friend Julius used to play (equal, equally) well.

7. But Roberto practiced (more diligent, more diligently).

8. Eventually Julius took up golf since Roberto beat him so (consistent, consistently) in tennis.

9. Roberto (enthusiastic, enthusiastically) entered the conference tournament.

10. He accomplished the (better, best) record of anyone who had ever entered.

Using Nouns as Modifiers

Writer's Tip Some writers awkwardly use nouns as adjectives. In a sentence such as *Marlene Draughn is interested in theater history,* the noun *theater* is used as an adjective modifying *history*. The sentence is effective. However, in a sentence like *Jack Nelson is a mayor candidate,* the use of the noun *mayor* as an adjective modifying *candidate* is ineffective. The correct word is the adjective *mayoral, a mayoral candidate.*

EDITING PRACTICE 10-5

In the space provided, rewrite each of the following sentences using the proper adjective form of the word incorrectly used as a noun.

Example: Jeff protested what he called idiot laws.

Jeff protested what he called idiotic laws.

1. The governor candidate passed the lie detector test.

_____

_____

2. The judge branch of the government is perhaps the one citizens understand the least.

_____

_____

3. The high school teacher reprimanded a student for his child behavior.

_____

_____

4. The United States has a long history of race prejudice.

_____

_____

5. The candidate was having trouble getting donations for his Senate campaign.

_____

_____

6. Some adults are not serious enough about their parent responsibilities.

_____

_____

7. Sergeant Preston was a member of the Royal Canada Mounted Police.

_____

_____

8. Suzy got a job as a medicine technologist.

_____

_____

9. The mayor candidate filed for the election this morning.

_____

_____

10. For three years now, the dentist has operated his office without a dentist assistant.

_____

_____

REVIEW EXERCISE 10-A   USING ADJECTIVES AND ADVERBS CORRECTLY

Underline the correct word in the following sentences.

Example: Gregory is not the (better, <u>best</u>) employee at the college.

1. He responds (slow, slowly) to orders that come through his department.

2. He often gets (angry, angrily) when people question his diligence.

3. He has a reputation for drinking too (heavy, heavily).

4. He has kept his job (consistent, consistently) over the years because he is related to the college president.

5. Nevertheless, he was told (recent, recently) that he would have to shape up.

6. He started taking inventory (more careful, more carefully).

7. He even made more of an effort to work (better, best) with the faculty and staff.

8. The president considered Gregory the (better, best) employee at the college.

9. He made (few, fewer) mistakes than any other staff member.

10. Unfortunately Gregory was fired last week for having the (worse, worst) records in the university system.

EDITING TEST 10-A USING ADJECTIVES AND ADVERBS CORRECTLY

In the space provided, rewrite each of the following sentences correctly.

Example: Cheryl is the better beautician in the freshman class.

Cheryl is the best beautician in the freshman class.

1. She treats all her customers polite.

_____

_____

2. She is most patient with her customers than the other students.

_____

_____

3. Cheryl washes each customer's hair thorough.

_____

_____

4. Each customer's hairdo is the most unique.

_____

_____

5. Cheryl wants the customer to feel beautifuller than when she came in.

_____

_____

6. She works real hard with each customer.

_____

_____

7. She sure sets ambitious goals for herself.

_____

_____

8. She plans to complete operate her own shop upon graduation.

_____

_____

9. The other students think she is definite crazy.

_____

_____

10. Her teachers, however, are confidently that she will succeed.

_____

_____

Writing Assignments

Assignment 10-1 In one paragraph (about half a page), explain how you would describe (over the phone or in a letter) a hot dog to someone from a culture where hot dogs are unknown. Do you think it would sound gross to this person? Appealing? What words would you use and what words would you avoid? Why?

Assignment 10-2 Write three paragraphs (about one and a half pages) on the following: How would you describe the view out your window to someone who could not (and never was able to) see? What would make this task challenging? What phrases would you have to use? How would you explain things like colors? Would you have to relate them to flavors or sounds?

Go Electronic!

For additional readings, exercises, and Internet activities, visit the Longman English pages at:

    http://longman.awl.com/englishpages

If you need a user name and password, please see your instructor.

More Practice with Your Writing and Grammar Skills

For additional practice with your writing and grammar skills, use the Writer's ToolKit CD-ROM included with this text. The ToolKit provides a wealth of computerized tutorials and practice activities.

part II

Punctuation and Mechanics

chapter 11

Commas

The comma is the most frequently used mark of punctuation. It is also the most frequently misused. Any punctuation mark that is used for as many different purposes as the comma is bound to create problems. The comma separates, introduces, and shows omission.

Though a comma indicates only a brief pause, its presence or absence can have a strong effect on the clarity of a sentence. If a writer fails to put a comma where it is needed, the reader might misinterpret the sentence.

> The government supplied guns, tanks, bulletproof cars and trucks.
>> Were the trucks also bulletproof? They would seem to be, judging by the punctuation.

As always, though, language and punctuation are changing. The trend in recent years has been "When in doubt, don't." In other words, if you cannot think of a specific reason why the comma should be used, leave it out. In this chapter we will explain the specific instances where commas should be used. If you master these rules, you should have little trouble with the comma. In order to help you group the numerous rules under a few general headings, the uses of the comma have been subdivided as follows:

1. Main clauses
2. Introductory elements
3. Items in a series and coordinate adjectives
4. Nonessential, parenthetical, and contrasting elements
5. Dates, degrees, place names, and long numbers
6. Unnecessary commas

Main Clauses

> Use commas to separate main clauses when they are joined by *and, or, nor, but, for, yet,* and *so.*

I find the study of the English language interesting, but I do not understand the confusing spelling rules.

Mr. James Fincaster is a lawyer in New York City, and his son is an accountant there.

Note: Some writers do not use a comma before a coordinate conjunction connecting two short main clauses, especially if the subject is the same in both clauses.

Mary washed her hair and then she blow-dried it.

EDITING PRACTICE 11-1

In the following sentences, insert commas where they are needed.

Example: Daphne and her sister got into an argument, and they have not made up yet.

1. Some teachers strongly encourage students to write journals but most students don't like the idea at first.

2. Eugene wanted to become a police officer yet he didn't have time to go through the training program.

3. The moon will be full tomorrow night so it should be perfect for camping.

4. The flat roofs on the buildings are interesting but they leak.

5. Nadine got interested in playing chess and she apparently has an aptitude for it.

6. Eric went with his wife to a yard sale and he was surprised at some of the bargains.

7. The horticulturalist drew up landscape plans for Jim's yard but he was not satisfied with them.

8. Mariano thought that the coin he had purchased was valuable but he was disappointed when he found out it wasn't.

9. Mikail wants to get married and settle down but he hasn't found the right woman yet.

10. Ted Bundy claimed that pornography caused him to commit his crimes yet most people feel he was just trying to delay the death penalty.

Introductory Elements

> **1.** Use commas to set off long (one-half line or more) introductory adverb clauses.

Although the weather was ideal, Jane wouldn't leave the house.

If the aldermen would only act, the problem would be resolved.

Notice that adverb clauses tacked onto the end of a sentence do not have to be set off with commas:

Jane wouldn't leave the house although the weather was ideal.

> **2.** Use commas to set off introductory verbal phrases.

Plying his trade expertly, the salesman sold the woman a car she couldn't afford.

To be perfectly honest, Gerald Smitherman cannot handle that job.

> **3.** Use commas to set off long (one-half line or more) introductory prepositional phrases.

In the dugout after the second game of a doubleheader, the catcher looked as if he couldn't even stand up.

After eating three sixteen-inch pizzas in twenty minutes, Bob was still hungry.

> **4.** Use commas to set off absolute constructions that come at the beginning of a sentence. An **absolute construction** is a word or group of words that relates to the thought of the sentence in which it is found but is not grammatically related to any particular word in the sentence.

Adverb absolute: Interestingly enough, no one had any desire to lead the new club.

Nominative absolute: The gate not yet being open to the public, Dale and Yvonne had to park three blocks away.

> **5.** Use commas to set off nouns of direct address.

John, did you go to the Kiwanis Club meeting last night?

Barbara, please pick up two king-size sheets for me if they are on sale.

> **6.** Use commas to set off mild interjections and *yes* or *no* answers followed by more explanation.

Well, I guess I could have done a better job if I had prepared more thoroughly.

Yes, I believe Bob does intend to go to the district meeting.

> **7.** Use commas to set off introductory conjunctive adverbs and transitional phrases. (See Chapter 8.)

Nevertheless, Jane is still the best person for the job even though she does work slowly.

On the other hand, the commissioners could just rezone the whole area.

> **8.** Use commas to introduce short quotations.

Mary said, "Nellie Forbush has to wash her hair in every performance of *South Pacific.*"

The young quarterback whispered to the coach, "Some of the starters broke the team rules last night."

9. Use commas to set off some introductory expressions in order to prevent misreading.

A few days before Bob set out on a trip and wrecked his car.
    The sentence needs a comma after *before* to prevent misreading.

A few days before, Bob set out on a trip and wrecked his car.

In 1979 273 people were killed in a DC-10 crash.
    The sentence needs a comma between the numbers.

In 1979, 273 people were killed in a DC-10 crash.
    Better yet, rewrite it.

The crash of a DC-10 in 1979 killed 273 people.

EDITING PRACTICE 11-2

In the following sentences, insert commas where they are needed.

Example: The doctor said, "Be sure to take your medicine regularly."

1. Although I studied for the test I did not do well.

2. The plane having already taken off I had to reschedule my flight.

3. Not many hours before the polls closed.

4. Interestingly enough everything we planned went off without a hitch.

5. On graduation day Yvette threw her cap in the air and yelled "I made it."

6. If I can get the parts by Wednesday I will have your car ready Friday.

7. Nanette did you get the new outfit you wanted?

8. Yes I think Howard would be perfect for the job.

9. In the center of the pet store we found the cat we wanted.

10. Gluing the vase as carefully as possible I was able to repair it adequately.

Items in a Series and Coordinate Adjectives

---
1. Use commas to separate words, phrases, and clauses in a series.

I like apples, oranges, bananas, and pears.
> Use the comma before the *and* unless the last two items go together: Jim's favorite entertainers are the Bravos, James Pawn, and Donna Gilbert and the Tonsils.

The driver lost control of his car and drove it over the guardrail, through the crowd, and down the embankment.

You need to watch your budget when you are constantly in debt, when you have to borrow to cover routine expenses, and when you feel compelled to buy clothes you don't need.

Go to the bookstore, buy an interesting-looking best-seller, and read it over the weekend.

---
2. Use a comma to separate coordinate adjectives. (**Coordinate adjectives** are equal adjectives that modify the same noun.)

A college student receives a meaningful, versatile education that will provide a broader view of life than could be obtained from on-the-job training.

Walden is an interesting, thought-provoking book.

Note: Many adjectives that refer to the number, age *(old, young, new),* origin, size, color, or location of the noun are so closely related to the nouns they modify that commas are not necessary. A useful rule of thumb is that if the word *and* can replace the comma without creating an awkward effect, then the comma is appropriate.

Sandra is a beautiful American girl.
> The sentence would be awkward if it read *Sandra is a beautiful and American girl;* therefore it would be equally awkward with a comma: *Sandra is a beautiful, American girl.*

There were many satisfied senior citizens when the Social Security increase came into effect.
> The sentence would be awkward indeed if it read, *There were many and satisfied and senior citizens when the Social Security increase came into effect.* Similarly, commas would only be distracting: *There were many, satisfied, senior citizens when the Social Security increase came into effect.*

EDITING PRACTICE 11-3

In the following sentences, insert commas where they are needed.

Example: Go to bed early, get up early, and eat a nutritious breakfast.

1. The customer wanted a good dependable truck.

2. Tommy, Jason and Lewis were the three winners.

3. All he had in his pockets were two quarters and a pocketknife.

4. The company hired an intelligent charming manager.

5. If you cannot sleep, get out of bed, read a book or watch television.

6. The students said it was an unfair even tricky test.

7. The new Spanish teacher spoke with a southern accent.

8. Drive the car to the shop, park it in front of the service door and explain the problem to the service manager.

9. Sue Ellen is a graceful versatile athlete.

10. Anne told Julian that he was rude to his parents, crude to women and generally obnoxious to everyone.

Nonessential, Parenthetical, and Contrasting Elements

> **1.** Use commas to set off nonessential adjective clauses and phrases. A **nonessential (or nonrestrictive) clause or phrase** is one that is not necessary to *identify* the noun it modifies.

Karen and Pam, with their bathing suits on and their suitcases in the trunk, headed for the beach.

The phrase *with their bathing suits on and their suitcases in the trunk* is not necessary to identify the nouns *Karen* and *Pam*.

Mr. Thomas Atkins appears to be very rich, always wearing cashmere topcoats and Brooks Brothers' suits.

Always wearing cashmere topcoats and Brooks Brothers' suits is a nonessential participial phrase placed at the end of the sentence. The phrase is not necessary to identify Mr. Atkins.

The Carthage High School cheerleaders, who were dressed in their cheer-leading uniforms, had to be at the stadium an hour before game time.
The clause *who were dressed in their cheerleading uniforms* is not necessary to identify the noun *cheerleaders*.

Note that essential (or restrictive) adjective clauses and phrases are *not* set off by commas.

The workers participating in the walkout were fired.
The phrase *participating in the walkout* is necessary to identify the noun *workers*. All workers were not fired, only those participating in the walkout. The phrase restricts the meaning of the sentence.

Students who cheat on tests are not respected by their teachers.
Teachers do respect most of their students. It is the ones who cheat that are not respected. Thus the clause *who cheat on tests* is essential and should not be set off with commas.

Adjective clauses beginning with the word *that* are essential.

Daisy Miller bought a novel that was written by Henry James.

Most adjective clauses following proper names are nonessential.

Susan B. Anthony, who was outspoken on the issue of women's rights, is now honored on a U.S. dollar coin.

Most adjective clauses following references to one's parents are nonessential.

My mother, who is a fine woman, lives in Portland, Maine.

Sometimes adjective clauses and phrases can be either essential or nonessential depending on what is meant.

The truck driver is very concerned about the Arabian horses, which were killed in the wreck.
With the comma the sentence indicates that all of the Arabian horses were killed.

The truck driver is very concerned about the Arabian horses which were killed in the wreck.
Without the comma the sentence indicates that only some of the Arabian horses were killed.

---

2. Use commas to set off nonessential appositives.

The owner, a self-made man, would not pay any player more than $250,000 a year.

She photographed Mount St. Helens, the only active volcano in the continental United States.

> Most one-word appositives are not set off with commas.

My son Tommy is a fast learner.

Roy Rogers' horse Trigger is stuffed.

> **3.** Nonessential titles are set off with commas. Essential titles are not set off.

Some Hemingway short stories, such as "The Killers" and "The Short Happy Life of Francis Macomber," are often anthologized.
  The phrase containing the titles is not essential to the meaning of the sentence.

The Yeats poem "Sailing to Byzantium" is one of the finest poems of the twentieth century.
  The title is essential to the meaning of the sentence; without it the reader would not know which poem by Yeats was meant.

> **4.** Use commas to set off parenthetical elements. (A **parenthetical element** is any word or expression that abruptly interrupts the flow of a sentence.) Parenthetical elements are not always introducers.

The project, of course, needs more study.

James Rein was unable to finish the book by the deadline, however.

 Most writers use commas to set off the longer conjunctive adverbs such as *however, moreover, furthermore, consequently,* and *nevertheless.* The shorter ones, such as *also, too, still, then,* and *thus,* are not always set off.

Thus the exercise was never actually completed.

---
5. Use commas with direct quotations to set off expressions such as *he said, she replied,* and *I shouted.*

"The main problem," he said, "is with the compressor."

"The lens is made in Germany," the photographer said, "and it should be just what you need."

---
6. Use commas to set off contrasted elements.

Give the job to Ensign Davis, not Sergeant Parker.

Margaret could give up cigarettes, but not fattening foods.

EDITING PRACTICE 11-4

In the following sentences, insert commas where they are needed.

Example: Miguel's daughter, Maria, is very imaginative.

1. The store's owner a self-made man is proud of his accomplishments.

2. One actress that I really enjoy watching is Jessica Tandy.

3. Drive the truck across the field through the creek and up the muddy slope.

4. The challenging motivational telecourse was popular with most students.

5. In 1998 153 people were killed in the mudslide.

6. Lauren's daughter Susie refused to vote for the same candidates as her parents.

7. Tommy said "I feel as if everyone depends on me."

8. Camille please sort your own laundry.

9. Interestingly enough the cheaper blender was the better one.

10. Keats's poem "On First Looking into Chapman's Homer" is one of his most famous.

Dates, Degrees, Place Names, and Long Numbers

---
1. Use commas to set off the items in a date.

On January 5, 1989, Leroy Holrod celebrated his eighty-fourth birthday.

Note: Commas are optional when only the month and year are given.

In May 1988 Nelson Swaim received his Ed.D. degree.

---
2. Use commas to set off titles and degrees after proper names.

N. P. Acumen, C.P.A.
Dr. Sharon Everett, Dean of Financial Services
Mr. Carl Brim, Chairperson

---
3. Use commas to set off geographical locations.

South Bend, Indiana, is the home of Notre Dame.
My mother lives at 2102 Seacrest Lane, Duluth, Minnesota.

---
4. Use commas after every group of three digits, counting from the right, in figures of one thousand or more.

2,394
9,643,298
$259,128

EDITING PRACTICE 11–5

In the following sentences, insert commas where they are needed.

Example: The party was scheduled for Tuesday, December 20, 1994.

1. John visited Portland Maine during the middle of winter.

2. Beth Westbrook President of the College attended the Governor's Ball.

3. Meredith celebrated her graduation on May 21 1995.

4. Richard Kildare M.D. is popular with his patients.

5. William McKinnon Vice President of Marketing has been ill all week.

6. On Monday August 14 1995 the largest factory in town closed down.

7. Brenda Davenport D.D.S has an office in the Nalle Clinic.

8. The meeting is to be in Dallas Texas on April 21 1995.

9. Walker Barnett Chairman of the Board does not tolerate dissension.

10. On Wednesday November 15 1995 the new stretch of highway will be opened.

Unnecessary Commas

Writer's Tip

Now that you have studied the basic comma rules, you should feel more confident about when to use commas. At this point, however, a reminder of where not to use commas may be helpful. Too often commas are carelessly put in places they do not belong. A comma indicates a pause, but not every pause needs a comma. In fact, there are certain brief pauses that should not have commas. In the following examples, the circled commas are unnecessary:

---

1. Except when there are intervening elements, do not use a comma to separate a subject from its verb.

The blind man with the white cane‚) walks downtown and back every Sunday.

---

2. Do not use a comma to separate a verb from its object.

Betty Ann honestly believed‚) that she could defeat her boyfriend in a wrestling match.

---

3. Do not unnecessarily use a comma before a coordinate conjunction.

Jennifer is both an excellent golfer, and a fine tennis player.

> **4.** Do not use a comma to set off most introductory words or short phrases.

At lunch, Bob and Jim signed the partnership papers.

In 1964, Muriel Thomas graduated from Mount Park High School.

Today, forty men completed their annual two weeks of training camp.

> **5.** Do not use commas to set off restrictive phrases, clauses, and appositives.

The men, putting up the fence, are with the local building supply company.

People, that drink too much, often have serious family problems.

John Gardner's book, *Grendel*, received many favorable reviews.

> **6.** Do not use a comma before the first item in a series or after the last item.

Barbara reads such books as, *Evelina, Emma,* and *Middlemarch.*

Not surprisingly, Barbara is an intelligent, sophisticated, and poised, woman.

EDITING PRACTICE 11-6

Circle the unnecessary commas in the following sentences.

Example: The driver of the 1965 Mustang, was arrested for speeding.

1. The woman, who is responsible for the accident, cannot be found.

2. Voters, that take their citizenship seriously, are well-informed about every election.

3. Carl is both a good athlete, and a good student.

4. At dinner, Jeremy always serves a fine wine.

5. Roseanne believes, that her plan will work.

6. Bob is an intelligent, polite, and handsome, administrator.

7. The man tried hard to be heard, and spoke as loudly as he could.

8. The young instructor with the air cast on his leg, broke his ankle last week.

9. The local postal supervisor says, that the mail is distributed quickly, but carefully.

10. The employees, gathering in the break room, are circulating a petition.

Name _____

Class _____

Section _____ Score: _____

EDITING TEST 11-A USING COMMAS CORRECTLY

Insert commas where they are needed in the following paragraph.

Example: After the committee debated for over two hours, the new student activity fee was increased.

1. Nigel Newton Chairman of the Committee knew that the increase in the fee would not be popular. 2. He also knew that the students who lived on campus demanded more social events. 3. Adrian who was Vice President of the Committee disagreed with any increase. 4. Adrian said "We must do more with what we have." 5. Adrian believed there should be less spent on student elections less spent on advertising events and less spent on travel. 6. Nigel and Adrian who were friends were able to discuss their differences. 7. Seeing how disturbed some of the students were, the two friends discussed the matter maturely. 8. Adrian agreed to support the increase but Nigel would have to handle the protest. 9. When the increased fee became official the protest became very vocal. 10. After two months had gone by though the entire incident was forgotten.

Writing Assignments

Assignment 11-1 Pick someone who was a role model for you in your childhood and write one paragraph (about half a page) about why that person was a role model. What did he or she do that was helpful to you and that you would like to be able to do? What characteristics of this person would you like to have? Was it a person or was it perhaps a favorite animal (a courageous dog, for example)? Was the role model a blend of different people? If you did not have a role model, why? Did or do you prefer to be the model for your own behavior?

Assignment 11-2 Think about an anti-substance-abuse (cigarettes, alcohol, drugs) advertisement you have seen on television or heard on the radio. Write three paragraphs (about one and a half pages) about the following: Who do you think is the target audience for the advertisement? Do you think it is reaching this audience effectively or not? Why? Use specific examples from the advertisement to support your ideas.

Go Electronic!

For additional readings, exercises, and Internet activities, visit the Longman English pages at:

    http://longman.awl.com/englishpages

If you need a user name and password, please see your instructor.

More Practice with Your Writing and Grammar Skills

For additional practice with your writing and grammar skills, use the Writer's ToolKit CD-ROM included with this text. The ToolKit provides a wealth of computerized tutorials and practice activities.

Semicolons

The semicolon is an important mark of punctuation. It is not used often, but when it is used, it must be used correctly. A reader will expect equal grammatical constructions on either side of the semicolon. If they are not there, the reader will be confused.

---

1. Use the semicolon between main clauses not connected by *and, or, nor, but, for, yet,* or *so.*

The Music Man is a fine musical; its best-known song is "Seventy-Six Trombones."

Most employees are covered by medical insurance; however, relatively few are covered by dental insurance.

---

2. Use semicolons to separate main clauses that themselves contain commas.

Betty Collins, a most unlikely candidate, was nominated on the first ballot; but, she told reporters, the party would be pleased with her nomination when she won the election in November.

The coordinate conjunction *but* indicates the break between the main clauses. Since the break between main clauses is more important than the breaks indicated by the four commas, the conjunction needs a semicolon before it to stress this importance.

Though there is no absolute rule for when the coordinate conjunction needs a semicolon before it at the break between main clauses, an acceptable practice would be to use the semicolon before a coordinate conjunction connecting main clauses when there is a total of two commas in the main clauses. This could mean two commas in the first main clause, two commas in the second main clause, or one comma in the first main clause and one comma in the second.

Two commas in first main clause: Andrew Carnegie, as well as John Rockefeller, made a fortune from the American capitalistic system; and Carnegie became one of America's most famous philanthropists.

Two commas in second main clause: Quite a few writers rebel against establishment values; but many of these authors, surprisingly enough, are shocked when the establishment rejects their revolutionary ideas.

One comma in both the first and second main clauses: Evaluating the track conditions closely, the trainer decided the horse should run; but the valuable animal received a debilitating injury, unfortunately.

---

3. Use semicolons to separate items in a series that itself contains commas.

Mr. William Engel was accompanied by his son John Engel, a buyer for Nichol's Mills; his daughter Joan Shaw, an executive with Person's Bank; and his wife, a board member of the Utah Power and Light Company.

A reminder: Do *not* use the semicolon to connect unequal grammatical constructions.

Having judged all the evidence available to him at the courthouse; James decided that the real estate cooperative was a rip-off.

The semicolon is used *incorrectly* to divide a participial phrase from a main clause.

Although the governor said he feared the decision would contribute to inflation; he kept salaries at the same level as the previous year.

The semicolon is used *incorrectly* to divide a subordinate clause from a main clause.

The incumbent tried hard to get the votes of all state employees; a task that he could never accomplish.

The semicolon is used *incorrectly* to divide a main clause from a noun modified by an adjective clause.

EDITING TEST 12-A USING SEMICOLONS CORRECTLY (I)

Insert semicolons where they are needed in the following sentences.

Example: Charles Darwin said that the fittest survive; he was a naturalist who desired to publish his findings.

1. Darwin also said that humans are derived from the primates many religious leaders were upset by the idea.

2. Huxley and Spencer supported Darwin's views they wrote many articles advancing his theories.

3. Darwin, on the other hand, did not try to advance his beliefs he was simply a scientist reporting what he discovered.

4. Nevertheless, church groups attacked Darwin they tried to discredit him.

5. Darwin was similar to Copernicus both of them reported their findings objectively.

6. But the church was not objective the Catholic church felt men like Darwin and Copernicus were undermining church dogma.

7. It has been said Darwin lamented his theories on his deathbed this statement may be little more than conjecture, however.

8. Darwin's theory is known as evolution the biblical interpretation is known as creationism.

9. Most scientists tend to agree with Darwin's theories they do not agree, however, that evolution follows a direct line from the primates.

10. Schools must decide what they will teach they must decide between evolution and religious tradition.

EDITING TEST 12–B USING SEMICOLONS CORRECTLY (II)

Insert semicolons where they are needed in the following paragraph.

Example: Some families like to go out to movies; other families would rather rent videos.

1. Juliane's parents would like her to go to medical school she would rather specialize in research. 2. She has always liked working in laboratories she enjoys empirical research. 3. Her parents are doubtful about her interest in research they think it is too isolated. 4. They would like to see her more active in society moreover, they would like to see her married. 5. Juliane is not currently interested in any particular man she is more concerned with her work. 6. Fortunately, her parents are open-minded they will not force their views on her. 7. Last week Juliane enrolled at MIT as a research technologist she was excited. 8. Her professors say she has great promise they encourage her in her studies. 9. Her parents have changed their minds they realize that Juliane really did know what she wanted. 10. After graduation Juliane married one of her professors they have a fine laboratory near a big hospital.

EDITING TEST 12-C USING SEMICOLONS CORRECTLY (III)

In the space provided, rewrite each sentence, correcting the semicolon errors.

Example: Ernie had a rough time at the dentist; because he had not taken care of his teeth.

   Ernie had a rough time at the dentist because he had not

   taken care of his teeth.

1. If the weather clears up soon; we should be able to get some yardwork done.

   _____

   _____

2. Trying hard to control her temper; Becky nearly bit off her thumb.

   _____

   _____

3. Lucille came back to the United States; because she wanted her unborn child to be an American citizen.

   _____

   _____

4. Even though the garden is carefully maintained; many plants are diseased.

   _____

   _____

5. Working in the lab late one night; Dr. Frankenstein received a fright.

_____

_____

6. Stella is a fine podiatrist; podiatry being a field she was introduced to by her father.

_____

_____

7. Dribbling down the court with the basketball; Jody was called for traveling.

_____

_____

8. Do not drop out of school early; if you can possibly avoid it.

_____

_____

9. Washington, D.C., is a beautiful city; one that I love to visit whenever I can.

_____

_____

10. Whenever the equipment arrives; we can begin regular practices.

_____

_____

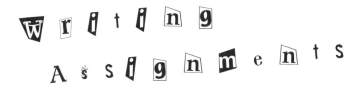

Writing Assignments

Assignment 12-1 Sit outside or at your window and watch a stranger on the street (or in the park, etc.). In one to two paragraphs (about a half to one page), make up a story about him or her. Where does this person come from? How did he or she grow up? What is the most important event that occurred in this person's life? You don't have to write your story based on the above questions; you can make up an incident that the person was involved in or a description of this person's character and personality, for example. The point is to use your imagination.

Assignment 12-2 Fear of the unknown is related to the prejudices we may feel about people, things, places, and so forth. In three paragraphs (about one and a half pages), discuss someone or something that you have been prejudiced about. For example, you might have very negative feelings about writing, reading, or exercise. You may dislike someone because he or she reminds you of someone who treated you badly once. You may feel negatively about someone or something simply because you know nothing about him or her or it. How is fear of the unknown a part of this negative feeling? If you knew more about the thing or person, do you think your feelings would change? Are you basing your feelings on past experiences or on what others have told you?

Go Electronic!

For additional readings, exercises, and Internet activities, visit the Longman English pages at:

   http://longman.awl.com/englishpages

If you need a user name and password, please see your instructor.

More Practice with Your Writing and Grammar Skills

For additional practice with your writing and grammar skills, use the Writer's ToolKit CD-ROM included with this text. The ToolKit provides a wealth of computerized tutorials and practice activities.

chapter 13

Apostrophes

The apostrophe is a somewhat distracting mark of punctuation, and it is not used consistently by all writers. Some languages avoid the problem by having a special ending for possessive nouns. In Latin, for example, the word *terra* means "land" and is used as a subject. When the word is *terrae*, however, it means "of the land" or "land's." Thus Latin uses what is called the *genitive case* and therefore does not need apostrophes. English could be written without apostrophes, too, but the expressions would be clumsy and wordy:

> the hat of the girl
> the bats of the boys
> the plays of Seneca
>> *Girl's hat, boys' bats,* and *Seneca's plays* would be much better.

Nevertheless, you must realize that English expressions containing apostrophes to indicate possession can be rewritten in phrases consisting of nouns followed by prepositional phrases. Restructuring the expressions in such phrases often helps clarify meaning. For example, if you were asked to put the apostrophe where it is needed in the expression *the guests attire,* you would need to know whether the expression means "the attire of the guest" or "the attire of the guests." *The guest's attire* means the attire of one guest, and *the guests' attire* means the attire of more than one guest. Once you have mentally restructured the expression in its correct form (noun plus prepositional phrase), you simply put the apostrophe where it belongs.

Also, many expressions containing apostrophes can be rewritten as nouns followed by prepositional phrases, but these expressions are not necessarily possessive. For instance, the expression *tomorrow's assignment* does not mean tomorrow possesses the assignment. Similarly, the expression *a good day's work* does not mean the day owns the work. Such constructions result from the fact that the English apostrophe substitutes for the genitive case of other languages, such as Latin. Therefore, the apostrophe in English can be used in the same manner as the genitive case in Latin. Since the genitive case is sometimes used for purposes other than indicating possession, the apostrophe is, too. Nevertheless, such an expression as *tomorrow's assignment* can still be rewritten as a noun plus a prepositional phrase: *the assignment for tomorrow.* Remembering that such nonpossessive uses of the apostrophe can be written out in the same manner as possessive constructions should help you better understand the use of the apostrophe.

Not all apostrophes in English even pertain to the genitive case of other languages. Sometimes apostrophes are used to indicate omissions, and sometimes they are used to form plurals. To simplify the uses of the apostrophe, we have divided this chapter into three sections: **possession, omission,** and **plurals.**

Possession

> **1.** To form the possessive of most singular nouns not ending in -*s*, add an apostrophe and -*s*.

the mayor's son
the team's coach
the student's test

> **2.** To form the possessive of singular nouns of one syllable ending in -*s*, add an apostrophe and -*s*.

the boss's secretary
Keats's poem
James's car

---

3. To form the possessive of singular nouns of more than one syllable ending in *-s*, add just an apostrophe.

---

the mattress' label
Socrates' philosophy
Aeschylus' trilogy

---

4. To form the possessive of plural nouns ending in *-s*, add only an apostrophe.

---

the players' contracts
the Smiths' house
the wives' meeting
the Joneses' vacation

---

5. To form the possessive of plural nouns not ending in *-s*, add an apostrophe and *-s*.

---

the men's organization
the children's magazine
the women's project

---

6. Use an apostrophe and *-s* to form the possessive of indefinite pronouns.

---

anybody's
everybody's
someone's
somebody's

But notice that no apostrophe is needed with personal pronouns, relative pronouns, or possessive pronouns.

ours, **not** our's
yours, **not** your's
hers, **not** her's
whose, **not** who's
its, **not** it's
their, **not** their's

7. Add an apostrophe and *-s* to the last word to indicate the possessive of compounds and word groups.

my mother-in-law's bookstore
anyone else's rights

8. Use an apostrophe to indicate authorship.

Oliver Goldsmith's *She Stoops to Conquer*
Herman Melville's *Moby Dick*
Ernest Hemingway's "The Killers"
Euripides' *Iphigenia at Aulis*

9. Use an apostrophe and *-s* with a noun or with an indefinite pronoun preceding a gerund.

Diana Nyad's swimming from the Bahamas to Florida required unbelievable endurance.

Someone's stealing the Christmas bell upset the townspeople.

10. Add an apostrophe and *-s* to the last name in a series to denote possession by two or more jointly.

Betty and Sue's piano
Lewis and Clark's expedition

11. Add an apostrophe and *-s* to each name to denote individual ownership.

John's and Robert's cars
Martha's and Paula's grades
Pam Smith's and Elizabeth Hardy's pianos

> **12.** Use the form accepted by tradition and law in indicating geographical terms, as well as names of firms, organizations, institutions, clubs, and titles.

Harpers Ferry
Lions Club
King's College
Gilbert's Fine Furniture, Inc.

EDITING PRACTICE 13-1

Insert apostrophes where they are needed in the following sentences.

Example: The cat's collar is bright red.

1. Sophocles play *Antigone* is in many freshman English anthologies.

2. The shows star was difficult to get along with during the filming.

3. Sherrie and Diannes apartment is quite expensive.

4. Someones mail-order purchase was left on the front lawn.

5. The dining-room tables finish is in poor condition.

6. The Alexanders home has been vandalized.

7. Samuel Johnsons *Rasselas* is an enjoyable book to read.

8. The faculty members vote clearly showed their support for the proposal.

9. Ladies watches are not as small as they used to be.

10. Margarets helping the injured child was a humane response to an unfortunate situation.

Omission

> **1.** Use an apostrophe to mark the omission of a letter or letters in a contraction.

don't   (do not)
can't   (cannot)
I'm   (I am)
o'clock   (of the clock)
it's   (it is)
who's   (who is)

Be sure to put the apostrophe in the proper place.

they're, **not** theyr'e
didn't, **not** did'nt

Do not confuse the contractions *it's* and *who's* with the possessive pronouns *its* and *whose*.

It's a beautiful day.
    It's means "it is."

The old car needs its engine overhauled.

Who's at the front door?
    Who's means "who is."

Whose books did you buy?

---

2. Use apostrophes to indicate the pronunciation of dialectical speech.

Watch you w'en your gittin' all you want. Fattenin' hogs ain't in luck.
                                            —JOEL CHANDLER HARRIS

---

3. Add an apostrophe where a figure or figures have been omitted.

---

class of '41 (1941)
spirit of '76 (1776)

EDITING PRACTICE 13-2

Insert apostrophes where they are needed in the following sentences.

Example: There's a huge pothole on Selwyn Avenue.

1. I dont think I can afford the house I had planned to build.

2. Theyre available to everyone that wants to attend the meeting.

3. Its not expected to be a big media event.

4. Whos expected to attend the convention in Washington, D.C.?

5. The CEO is expected to arrive at nine oclock.

Plurals

> **1.** Use the apostrophe and -*s* to indicate the plurals of letters used as letters.

His *l*'s look like *i*'s.
Her *e*'s look like *o*'s.
There are four *i*'s and four *s*'s in *Mississippi*.

> **2.** Use the apostrophe and -*s* to indicate the plurals of words used as words.

Mary often confuses her *and*'s and her *an*'s.
It is hard to tell the difference between his *ploy*'s and his *play*'s.

> **3.** Use an apostrophe and -*s* to indicate the plurals of figures used as figures.

The printer in the school shop has no more 3's.
The teacher writes 9's that look like 7's.

> **4.** Use the apostrophe and -*s* to indicate the plurals of symbols and of some abbreviations.

That model typewriter's #'s and $'s are very close to each other.
One English professor at Harvard has four *M.A.*'s and two *Ph.D.*'s.

Be careful not to use apostrophes carelessly when the noun is plural and not possessive.

The Joneses are good neighbors.

EDITING PRACTICE 13-3

Insert apostrophes where they are needed in the following sentences.

Example: Her *sword's* sounded like *ford's*.

1. The mathematics department was searching for candidates with M.A.s in physics and astronomy.

2. The division secretary said my *plays* looked like *ploys*.

3. The 7s and 9s in the manuscript looked similar.

4. The words *son*s and *sun*s sound alike.

5. The *g*s on the printer did not print properly.

6. Tommy made three *A*s and two *B*s last semester.

7. The *i*s and the *l*s looked too much alike.

8. My handwriting does not distinguish well between *a*s and *o*s.

9. The University of Minnesota granted 286 MAs last semester.

10. On my computer keyboard I often strike *q*s for *w*s.

EDITING TEST 13-A   USING APOSTROPHES CORRECTLY

Insert apostrophes where they are needed in the following paragraph. Add an s *if necessary.*

Example: Jane's cap

1. Jeremy wife Sarah noticed a leak in the basement. 2. Its not a pleasant sight to see your carpet damp, possibly being ruined. 3. She didn't know any plumbers. 4. She looked through the telephone book listings for plumbers. 5. She didn't know the plumber she called. 6. The plumbers shop was close to her home. 7. "It's going to be an expensive repair job," the plumber told her. 8. "Your copper pipes arent in good shape. 9. In fact, theyre worn out. 10. "You shouldve had them replaced with plastic pipe years ago."

Writing Assignments

Assignment 13-1 What is your favorite style of music? In one paragraph (about half a page), discuss the band, singer, composer, etc., who best performs this music. What is it about the music that you like? Use specific examples from the lyrics, tune, instruments, etc., to support your ideas.

Assignment 13-2 Often, we confuse words that are spelled differently but that sound the same. Look up the following words in the dictionary, then, in two to three paragraphs (about one to one and a half pages), explain what each word means and use it in a sentence. Are there words that you often misuse? What are they? Most of us have at least a couple of words that we don't always use correctly. Have you figured out a way to remember which word should be used in which way? If so, what is your memory device?

accept/except
affect/effect
to/too/two

Go Electronic!

For additional readings, exercises, and Internet activities, visit the Longman English pages at:

http://longman.awl.com/englishpages

If you need a user name and password, please see your instructor.

More Practice with Your Writing and Grammar Skills

For additional practice with your writing and grammar skills, use the Writer's ToolKit CD–ROM included with this text. The ToolKit provides a wealth of computerized tutorials and practice activities.

Quotation Marks

Unlike the rules concerning some marks of punctuation, the rules concerning quotation marks are fairly well standardized.

> The main rule is always "Quotation marks come in pairs." Whenever you use an opening set of quotation marks, you must remember that a closing set will be required.

Since quotation marks serve more than one purpose, this chapter is divided into four parts: "Direct quotations," "Titles," "To Indicate" "Special Sense," and "With Other Marks of Punctuation." If you follow the rules presented in these four sections, you should not have any trouble using quotation marks correctly.

Direct Quotations

> **1.** Use double quotation marks to enclose direct quotations. Capitalize the first letter of the first word of a quoted sentence.

Plutarch said, "It is indeed a desirable thing to be well descended, but the glory belongs to our ancestors."

Do not capitalize the first letter of the first word of a quotation if what is quoted is not a complete sentence and the letter would not ordinarily be capitalized.

Plutarch said that it is fine for us to be descended from famous people but added that the fame "belongs to our ancestors."

Do not use quotation marks to set off an indirect quotation. An indirect quotation reflects the original thought but is not in the exact words of the original. Indirect quotations are often introduced by the word *that*.

Plutarch said that it is fine for us to be descended from famous people but added that the fame belongs to those who earned it.

---

2. Use single quotation marks to enclose a quotation within a quotation.

John said, "Many American soldiers in Vietnam did not agree with Nathan Hale's words, 'I only regret that I have but one life to lose for my country.'"

---

3. With a quotation within a quotation within a quotation, double quotation marks are used first, then single quotation marks, and then double quotation marks again.

"It is a brave man indeed," Jonathan said, "who believes Lieutenant Edward's sentiment: 'Every good soldier agrees with Nathan Hale's words, "I only regret that I have but one life to lose for my country."'"

Quotation marks should not get any more involved than quotations within quotations. When the sentence is more complicated than that, it should be rewritten.

Note: If you read books or magazines printed in the British Isles or in British territories, you will find that the use of double quotation marks and single quotation marks is exactly the reverse of what has been explained in this chapter. American usage, however, does not permit the use of single quotation marks by themselves except in headlines.

> **4.** The preferred way of reproducing long quotations is to omit the enclosing quotation marks and indent the entire passage of the quotation about a half inch. In a typed paper, you should double-space the indented quotation.

It is interesting that—like Allen Tate, T. S. Eliot, and Ezra Pound—Randall Jarrell never wrote a defense of poetry for the people who felt it needed one. He felt strongly that

> poetry does not need to be defended, any more than air or food needs to be defended; poetry—using the word in its widest sense, the only sense in which it is important—has been an indispensable part of any culture we know anything about. Human life without some form of poetry is not human life but animal existence.[1]

Because he believed poetry was necessary for human existence, he refused to jump on the bandwagon and condemn modern poetry because of its complexity.

> **5.** A two-line quotation from a poem can be handled in either of two ways.

You may incorporate the quotation into the text by enclosing it in quotation marks and using a slash to indicate the end of the first line.

Alexander Pope said in his *Essay in Criticism,* "A little learning is a dangerous thing / Drink deep, or taste not the Pierian spring." There are many such memorable statements in the poetic essay.

The quotation may be set off from the text and reproduced exactly as it appears in the original (with no quotation marks employed that are not in the original).

Alexander Pope said in his *Essay in Criticism,*

> A little learning is a dangerous thing;
> Drink deep, or taste not the Pierian spring.

There are many such memorable statements in the poetic essay.

---

[1] Randall Jarrell, "The Obscurity of the Poet," *Partisan Review* 18 (Jan.–Feb. 1951): 67.

> **6.** Longer passages from poems must be set off from the text and re-produced exactly as they are found in the original.

The well-known Scottish poet Robert Burns once wrote:

> My love is like a red red rose
>   That's newly sprung in June:
> My love is like the melodie
>   That's sweetly play'd in tune.

Many English teachers quote the stanza when they are explaining similes to their students.

> **7.** In dialogue remember to set off such expressions as *he said, she replied,* and *he asked* with commas.

Ellen asked, "Will Paul come to the meeting?"
"Paul cannot attend the meeting today," Jane replied.
"If Paul would come," Ellen said, "we could finish this project today."

EDITING PRACTICE 14-1

Insert quotation marks where they are needed in the following sentences.

Example: "Place your books in your lockers," the teacher said, "and we will begin work on the art project."

1. The golfer said to his caddy, Hand me the nine iron.

2. I would like to take some lessons in music theory, I told my mom, and then take some piano lessons.

3. Did you know that there are only three computers available in the Writing Center? said one student to another.

4. The instructor of the electrical applications class told the students, Be sure to turn off the power source before starting to work.

5. The timer for the bomb, the bomb squad leader said, was a simple drugstore alarm.

6. I need a new car, Tom said, but I don't know what kind I want.

7. Jorge knew that his company's bid would not be accepted.

8. Only three members of the team will be able to make the trip to New York, the debate coach told his squad.

9. The steaks are a little crisp, Blanche told her neighbors.

10. Willie, you must practice at least an hour a day if you expect to maintain and improve your skills, his coach told him.

Titles

Books and newspapers do not handle titles the same way. Newspapers use practically no italics at all, whereas books generally use italics for separate publications. The rule presented in this section reflects the usage of reputable book publishers.

> The general rule is to italicize (underline) the title of a long work and to enclose the title of a short work in quotation marks. Use quotation marks to enclose the titles of newspaper and magazine articles, essays, short stories, short poems, short musical works, and subdivisions of books.

"Dover Beach" is Matthew Arnold's best-known poem.

"The Unparalleled Adventure of One Hans Pfaall" is an interesting short story by Edgar Allan Poe.

One of T. S. Eliot's most famous essays is "Tradition and the Individual Talent."

A series entitled "The Community College: A Better Way" appeared in the *Montgomery Herald.*

The first big hit in America by the Beatles was "I Wanna Hold Your Hand."

Part 2 of Herman Wouk's *War and Remembrance* is entitled "Midway."

EDITING PRACTICE 14-2

Insert quotation marks where they are needed in the following sentences.

Example: The next poem on the list is "Mr. Flood's Party" by Edwin Arlington Robinson.

1. *The Washington Post* ran an article entitled Watergate Revisited.

2. Many readers are fond of Robert Frost's short poem Home Burial.

3. Ernest Hemingway wrote a short story about abortion called Hills like White Elephants.

4. I Am Born is the title of the first chapter of Dickens' novel *David Copperfield*.

5. Emily Brontë's novel *Wuthering Heights* is a classic.

To Indicate Special Sense

> **1.** Use quotation marks to call attention to an unusual word or phrase, a technical term, or a slang or dialectical expression that differs in style from the context.

The minister knew he was "right on" with his advice to the young.

An "erg" is a unit of energy.

> **2.** Use quotation marks to suggest that a word or phrase is being used ironically.

Jim's "valuable" prize turned out to be a cheap watch.

The "easy" economics exam caused Jerry to graduate a semester behind his classmates.

 Because enclosing an expression in quotation marks really makes it stand out, be sure not to overuse quotation marks to indicate that a word or phrase is used in a special sense. To overuse the device merely weakens its effectiveness.

With Other Marks of Punctuation

---
1. Place the period and the comma inside the quotation marks.

"You know," the Senator said, "I think I'll run for president."

"Please get off my foot," Kathy asked nicely.

---
2. Place the colon and the semicolon outside the quotation marks.

One of Poe's best stories is "The Gold-Bug"; the story takes place in South Carolina.

There are four important characters in "The Open Boat": the cook, the captain, the oiler, and the correspondent.

---
3. Place the question mark and the exclamation point inside the quotation marks when they apply to the quoted matter.

Barbara asked, "Are you ready?"

Did he ask, "What is reality?"

"Tackle him! Tackle him!" the coach shouted from the sidelines.

"Can we stay here?" she asked.

Notice in the last two sentences that no comma follows a question mark or an exclamation point.

---
4. Place the question mark and the exclamation point outside the quotation marks when they apply to the whole sentence.

Stop singing "Dixie"!

Do you like "Yankee Doodle"?

Sometimes the proper use of quotation marks can be complicated. For instance, the following sentence contains a quotation within a quotation; the overall quotation is a question but the quotation within a quotation is a statement.

Bob asked his neighbor, "Did my wife say, 'I'm leaving'?"

EDITING PRACTICE 14-3

Put quotation marks where they are needed in the following sentences.

Example: The policeman shouted, "I cannot hear where the sound is coming from. Hush!"

1. Erwin asked, Will the new sandwich shop open on time?

2. Jean yelled in pain, I think I broke my leg!

3. Young Goodman Brown is a well-known short story by Nathaniel Hawthorne.

4. The teacher, who was nearly in a panic himself, shouted to the students, Don't panic.

5. A hertz is a unit of frequency.

6. Sari yelled, Turn off the power!

7. Ernie said, Do you really think the new parking proposal will pass?

8. John asked, Do you know the words to the famous western song The Streets of Laredo?

9. The drivers' license examiner told the group, Bring your test papers to the front of the room when you finish.

10. Ozymandias is a fine short poem by Shelley.

EDITING TEST 14–A   USING QUOTATION MARKS CORRECTLY (I)

Insert quotation marks where they are needed in the following paragraph.

Example: The author asked the student, "Have you read my short story 'Barefoot in the Bermuda Triangle'?"

1. Mitchell asked Jackie, Have you read Virginia Woolf's novel *To the Lighthouse?* 2. Yes, Jackie said, I have. 3. Which of the three sections did you like the best? Mitchell wanted to know. 4. Jackie replied, I only remember the middle section called Time Passes. 5. Then she asked, What were the titles of the other two sections? 6. Mitchell told her that the first section was The Window and the third section was The Lighthouse. 7. Then he said, I'm not surprised that you remembered the Time Passes section. 8. That entire portion is beautiful prose describing the passage of time and the indifference of Nature to human suffering, Mitchell explained. 9. Yes, Jackie agreed, it is. 10. It seemed to me more like poetry than prose, she said.

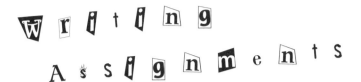

Writing Assignments

Assignment 14-1 Look up argument and debate in the dictionary. In one paragraph (about half a page), explain the difference between the two. Give an example of how and where each occurs. What makes the two different?

Assignment 14-2 Pick a country you have heard or read about but have never visited. Imagine that you are riding a bus through this country (limit the ride to a city, village, part of the countryside, etc.), and in three paragraphs (about one and a half pages), describe what you see on this imaginary trip. How do the people look? What are they doing? What does the land, city, etc., look like? How is it different from and similar to the place where you live?

Go Electronic!

For additional readings, exercises, and Internet activities, visit the Longman English pages at:

http://longman.awl.com/englishpages

If you need a user name and password, please see your instructor.

More Practice with Your Writing and Grammar Skills

For additional practice with your writing and grammar skills, use the Writer's ToolKit CD–ROM included with this text. The ToolKit provides a wealth of computerized tutorials and practice activities.

chapter **15**

Capitalization and Italics

Capitalization

It is difficult to formulate a definitive set of capitalization rules for the English language. Capitalization usage changes with time, meaning, and purpose. The current trend, for instance, is toward fewer capital letters than were used in the past. Just a hundred years ago a newspaper such as *The New York Times* would have capitalized many words that a modern issue of the paper would not. Also, the meaning of a word in the context of a sentence can affect capitalization. You may live on Main Street, for example, and it could be the main street in the town. Capitalization usage varies with purpose, too. Thus newspaper headlines are not always capitalized the same way as newspaper articles. At best, capitalization rules serve only as guides. Since it is important, however, to be as consistent as possible, use capital letters only for a specific purpose and with a particular rule in mind.

In this section the rules of capitalization are divided into three units to make them easier to remember: (1) "Mechanics"; (2) "Places, Times, and Kinds"; and (3) "Government and Social, Publishing and Personification."

Mechanics

1. Capitalize the first word of every sentence.

The amateur defeated the professional in the pro-am tournament.

> **2.** Capitalize a word or the first word of a phrase that stands alone as a sentence.

Thanks.
Objection overruled.

> **3.** Capitalize the first word of a direct quotation within a sentence (but not if the quotation is a fragment).

Kahlil Gibran said, "Let there be spaces in your togetherness."
Kahlil Gibran says you must have "spaces in your togetherness."

> **4.** Capitalize the first word of each line of poetry (unless it isn't capitalized in the original).

The woods are lovely, dark and deep
But I have promises to keep,
And miles to go before I sleep.
　　　　　—ROBERT FROST

But some poets prefer not to capitalize:

it's just like a coffin's
inside when you die,
pretentious and
shiny and
not too wide
　　　　　—e. e. cummings

> **5.** Capitalize a common noun when it is used alone as a well-known short form of a specific proper name.

the Gulf (Gulf of Mexico)
the Capitol (in Washington, D.C.)

---
6. Capitalize the interjection *Oh* and the pronoun *I*.

Come forward, Oh dear friends; I need your help.

---
7. Capitalize all proper nouns and adjectives.

Faculty Senate
Surry Community College
Louisville Country Club
Lookout Dam

But notice:

a college
an avenue
a dam
a democracy

---
8. Capitalize the first word and any nouns in the salutation of a letter.

Gentlemen
Dear Mr. Smith
My dear Gloria

But only the first word of the complimentary close is capitalized:

Very truly yours
Sincerely yours

---
9. Capitalize calendar designations.

Monday
August
Thanksgiving Day

But notice:

twentieth century
winter

10. Capitalize the abbreviations of many titles and degrees and some common one- or two-letter abbreviations.

James Alfred Draughn, Ph.D.
Theodore N. Swaim, Jr.
TV, CB, F (Fahrenheit)

11. Capitalize the numerals used to refer to organizations or to periods of time. Spell out numerals preceding a name. Often, numerals following a name are put in Roman numerals.

First World War
Second Army
World War II
Edward VII
Fifty-first Congress

12. Capitalize expressions of time such as *A.M.*, *P.M.*, *A.D.*, and *B.C.* (Some writers prefer not to use capital letters for *A.M.* and *P.M.*)

55 B.C.
6:20 A.M.
A.D. 449

EDITING PRACTICE 15-1

Supply capital letters where they are needed.

Example: the class meets every tuesday night.

1. churchill downs in louisville, kentucky, is the site of the kentucky derby.

2. the united states entered world war ii in 1941.

3. christmas day is a sad time for many lonely people.

4. in 55 b.c. julius caesar invaded england.

5. it was f.d.r. who said, "we have nothing to fear but fear itself."

6. the lincoln memorial in washington is very impressive.

7. the meeting will begin promptly at 10:00 a.m.

8. the temperature was 3°f this morning.

9. steve's mother said, "please close the door."

10. dry wells is a ghost town.

Places, Times, and Kinds

---

13. Capitalize geographical terms.

Hudson River
Irish Sea
Pike's Peak
Rocky Mountains
Lake Erie

But notice:

the Erie and Huron lakes

---

14. Capitalize descriptive terms used to designate a definite region or locality.

---

the North Atlantic States
the South
Eastern Hemisphere
the Promised Land

Directional parts of states are not capitalized, however.

eastern Kentucky
southern Idaho

Also, compass points are not capitalized when indicating direction.

The Smiths drove west for ten miles and then headed northwest for the next twenty-five miles.

15. Capitalize the names of specific streets, roads, highways, toll roads, etc.

Highway 66
Road 2249
West Virginia Turnpike

16. Capitalize proper names.

John Conklin
Spain
Paris

17. Capitalize the derivatives of proper names used with a proper meaning.

Miltonic style
Jeffersonian democracy
Spanish
Parisian
American

Words derived from proper names that now have independent meanings are *not* capitalized.

china (meaning "porcelain")
pasteurize
bohemian
volt

18. Capitalize nouns of kinship when used as substitutes for proper names.

I would like to introduce you to Dad.

But *do not* capitalize nouns of kinship that are preceded by an article or a possessive.

She is my mother.

---

19. Capitalize a course of study if the name of the subject is derived from a proper noun or if you are referring to a specific course title.

French
German
Piaget's Theory of Cognition
History 101
Shorthand II

But:

history
shorthand

---

20. Capitalize the word *the* only when it is part of an official name or title.

The Hague
The Tempest

But the word *the* is not generally capitalized in references to newspapers, magazines, vessels, and companies unless it is part of the actual name (and even then sometimes not capitalized):

the Atlantic Monthly
the U.S.S. *America*
the *Winston-Salem Journal*
the Fuji Film Co.

---

21. Capitalize the scientific name of a genus, but not the name of a species.

Acer saccharinum (genus and species)

---

22. Capitalize religious feast, festival, and fast days as well as historic events and eras.

Feast of the Passover
the Renaissance
Yom Kippur
Christmas Day

Battle of Salamis
Korean War
Kwanza
the Treaty of Versailles

---

23. Capitalize names for God or the Trinity, both nouns and adjectives, and pronouns referring to the Deity.

---

the Messiah
Our Father
His mercy
Allah

---

24. Capitalize the names of sacred writings.

Holy Bible
Genesis
Koran

EDITING PRACTICE 15-2

Correctly supply capital letters where they are needed.

Example: *war and peace* is a famous novel by ~~l~~eo ~~t~~olstoy.
(W and P above *war* and *peace*; L and T above *leo tolstoy*)

1. the masters is a famous golf tournament.

2. andrew jackson was the american general at the battle of new orleans.

3. highway 21 has a hugh pothole about two miles from stokesbury.

4. i have studied *wuthering heights* at least three times.

5. the mitchell river is perhaps the cleanest river in surry county.

6. lauren studied german at syracuse university.

7. i named my boat the *suzy q.*

8. my aunt lives in racine, wisconsin.

9. stone mountain is an interesting place to visit.

10. Huan subscribes to *people, life,* and *time* magazines.

Government and Social, Publishing, and Personifying

> **25.** Capitalize the names of administrative, legislative, and judicial bodies and departments.

House of Representatives
Supreme Court
Department of Commerce
General Assembly of North Carolina

> **26.** Capitalize the names of organizations, political parties, alliances, institutions, religious groups, races, movements, classes, nationalities, athletic teams, civic groups, etc.

Lions Club
Young Men's Christian Association
Republican party
Princeton University
Catholics
Jews
Dallas Cowboys

But:

democracy
club

> **27.** Capitalize any titles preceding a person's name.

President Kennedy
King Charles
Ambassador Smith
Professor Wiles

> **28.** Capitalize a common-noun title immediately following a name or used alone as a substitute for it to indicate preeminence or distinction.

Jim Rawlings, Governor
the President (of the United States)
the King (referring to a specific one)
the Pope

---

29. Capitalize the first and last words of the titles of books, articles, student compositions, etc., and capitalize all other important words (nouns, verbs, adjectives, and adverbs). Do not capitalize articles (*a, an, the*) or short (four letters or less) prepositions or conjunctions.

Gone with the Wind
A Raisin in the Sun
"An Analysis of Roderick Usher"

But notice:

"The Man Against the Sky"
Desire Under the Elms

The prepositions *against* and *under* contain five letters or more.

---

30. Capitalize trade names, variety names, and names of market grades.

Corning Ware (trade name)
Golden Delicious apple (variety)
USDA Choice (market grade)

---

31. Capitalize all personifications. (Personification is the granting of human attributes to abstract ideas and inanimate objects.)

Suddenly and unexpectedly, Death crept into the room during the night.

The Chair recognizes the representative from Guilford County.

EDITING PRACTICE 15-3

Supply capital letters where they are necessary.

$$\overset{M}{} \qquad \overset{H}{} \qquad \overset{R}{}$$

Example: ~~m~~ary served in the ~~h~~ouse of ~~r~~epresentatives for two terms.

1. herman wouk scored two hits with *the winds of war* and *war and remembrance.*

2. i like the morning flower pattern for everyday china.

3. the oakland a's are trying to get into the playoffs.

4. *invisible man* is a fine novel by ralph ellison.

5. the woman thought death stalked her constantly.

6. "the cask of amontillado" is a short story by poe.

7. eliot ness worked for the treasury department.

8. michael jordan was a star for the chicago bulls.

9. have you ever read the book *my brother was an only child?*

10. carla thinks professor reece is an excellent teacher.

Italics (Underlining)

There is no definitive set of rules for the use of italic type. Different publishers follow different rules. Nevertheless, the rules presented in this chapter generally reflect the usage recommended by the *U.S. Government Printing Office Style Manual* and most authorities. In typewritten and handwritten papers you should underline in all cases where printers use italics.

> **1.** Italicize all titles of separate publications (books, magazines, newspapers, plays, long musical compositions, long poems, etc.).

U.S. Government Printing Office Style Manual (book)
Rosencrantz and Guildenstern Are Dead (play)
Paradise Lost (epic poem)
La Bohème (opera, long musical work)
Moby Dick (novel)
U.S. News & World Report (magazine)
the *Chicago Tribune* (newspaper)

> **2.** Italicize the names of ships, trains, aircraft, and spacecraft.

The *Queen Elizabeth II* is a beautiful ship.

Lindbergh's *Spirit of St. Louis* was small and fragile.

The moon-mission of *Apollo IX* will never be forgotten.

> **3.** Italicize the titles of motion pictures and works of art.

Star Wars was a movie with magnificent special effects.

Michelangelo's *David* is one of the most famous sculptures in the world.

Leonardo da Vinci's *Mona Lisa* is perhaps the most famous painting in the world.

> **4.** Italicize the Latin names of genus and species.

Osmunda cinnamomea (cinnamon fern)
Canis familiaris (dog)

> **5.** Italicize foreign words and expressions.

raison d'être (French for "reason for being")
e pluribus unum (Latin for "from many, one")

Note: Many foreign words and expressions are so commonly used they are said to be Anglicized; such words and expressions are not italicized. To eliminate doubt, consult a dictionary.

patio (Spanish)
hors d'oeuvre (French)
bona fide (Latin)

> **6.** Italicize a letter, word, number, or expression when it is spoken of as such or is used as an illustration.

The *i*'s on that make of typewriter look like *l*'s.

The words *adapt* and *adopt* confuse many readers.

Please form your *Z*'s and *3*'s distinctly.

---

7. Italicize—sparingly—to emphasize a word or expression.

Write all essays in *ink!*

Do not overuse italicizing in this manner.

EDITING TEST 15-A USING CAPITAL LETTERS AND ITALICS CORRECTLY (I)

Supply capital letters and underlining where they are needed in the following paragraph.

Example: ~~h~~erman ~~m~~elville's ~~m~~oby ~~d~~ick
<small>H   M   M   D</small>

1. ernest hemingway was a popular american writer. 2. he wrote a collection of short stories called men without women. 3. he also wrote a book about bullfighting called death in the afternoon. 4. for whom the bell tolls is one of his popular titles. 5. some readers consider a farewell to arms his best work. 6. interestingly enough, women readers seem to like this macho writer. 7. hemingway was fond of hunting and fishing. 8. he won the nobel prize shortly after publishing the old man and the sea. 9. Hemingway lived life to the fullest and shared his experiences with his readers. 10. Unfortunately, he lost some of his confidence late in life.

EDITING TEST 15-B USING CAPITAL LETTERS AND ITALICS CORRECTLY (II)

Supply capital letters and underlining where they are needed in the following paragraph.

Example: ~~uss~~ <u>c</u>onstitution

1. marie recently developed an interest in renaissance art. 2. she began keeping a list of her favorite works. 3. she likes leonardo da vinci's famous portrait entitled mona lisa. 4. her favorite artist, though, is michelangelo. 5. she especially likes his statue david and his painting on the ceiling of the sistine chapel. 6. marie also likes the work of raphael, especially his painting the school of athens. 7. she has titian's portrait man with the glove on her list. 8. other items are michelangelo's statue moses and raphael's painting galatea. 9. marie likes the work in marble by donatello, especially the two statues st. mark and st. george and the dragon. 10. marie certainly shows good taste in her selections.

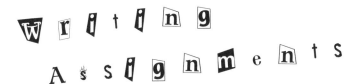

Writing Assignments

Assignment 15-1 In one paragraph (about half a page), give instructions to an alien from another planet on how to put on, lace, and tie shoelaces. How would you talk to the alien through this process? What words and phrases would you use to explain it? Would you break the process into steps? If so, what steps?

Assignment 15-2 Watch a local news broadcast about some controversial issue in your neighborhood or fairly close to where you live. Write a brief letter of three paragraphs (about one and a half pages) to the editor of your local newspaper. In the letter represent yourself as either for or against the issue and carefully explain and support your ideas. In an editorial letter it is important to be persuasive (to keep your reader's attention and encourage him or her to think about your ideas). Simply saying something is right or wrong, good or bad doesn't explain anything. Present your ideas thoughtfully, and support them with specific examples from either your own experience or the experiences of others.

Go Electronic!

For additional readings, exercises, and Internet activities, visit the Longman English pages at:

> http://longman.awl.com/englishpages

If you need a user name and password, please see your instructor.

More Practice with Your Writing and Grammar Skills

For additional practice with your writing and grammar skills, use the Writer's ToolKit CD–ROM included with this text. The ToolKit provides a wealth of computerized tutorials and practice activities.

chapter 16

Abbreviations and Numbers

Abbreviations

Standard English usage is rather conservative and permits few abbreviations. As might be expected, there is little consistency in the abbreviations it does accept. Also, the acceptability of abbreviations varies according to the purpose of the writing. For instance, a chart in a technical report and the bibliography of a scholarly article will use far more abbreviations than the standard prose of most popular magazines and books written for a general audience. Naturally, the audience aimed at will largely determine the acceptability of abbreviations. Technical matter aimed at specialists who share a similar background and who are expected to know the jargon of the field contains numerous abbreviations. In fact, the abbreviations, symbols, and equations of some technical writing are practically a form of shorthand. On the other hand, abbreviations are kept to a minimum in popular magazines such as *Time, Newsweek,* and *Reader's Digest.* In these magazines the purpose is clarity. Your compositions for your English class are written in standard English. Like popular magazines, you should have clarity as a goal. You do not want to use any abbreviations that might confuse your reader.

Though lists of acceptable abbreviations might differ greatly from one magazine to another, some conventions in abbreviating have developed over the years. This chapter presents the conventions most often accepted in standard English writing for nontechnical audiences.

---

1. Use the abbreviations *Mr., Mrs., Miss, Ms., St.,* and *Dr.* whenever these titles precede a proper name.

Dr. Alice Smith
Mr. Jones
Mrs. Alistair
Ms. Frances Ingram
St. Christopher

---

2. Use the abbreviations *Gen., Sgt., Prof., Gov., Rev., Hon., Sen., Rep.,* and *Capt.* if the title is followed by a first name or an initial as well as a surname.

Gen. George Patton
The Rev. J. Hutton
Prof. H. Kissinger

But:

Captain Adams
Sergeant Brown

---

3. Use the abbreviations *Jr.* and *Sr.* when preceded by a proper name.

William E. Edmonds, Jr.
Edward J. Pendleton, Sr.

---

4. Use the abbreviations *D.D., Ph.D., M.A., B.A., M.D.,* and *C.P.A.* when preceded by a proper name or alone if the context is clear.

June R. Mandell, Ph.D.
William C. Ludwig, C.P.A.
He earned an M.A. degree before he sat for the C.P.A. exam.

---

5. Use the abbreviations *Co., Corp., Inc., Bros., Ltd.,* and symbols such as the ampersand (&) in describing business firms only when the abbreviations are part of the legally authorized name.

Grosset & Dunlap, Inc.
Jones Bros. & Co.
Radio Corp. of America
A & P Company

---

6. The abbreviations *i.e., e.g., cf., et al., etc.,* and *vs.* or *v.* may be used in any type of writing.

---

i.e. (that is)   et al. (and others)
e.g. (for example)   etc. (and so forth)
cf. (compare)   vs. or v. (versus)

The artist brought several examples of his craft, e.g., silver pitchers and pewter sconces.

---

7. Use the following abbreviations for states when they immediately follow any capitalized geographical term. Alaska, Hawaii, Idaho, Iowa, Maine, Ohio, and Utah are spelled out. Do not abbreviate the name of the state when it stands alone.

Ala.	Del.	Ky.	Miss.
Ariz.	Fla.	La.	Mo.
Ark.	Ga.	Mass.	Mont.
Calif.	Ill.	Md.	N.C.
Colo.	Ind.	Mich.	N. Dak.
Conn.	Kans.	Minn.	Nebr.
Nev.	Okla.	S. Dak.	Wash.
N.H.	Oreg.	Tenn.	Wis.
N.J.	Pa.	Tex.	W. Va.
N. Mex.	R.I.	Va.	Wyo.
N.Y.	S.C.	Vt.	

Albany, N.Y.
Nashville, Tenn.
Portland, Maine
Provo, Utah
Little Rock, Ark.

But:

She was born in South Carolina.

> **8.** Spell out the names of most countries.

in Brazil
in London, England

> **9.** Use the abbreviation *U.S.* as an adjective but not as a noun.

U.S. Navy
U.S. Government Printing Office
in the United States

> **10.** Use the abbreviations A.D., B.C., A.M., P.M., *no.* or *No.*, and the symbol $ only with dates or figures.

A.D. 1066
350 B.C.
4:50 P.M.
$105
No. 3

> **11.** Use the abbreviation *D.C.* for District of Columbia.

Washington, D.C.

> **12.** Use abbreviations for things normally referred to by their capitalized initials. Do not use periods.

CB
TV

> **13.** Use commonly accepted acronyms (words derived from the initial letters or syllables of successive parts of a term). Do not use periods.

Amoco (American Oil Company)

UNESCO (United Nations Educational, Scientific, and Cultural Organization)

© 2000 Addison–Wesley Educational Publishers Inc.

EDITING PRACTICE 16-1
Correct all abbreviation errors.

                              number

Example: A large ~~no.~~ of potential lawyers failed the bar exam.

1. Rev. Miller will conduct services at eleven P.M., Sunday.

2. Geo. Washington served the country well as the first president.

3. Capt. Adams is from Helena, Mon.

4. Columbus discovered America in A.D. 1492.

5. The U.S. is in good shape economically.

6. Victor Hugo was a famous Fr. novelist.

7. Mary & Jane spent all day at the fair.

8. Raleigh is the capital of No. Car.

9. Julius Caesar invaded Eng. in 55 B.C.

10. Clark has a cb radio in his car as well as a ham rad.

---

14. Spell out months, days of the week, and units of measurement.

Monday
September
Mary is nearly six feet tall.
163 pounds

---

15. Spell out the words *street, avenue, boulevard, road, square, court, park, mount,* and *river* used as an essential part of proper names.

Fifth Avenue
Hampton Court
Washington Square
East Boulevard

---

16. Spell out the names of courses of study and the words for *page, chapter, volume, part, book,* and *canto.*

I studied physical education and chemistry.
page 15
Chapter 3
canto XXXI

---

17. Spell out first names.

George Washington, **not** Geo. Washington
William Penn, **not** Wm. Penn
Thomas Jefferson, **not** Thos. Jefferson

---

18. For an abbreviation that is not generally known, write out the full form in parentheses immediately following its first use.

---

b.h.p. (brake horsepower)
F.S.L.N. (Sandinista National Liberation Front)

---

19. Do not use a period after chemical symbols.

$C_8H_{15}N$
H_2O

---

20. Do not use a period after initials of military services and specific military terms.

USN   United States Navy
MP   Military Police
MIA   Missing in Action
AWOL   Absent Without Leave
PX   Post Exchange

---

21. Do not use a period after the acronyms of certain governmental agencies or call letters of television and radio stations.

DOE   Department of Energy
FBI   Federal Bureau of Investigation
CIA   Central Intelligence Agency
WXII   television station call letters
WB4EIV   amateur radio operator's call letters

EDITING PRACTICE 16–2
Correct all abbreviation errors.

              William   American
Example: ~~Wm.~~ Bradford is an early ~~Am.~~ writer.

1. Tammy is a patient at Charter Hosp.

2. The radio station's call letters are W.A.Y.S.

3. The chemical symbol for salt is Na.Cl.

4. The bag of kitty litter weighed over twenty lbs.

5. The stockholders' meeting is planned for Tu., Sept. 6th, 1999.

6. The abortion clinic on E. Blvd. was bombed last Thurs.

7. The bag of fertilizer weighed over eighty lbs.

8. The young soldier went A.W.O.L.

9. The committee headquarters is on 5th Ave.

10. Pg. 4 of ch. 5 has a famous misprint.

Numbers

There seems to be a growing trend these days toward the use of more figures in writing. It is a known fact that readers can comprehend figures more quickly than they can comprehend the written-out forms of numbers. And, of course, figures are vastly preferable in much technical and scientific material. Nevertheless, some rules governing the use of figures are applicable in most standard English prose written for the general reader; those rules are presented in this chapter.

> **1.** Use figures for numbers that require more than two words to spell out.

    153
    4,289

But notice:

    twenty-four
    ninety-six
    ten

2. Use figures for time designations used with A.M., P.M., B.C., and A.D.

8:01 A.M.
55 B.C.
11:53 P.M.
A.D. 1066

But not:

ten A.M.
thirty-three B.C.

3. Use figures in addresses.

Route 2
1128 Belgrade Drive
P. O. Box 531
Room 374

4. Use figures for most dates but not all.

May 1849
January 5, 1946, **or** 5 January 1946
August ninth **or** the ninth of August **or** August 9 **or** August 9th
the sixties **or** the 1960s **or** the 1960's
the twentieth century
1600 **or** 1632–1638 **or** 1632–38
from 1941 to 1945

But not:

May, 1849
    The comma is not needed.

January 5th, 1946
    Do not use *th* when the year follows.

from 1941–1945
    From must be accompanied by the complementary word *to*.

5. Use figures for serial numbers.

Newsletter 63
page 154
Chapter 4
paragraph 2
Document 12

6. Use figures (normally Roman numerals) to differentiate kings, emperors, and popes with the same names.

Edward VIII
Charles V
Elizabeth II
Boniface VI

7. Use figures (generally Roman numerals) in denoting vehicles.

Courageous II
Pioneer I
Apollo IX

8. Use figures (Roman numerals) to designate family members of the same name beyond the second generation.

Ralston M. Ounce, III
John R. Dobbins, IV

9. Use figures to designate local branches of labor unions and fraternal lodges.

Teamsters Local 391
American Legion Post 266

> **10.** Use figures to designate state and interstate highways.

North Carolina 52
Interstate 77

> **11.** Use figures with decimals, degrees, percentages, money, and pro-
> portion.

35.6 inches
$912.69
longitude 51°05′01″W
33 percent
odds of 4 to 1

> **12.** Use figures with game scores, election results, statistics, and items
> in a series.

a score of 50 to 6
a vote of 321 to 9 against
4 hammers, 7 screwdrivers, and 1,268 nails

> **13.** Use figures in parentheses to repeat numbers in legal or commer-
> cial writing.

The cashier keeps two hundred (200) dollars of ready cash on hand.

or

The cashier keeps two hundred dollars ($200) of ready cash on hand.

EDITING PRACTICE 16–3

Make any necessary corrections in the use of numbers.

1. The address of the courthouse is five-three-one-four Main Street.

2. The project took three men, two women, five typewriters, and five
   thousand six hundred and fifty-three sheets of paper.

3. Sam Duff decided not to run for reelection as representative from the 8th District.

4. Theodore was born on September 25th, 1977.

5. Alfred Norton has already had 5 wives.

6. Chapter twelve needs to be rewritten.

7. The Mustangs defeated the Greyhounds eighty-six to seventy-three.

8. Highway four sixty-two is nearly complete.

9. The committee met regularly from 1986–1992.

10. Over 62% of those solicited responded to the questionnaire.

---

14. Large round numbers may be either spelled out or put in figures.

---

thirty million dollars
$30,000,000
$30 million

---

15. Spell out numbers beginning sentences.

Ninety men volunteered for the assignment.
Five percent of the Conservative Party are actually Marxists.

When possible, rewrite sentences so that numbers do not come at the beginning.

---

16. Spell out ordinal numbers preceding the noun of successive dynasties, governments, and governing bodies.

Third Reich
Eighty-second Congress
Twelfth Dynasty

---

17. Spell out ordinal numbers less than one hundred that designate political divisions and military units.

Fifth Congressional District
Third Ward
Ninety-fourth Precinct
Second Army
Forty-fifth Regiment
Seventeenth Battalion

18. Spell out numbered streets under one hundred.

Fifth Avenue
Thirty-second Street

19. Spell out numbers designating churches or religious organizations.

First Presbyterian Church
Seventh-Day Adventists

20. Spell out numbers preceding the expression *o'clock*.

eight o'clock

EDITING PRACTICE 16-4

Make any necessary corrections in the use of numbers.

Example: Election returns from the ~~9th d~~istrict were lost.
(Ninth D)

1. One mile is 1760 yards.

2. The 42nd Regiment is ready to go.

3. The fire started at 8 o'clock at night.

4. The offices of Flagler & Sharp are located on 7th Avenue.

5. Nobert is to meet the preacher at the 1st Baptist Church tonight.

6. There were 2523 suggestions in the suggestion box.

7. 93 percent of the women favored the new maternity leave policy.

8. The 99th Congress was embroiled in controversy.

9. 15 couples returned from their vacation early.

10. The concert is scheduled to begin in the park at 2 o'clock.

EDITING TEST 16-A USING ABBREVIATIONS AND NUMBERS CORRECTLY

Make any necessary changes in the use of abbreviations and numbers.

Example: eight o'clock in the morning

1. Thos. Jefferson was a very interesting man. 2. He lived at Monticello in VA. 3. He loved his home and his st. 4. Govt. work was more of an obligation than a pleasure. 5. He was drafted to write the Dec. of Ind. 6. Benj. Franklin felt Jefferson was the best author. 7. Jefferson was also interested in relig. freedom in VA. 8. He considered religious freed. very important. 9. In addition, he founded the Univ. of VA. 10. He wanted the Univ. to separate the secular and the religious.

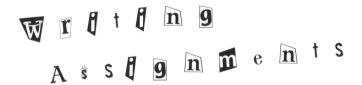

Writing Assignments

Assignment 16-1 Write one paragraph (about half a page) about what you think the positive and negative aspects of computers are. How are computers helpful? How are computers a problem? Or do you think computers are all good or all bad? Why?

Assignment 16-2 Write two to three paragraphs (about one to one and a half pages) about the following: Humor is found in many parts of life, and it is based on the unexpected. Often, however, funny actions or words are embarrassing (or even harmful) to the person who did or said them. Why do we laugh at things that are not completely funny (like someone's tripping and falling)? Is it because we could be—or have been—in that person's shoes? Think of a moment in your life that is humorous to you now but was a bit embarrassing to you when it happened. What makes it funny? Why is humor sometimes a valuable tool for dealing with embarrassing moments?

Go Electronic!

For additional readings, exercises, and Internet activities, visit the Longman English pages at:

http://longman.awl.com/englishpages

If you need a user name and password, please see your instructor.

More Practice with Your Writing and Grammar Skills

For additional practice with your writing and grammar skills, use the Writer's ToolKit CD–ROM included with this text. The ToolKit provides a wealth of computerized tutorials and practice activities.

chapter 17

Other Marks of Punctuation

In this chapter we present the punctuation marks that have not previously been discussed. The punctuation marks in this chapter are no less important than other punctuation marks that may have more rules governing their usage. In fact, some of the marks discussed here are so specialized that any incorrect use of them could confuse your readers.

Periods

> **1.** Use a period to mark the end of a declarative sentence (one that makes a statement) or a mildly imperative sentence (one that expresses a command or makes a request).

Matt Davis is the best blocker on the team.
    The sentence makes a statement.

Please close the door.
    The sentence makes a request.

Open the glove compartment and get my gloves.
    The sentence expresses commands.

But a strongly imperative sentence needs an exclamation point.

Put your hands over your head and lean against the wall!

---

2. Use a period to mark the end of an indirect question. Words such as *when* and *what* often introduce questions that are asked so indirectly that no question mark is necessary.

The Dean asked me when I could come by and speak with him.
Martha asked what Bob had said about her.

---

3. Use a period to mark the end of a polite request, even if it is worded as a question.

Business letters often reflect this use of the period. When a businessperson asks a question in a letter, the intent is often more a mild imperative than a question. Also, in such cases the answer is generally assumed to be *yes.*

Will you reply by return mail.
Will you see that the shipment is adequately insured.

---

4. Use a period for most abbreviations.

Mrs.
Dr.
P.M.
A.M.
etc.
e.g.

Use only one period if a declarative sentence ends with an abbreviation.

The new economics professor is from Washington, D.C.

Use a question mark or an exclamation point after the abbreviation period if an interrogative sentence (one that asks a direct question) or an exclamatory sentence (one that expresses strong feeling or surprise) ends with an abbreviation.

Is the pitcher from Charlotte, N.C.?
Don't hop a train to Chicago, Ill.!

Use whatever punctuation mark would normally be used to follow an abbreviation period inside the sentence.

Some writers use many abbreviations such as *i.e., e.g.,* and *etc.;* other writers, however, do not favor such Latin abbreviations.

---

5. Use a period to separate dollars from cents in writing figures.

$1.29
$36.94

---

6. Use the period as a decimal point in writing figures

98.6°
16.8 percent
$15.6 million

EDITING PRACTICE 17–1
Insert periods where they are needed in the following sentences.

Example: Mrs. Ruth Herman will lecture on "Mead and Samoa."

1. Penny asked me if she could borrow ten dollars

2. Please leave the room

3. Will you please credit my account for the returned merchandise

4. Evening classes at the college begin at 7:00 PM

5. Dr Jackson can see you today at 10:00 AM

6. The receipt for twenty-eight dollars and thirty cents should be written as $2830

7. Did you have a chance to visit with your sister in Richmond, Va?

8. Please close the window, Charles

9. Rev Van Rinegold is supposed to drop by today at 2:00 PM

10. Rick asked the coach if the team had been selected yet

Ellipses

There are several instances where "multiple periods" are employed in writing.

The most common use of multiple periods is the ellipsis. The ellipsis mark is three spaced periods in a row. It is sometimes, as in mathematics, used to indicate that a series, pattern, or listing continues beyond the last item cited.

The boy counted to one hundred: 1, 2, 3, 4 . . .

Sometimes an ellipsis is used to indicate the passage of time.

It was a beautiful morning . . . a cloudy afternoon . . . a stormy evening.

By far the most important use of the ellipsis mark, however, is to indicate that part of a quotation has been left out. Since quotations are normally supposed to be reproduced exactly as they appeared in the original, the ellipsis mark is important in that it lets you alter the quotation by omitting part of it. You should familiarize yourself with the following two rules:

> **7.** If the omission occurs at the beginning or in the middle of a sentence, use three periods.

". . . Wanting both government and liberty the writer . . . pointed out the relationship between the two."

Sometimes the ellipsis mark at the beginning of a quotation is omitted.

"Wanting both government and liberty the writer . . . pointed out the relationship between the two."

> **8.** If the last part of a quoted sentence is omitted or if entire sentences of a quoted passage are omitted, add a fourth period.

Original quotation: Literature is my Utopia. Here I am not disfranchised. No barrier of the senses shuts me out from the sweet, gracious discourse of my book-friends. They talk to me without embarrassment or awkwardness.

—HELEN KELLER

Quotation with ellipses: Literature is my Utopia. . . . No barrier of the senses shuts me out from the . . . discourse of my book-friends. They talk to me without embarrassment or awkwardness.

Ellipses should not be used to alter the meaning of the original source. If a reviewer says, "I do not think the book is very good," it would be misleading of you to reproduce the quotation leaving out the word *not* "I do . . . think the book is very good."

Brackets

Like ellipses, brackets can be useful in reproducing quotations. Ellipses permit us to omit words from quotations; brackets permit us to add words. Do not confuse brackets [] with parentheses (). Parentheses are used to enclose parenthetical material in your own work, whereas brackets are used to add your own parenthetical comments, corrections, and additions to the passage you are quoting.

> **1.** Use brackets to enclose an explanation that is inserted in quoted material and that is not part of the original text.

James Macke wrote, "She [Emily Dickinson] is the best female poet America has produced."

The newspaper reported, "Sebastian Coe now holds the world's record for each leg in the Triple Crown [800 meters, 1,500 meters, and the mile]."

> **2.** Use brackets enclosing the Latin word *sic* (meaning "thus") following errors in fact, spelling, punctuation, or grammar to indicate that you know the errors are present.

The book stated, "Abraham Lincoln was assassinated on April 14, 1965 [*sic*]."

The student wrote "The English coarse [*sic*] was very difficult."

> **3.** You can correct some errors in the original text by enclosing the correction in brackets.

The division manager wrote the owner, "You should get Roger Boyd inste[a]d of Bill Tompkins."

The newspaper summarized the election results with the headline, "McDonald To Be New Pres[id]ent."

EDITING PRACTICE 17-2

In the following sentences, insert brackets where they are necessary.

Example: John F. Kennedy was assassinated in 1964 [sic].

1. The critic wrote, "She Emily Dickinson was the finest American poet of the nineteenth century."

2. "Ernest Hemmingway *sic* won the Nobel Prize for literature," the article said.

3. The professor wrote, "He William Shakespeare is the finest dramatist the world has ever known."

4. The book stated, "It took some time before William Falkner *sic* was appreciated by the public."

5. The hostess left a note for her staff that said, "Their *sic* are not enough wine glasses."

Colons

The colon is a rather formal mark of punctuation. Some writers prefer not to use it. Nevertheless, there are some situations where the colon is the most appropriate mark of punctuation to use.

> **1.** Use the colon to introduce a series of examples or a list of items.

There are three kinds of extrasensory perception: telepathy, clairvoyance, and precognition.

Many schools are organized in the following way: Grades 1–6, Grades 7–9, and Grades 10–12.

> **2.** Use the colon to introduce a long formal statement, quotation, or question.

The book made one irrefutable point: Every good scholar is a good listener.

Speaking of labor, Abraham Lincoln said: "Labor is prior to, and independent of, capital. Capital is only the fruit of labor, and could never have existed if labor had not first existed!"

This is the real question: Should the judiciary be given more power than the President and Congress?

---

3. Use a colon after the formal salutation of a business letter or speech.

Dear Mr. Tolbert:
Ladies and Gentlemen:

---

4. Use a colon between the chapter and verse of a biblical reference.

Genesis 46:3
Job 11:20

---

5. Use a colon between the title and subtitle of a book.

College English: The First Year
Poe: A Collection of Critical Essays

---

6. Use a colon to separate hours from minutes in time references.

12:58 P.M.
6:45 A.M.

---

7. Use a colon to indicate that an initial clause will be further explained by the material that follows the colon. In such constructions the colon could be substituted for the expressions *namely* and *for example.*

The local government was famous for its inefficiency: the city councilmen were always duplicating the work of the county commissioners.

Be very careful not to confuse this use of a colon with the normal use of a semicolon. Though the two marks of punctuation may resemble each other in appearance, they do not serve the same function.

8. Do not use a colon between a preposition and its object.

Incorrect: He has always thought highly of: Henry James, Fyodor Dostoyevski, and Gustave Flaubert.

9. Do not use a colon after a verb, after the word *that*, or after the expression *such as*.

Incorrect: John has always enjoyed: tennis, golf, basketball, and handball.
Correct: John has always enjoyed tennis, golf, basketball, and handball.

Incorrect: His problems are: awkwardness, nervousness, and shyness.
Correct: His problems are awkwardness, nervousness, and shyness.

Incorrect: Martha enjoys some of America's classics, such as: *The Deerslayer, The Scarlet Letter, The Adventures of Huckleberry Finn, Moby Dick,* and *Light in August.*
Correct: Martha enjoys some of America's classics, such as *The Deerslayer, The Scarlet Letter, The Adventures of Huckleberry Finn, Moby Dick,* and *Light in August.*

EDITING PRACTICE 17-3

In the following sentences, insert colons where they are needed.

Example: 10:00 A.M.

1. Please listen for the following broadcasts the morning one at 800, the afternoon one at 100, and the evening one at 600.

2. *Thinking Critically A Beginner's Guide* was not a best-seller.

3. John 3 16 is a very popular passage from the Bible.

4. My English class meets from 1000 A.M. to 1120 A.M.

5. *Byron A Collection of Critical Essays* is a book of collected essays on the works of the poet Byron.

6. Be sure to follow these steps disconnect electrical appliances, raise windows slightly, go to a safe place in the basement away from all windows.

7. I set the VCR to begin taping at 815 P.M.

8. *Relativity An Introduction to Einstein* provides a useful introduction to relativity.

9. The meeting is scheduled to last from 1000 A.M. to 1130 A.M.

10. *Generations An Introduction to Drama* is a good beginning text on the subject.

Exclamation Points

Exclamation points should be used sparingly. Their correct uses are few and limited. An overuse of exclamation points makes them ineffective.

---

1. Use an exclamation point to express emphasis, surprise, or strong emotion.

The book advised—idiotic though it seems!—that everyone should strive for celibacy.

What an unbelievably ignorant remark!

"I'm in pain! I'm in pain! Please help me!"

---

2. Use the exclamation point to express a command or to make a fervent plea.

Pick your toys up this instant!

Please just let me be!

---

3. Use an exclamation point after strong interjections.

Ouch! That bowl was really hot.

Man! That was a close call.

Question Marks

Though a question mark is generally considered a terminal mark of punctuation (one that comes at the end of a sentence), it may appear within a sentence. But in any event, be sure not to overuse the question mark. The mark should be used sparingly and in accordance with the rules presented in this section.

---

1. Use a question mark after a direct question.

Did Orville Wright make the first successful flight?

Robert asked, "Is there any pay increase based on merit?"

Darius—or was it Xerxes?—beat the waves to make them obey his command.

Will I run? is the question every untested soldier asks himself.

But notice that a question mark is not used after an indirect question.

Mary asked what you were going to wear.

---

2. Use the question mark with what would ordinarily be declarative or imperative sentences to indicate doubt.

Close the windows?

I have been in the hospital for two days?

---

3. Use question marks to indicate a series of queries within the same sentence.

Who will survive? The oiler? The captain? The cook? The correspondent?

Which form of government do you prefer? Communism? Fascism? Capitalism? Socialism?

EDITING PRACTICE 17-4

Supply exclamation points and question marks where they are needed in the following sentences.

Example: Turn off the spigot!

1. Do you think Tammy is emotionally stable

2. Don't drop that sheet of glass

3. Did you notice that the flag was at half mast

4. Be quiet

5. Will the senator get the bill drafted on time

Dashes

Some writers and teachers consider the dash an amateurish mark of punctuation. And though the rules in this section indicate correct uses of the dash, you are advised to use the dash sparingly.

---

1. Use a pair of dashes to set off a parenthetical expression that you want to emphasize.

New York, Los Angeles, and Denver—but not Phoenix—are all acceptable convention sites.

If you do get the book finished on time—and I expect you to try—give me a call immediately.

Louis Diat—formerly a famous chef at the Ritz—published a book called the *Basic French Cookbook.*

---

2. Use a pair of dashes to indicate an abrupt change in thought or tone.

San Francisco—Mom, I wish you could be here—is a wonderful place. Words like *sesquipedalian* and *onomatopoeia*—two-dollar words that aren't worth two cents—pervade scholarly writing.

> **3.** Use a pair of dashes to set off an interpolated question.

Abraham Lincoln—or is it George Washington?—is generally recognized as America's greatest president.

> **4.** Use a pair of dashes to set off a parenthetical element that contains commas.

Four tragedies—*Hamlet, Macbeth, King Lear,* and *Othello*—are generally considered Shakespeare's best plays.

> **5.** Use a dash between an introductory series and the main part of the sentence that explains it.

Homer, Virgil, Dante, Shakespeare, Goethe—these were the men who made up his list of the world's greatest poets.

> **6 .** Use a dash to introduce a word or group of words that you want to emphasize.

There is one thing Bob enjoys more than eating—golf.

If we had some ham, we could have some ham and eggs—if we had some eggs.

> **7.** Sometimes a dash is used to indicate the omission of letters.

Representative G— is not likely to be well received when he returns to the district.

Sometimes Ed can be one genuine son of a b—

> **8.** Sometimes dashes are used to suggest a stuttering or halting speech.

I—er—really don't know what to say.

P—P—Please b—b—bear with m—m—m—me.

> **9.** Sometimes the dash is used in dialogue to indicate an unfinished word or statement.

Margaret said, "I don't care what you w—"

"Margaret, now just calm down," her husband warned.

"Little Jimmy was our whole life and now—" the bereaved mother burst into tears.

EDITING PRACTICE 17-5

Insert dashes where they are needed in the following sentences.

Example: Senator K— will probably have to stand trial.

1. Jodie, Jackie, Burt, and Ned these are the most promising students in this year's class.

2. The project thank heavens it was funded will employ many people.

3. Hector stuttered, "P P Please give m m me a ch ch chance."

4. I have only one more paper to grade the one on genetic experimentation.

5. Clive or was it Joel? made the best score of anyone ever to have taken the test.

6. The student speaker began, "I uh wish to talk to you uh about a matter of um great importance."

7. Judge K did not wish to be identified.

8. Three women Joan, Susan, and Alice decided to run for the office.

9. Otto asked Vivian, "Would you l l like a p p piece of c c candy?"

10. The wooden object or was it plastic? was found in the wreckage.

Parentheses

The main purpose of parentheses is to set off incidental explanatory information. Commas, dashes, and parentheses can all be used to set off parenthetical information, but the three punctuation marks are used in different ways. Commas are used to set off information that is closely related in thought and structure to the sentence in which the parenthetical information appears. Commas are mild separators; they neither emphasize the parenthetical element nor deemphasize it. Dashes, however, are used to set off more abrupt parenthetical elements. Dashes are informal marks of punctuation that really emphasize whatever is being set off. Parentheses, on the other hand, are used to set off information that is primarily provided for clarity or for the reader's information. Parentheses are noticeable marks that should not be overused. Parentheses tend to de-emphasize the information that is set off.

Ralph Waldo Emerson, one of the transcendentalists, is a major figure in American literature.

The commas are used here to set off the qualifying element in the least obtrusive manner.

Ralph Waldo Emerson—an outstanding Lyceum lecturer—is a major figure in American literature.

The dashes are used to emphasize the interpolated information.

Ralph Waldo Emerson (see also his contemporary Henry David Thoreau) is a major figure in American literature.

The parentheses are used to de-emphasize the parenthetical information, which is inserted merely for the benefit of readers who might be interested.

> **1.** Use parentheses to enclose incidental explanatory matter.

John Adams (1735–1826) was the second president of the United States.

Sentence fragments (see Chapter 7) are very annoying to readers.

The date of President Kennedy's assassination (November 22, 1963) has been forgotten by many Americans.

> **2.** Use parentheses to enclose a numerical figure used to clarify a spelled-out number that precedes it.

The dental bill was ninety-eight dollars ($98).

The book entitled *Byron's Complete Poetical Works* costs twenty-five (25) dollars.

> **3.** Use parentheses to enclose a fully spelled-out term in order to clarify an abbreviation that precedes it. Do this only the first time the abbreviation is used.

MIA (Missing in Action)
UNRRA (United Nations Relief and Rehabilitation Administration)

> **4.** Use parentheses to enclose numbers or letters that designate each item in a series.

The camp Bobby wants to go to is (a) too expensive, (b) too far away, and (c) too poorly supervised.

Five of America's most famous golfers are (1) Bobby Jones, (2) Ben Hogan, (3) Sam Snead, (4) Arnold Palmer, and (5) Jack Nicklaus.

Note: In your writing try to avoid this usage, as it tends to make your papers mere catalog lists.

> **5.** When the parentheses do not enclose a whole sentence beginning with a capital letter, place the necessary commas and periods after the closing parenthesis.

In *On the Origin of Species* by Charles Darwin (1809–1882), the author discusses the process of natural selection.

Your evidence (most of us consider it invalid) is purely circumstantial.

> **6.** When the parentheses enclose a whole sentence beginning with a capital letter, place the period or other terminal punctuation mark just before the closing parenthesis.

Are car sales representatives really ethical? (For that matter, are any sales representatives truly ethical?)

Answer one of the three questions. (Be sure to write neatly and in ink!)

Sandra did not like her physical science teacher. (But then Sandra hasn't liked any science teacher since she failed science in the seventh grade.)

EDITING PRACTICE 17-6

Insert parentheses where they are needed in the following sentences.

Example: Ulysses Grant (1822–1885) made a better general than he did a president.

1. The report see the enclosed photos covers the subject adequately.

2. Clarence Darrow 1857–1938 defended John Scopes.

3. Please consider three things: 1 cost, 2 location, and 3 reputation.

4. Mark Twain see also Samuel Langhorne Clemens is America's most noted humorist.

5. Members of the NCTE National Council of Teachers of English will meet in Denver this year.

6. I paid two hundred dollars $200 for the watch.

7. John Calvin 1509–1564 was a famous religious reformer.

8. The car my son wanted was a too expensive, b too old, and c too impractical.

9. The portfolio notice the oil paintings in particular represents three years' work.

10. Wyatt Earp 1848–1929 lived a long life during dangerous times.

Slashes (Virgules)

> **1.** Use the slash to indicate alternative expressions.

During the 1960s many colleges offered a pass/fail grading system.

The job requires a knowledge of typing and/or shorthand.

> **2.** Use the slash to indicate the end of a line of poetry when running two lines of a quoted passage in with the text.

Referring to the battles of Lexington and Concord, Ralph Waldo Emerson wrote, "Here once the embattled farmers stood / And fired the shot heard round the world."

In "The Deserted Village" Oliver Goldsmith said, "Ill fares the land, to hastening ills a prey, / Where wealth accumulates, and men decay."

EDITING PRACTICE 17-7

Insert slashes where they are needed in the following sentences.

Example: The umpires and/or the players will get their way.

1. Emily Dickinson said, "The soul selects her own society, Then shuts the door; On her divine majority, Obtrude no more."

2. My friend Williard took electronics on the pass fail system.

3. The female cadets and or the administration will take the matter to court.

4. Ralph Waldo Emerson wrote, "Rhodora! If the Sages ask thee why This charm is wasted on the earth and sky, Tell them, dear, that if eyes were made for seeing, Then Beauty is its own excuse for being."

5. The job requires knowledge of the Microsoft Word and or the Word Perfect word-processing system.

Hyphens

Compound Words

> **1.** Use a hyphen to connect two or more words serving as a single adjective before a noun.

The medic administered mouth-to-mouth resuscitation.

A two-thirds majority will be required to pass the bill.

Henry Price is not a well-known poet.

But notice that the hyphen is generally omitted when the adjective does not precede the noun it modifies.

John Keats's name is well known.

2. Use a hyphen to form compound nouns of two nouns that show the same functions in one person or thing.

player-coach
secretary-treasurer
AFL-CIO

3. Use a hyphen with numbers from twenty-one to ninety-nine.

thirty-six
eighty-four

4. Use a hyphen to express decades in words.

eighteen-twenties
nineteen-sixties

5. Use a hyphen or an en-dash on your computer to indicate a range of numbers.

the years 1832–1837
pages 164–189
Richard Brinsley Sheridan (1751–1816)

6. Use a hyphen to indicate the spelling of a word.

The number is spelled t-w-o and the adverb, t-o-o.
My name is J-o-n, not J-o-h-n.

7. Use a hyphen to prevent confusion in pronunciation when the addition of a prefix results in the doubling of a vowel.

re-elect
anti-imperialist
pre-empt

> **8.** Use a hyphen to join the following prefixes to proper nouns or adjectives.

anti-	anti-German
mid-	mid-America
non-	non-Japanese
pan-	Pan-Hellenic
pro-	pro-Israeli
un-	un-American

> **9.** Use a hyphen to form most, but not all, compound nouns and adjectives from the following prefixes.

all-	all-star
co-	co-worker
cross-	cross-examination
double-	double-breasted
ex-	ex-commissioner
great-	great-grandmother
heavy-	heavy-duty
ill-	ill-conceived
light-	light-hearted
self-	self-concept
single-	single-minded
well-	well-intentioned

Note: Ill- and well- compounds are hyphenated before a noun, but are two words after a noun.

EDITING PRACTICE 17-8

Insert hyphens in the following sentences where they are needed.

Example: The team's owner–manager was arrested for gambling.

1. There are at least twenty five ways to complete that project.

2. The verb is spelled d e v i s e, the noun, d e v i c e.

3. The team had a pre game meeting in the locker room.

4. The nineteen eighties was a time of political conservatism.

5. Ninety seven people applied for one job opening at the bank.

6. I read pages 491 543 in my history text last night.

7. The man made virus was barely contained.

8. There is much pro Israeli sentiment in the American government.

9. Joel Barlow (1754 1812) is a little known American poet.

10. The day to day figures looked good for the new company.

EDITING TEST 17-A USING THE OTHER MARKS OF PUNCTUATION (I)
Supply periods, brackets, colons, exclamation points, and question marks where they are needed in the following paragraph.

Example: *American Literature–The Makers and the Making*

1. The Dobson Book Club met at 700 PM 2. The book under discussion was written by Sen Dolph Sanders 3. Everyone enjoyed his book *Intrigue The Other Side of Politics* 4. The members wanted to know how the Senator knew so much about political corruption 5. Could he be dishonest himself 6. In the preface to *Intrigue The Other Side of Politics,* Sen Dolph Sanders said that nearly every politician in Washington is exposed to corruption daily. 7. He also added that most elected officials are honest 8. Of course, members of the book club wanted to believe him, but Wain's book *Temptation The Psychology of Greed* discusses the innate human weakness to temptation 9. What was shocking was how much Sen Dolph Sanders made from his book 10. In the first year he earned over $800,000

Name _____

Class _____

Section _____ Score: _____

EDITING TEST 17–B USING THE OTHER MARKS OF PUNCTUATION (II)

Insert dashes, parentheses, slash marks, and hyphens where they are needed in the following paragraph.

Example: It is an either/or choice.

1. Richard Brinsley Sheridan 1751 1816 is a well-known British dramatist.

2. *The Rivals* 1775 is one of his plays that is still produced frequently.

3. Another popular Sheridan play is *The School for Scandal.* 4. One of his famous characters is Mrs. Malaprop, from the French *malapropos,* "badly to the purpose." 5. One of his lesser-known plays is *The Critic* 1779. 6. *The Duenna* 1775 was a popular musical comedy for a while. 7. Sheridan, a man that considered opening night a dress rehearsal, often did not have his plays completed by opening night. 8. Sheridan, captured by the theater manager, was once forced to stay in a room by himself until he finished a play. 9. Once about 1777 he was finishing a play in one room in the theater while the actors were performing Act I on stage. 10. Truly Richard Brinsley Sheridan was not the most disciplined of authors.

EDITING TEST 17-C   USING THE OTHER MARKS OF PUNCTUATION (III)

Supply periods, brackets, dashes, exclamation points, question marks, parentheses, slash marks, quotation marks, and hyphens where they are needed in the following paragraph.

Example: Do not forget to put a period at the end of this sentence.

1. The teacher told the class, Try reading more and watching TV less 2. She continued, the John Gallup reports that reading levels in this country have been dropping for years 3. According to statistics, she explained, twenty one out of the thirty six of you in here do not read up to your grade level 4. She said, Furthermore, the report see page 15 indicates parents do not discourage TV watching 5. Books can be your best friends, she said 6. They can also exercise your imagination, she added 7. Television can often be such a mindless experience, she stated 8. Soap operas, cop shows, sitcoms, and reruns these are the programs to which many Americans are addicted, she bemoaned 9. Why not pick up a book and try something different she asked 10. Then the teacher exclaimed, Turn off those TVs now

Writing Assignments

Assignment 17-1 Read an article in a newspaper or magazine and summarize it in one paragraph (about half a page). When you summarize, you are pulling out the main points made in the article, but you don't pull out all the supporting details. The point is to have a summary of what the article is generally about. The article needs to be long enough to give you several main points for summary, so it should be at least two columns (newspaper) or one page (magazine) in length.

Assignment 17-2 Select an article in a newspaper or magazine and read it carefully three times. The article should be at least one or two columns (newspaper) or one page (magazine) in length. Read the article once without taking any notes. The second time you read the article, however, highlight the supporting ideas and examples that the writer uses to back up his or her main ideas. On your third reading, make notes about how well these ideas and examples support the writer's main ideas. Write two or three paragraphs (about one to one and a half pages) about the author's use of support. What kinds of support does the writer use? Is the argument convincing to you? If so, why? If not, why?

Go Electronic!

For additional readings, exercises, and Internet activities, visit the Longman English pages at:

http://longman.awl.com/englishpages

If you need a user name and password, please see your instructor.

More Practice with Your Writing and Grammar Skills

For additional practice with your writing and grammar skills, use the Writer's ToolKit CD-ROM included with this text. The ToolKit provides a wealth of computerized tutorials and practice activities.

Answers to Practice Sentences and Editing Practices

CHAPTER 1

PRACTICE SENTENCES 1-1

1. The club <u>sponsored</u> many projects.
2. It <u>sought</u> improvement in all areas of the community.
3. Cecil <u>joined</u> the community cleanup project.
4. He <u>collected</u> soda cans and other types of litter on the streets of the city.
5. Lupe <u>participated</u> in the community face-lift project.
6. She <u>painted</u> the inside and outside of several old buildings.
7. Cecil and Lupe <u>went</u> to lunch one day.
8. They <u>compared</u> notes on their community work.
9. They <u>considered</u> the work too hard.
10. Now they <u>learn</u> about property repairs by watching television.

PRACTICE SENTENCES 1-2

1. In high school Susan <u>became</u> an avid science student.
2. She <u>was</u> in the physics lab every afternoon.
3. In college, however, Susan <u>seemed</u> to lose interest in science.
4. She <u>became</u> aware of the beauty of the English language.
5. She <u>is</u> now very happy with a good novel.
6. Susan also <u>feels</u> the rhythm of a poem by John Keats.
7. Chaucer's *Canterbury Tales* <u>is</u> one of her favorite works.
8. She <u>appears</u> fond of the early form of the English language.
9. Her favorite poet, however, <u>is</u> Emily Dickinson.
10. No doubt, Susan <u>will be</u> an outstanding English teacher.

PRACTICE SENTENCES 1-3

1. He <u>has</u> obtained all the wood.
2. He <u>has</u> had all the necessary tools for many years.
3. He <u>has</u> planned an entire day for the project.
4. He <u>will</u> construct the frame first.
5. Then he <u>will</u> attach the floor.
6. After that he <u>will</u> assemble the sides.
7. Next he <u>will</u> work on the roof.
8. Finally he <u>will</u> attach the shingles.
9. The dog <u>will</u> be so proud.
10. But first John <u>must</u> begin the project.

PRACTICE SENTENCES 1-4
  1. At first I <u>was planning</u> a career as clerk in a local department store.
  2. But I <u>could</u> never <u>earn</u> a good salary in such a position.
  3. I <u>would</u> never <u>be promoted</u> in the family-owned business either.
  4. So, what <u>can</u> I <u>do</u>?
  5. I <u>have</u> always <u>enjoyed</u> working with numbers.
  6. In college I <u>could study</u> accounting.
  7. An accountant <u>can make</u> a good living.
  8. Accountants <u>can help</u> people with their financial problems as well.
  9. <u>Would</u> I <u>enjoy</u> a career in accounting?
  10. My teachers and my heart <u>are telling</u> me, "Yes."

PRACTICE SENTENCES 1-5
  1. The judge listened to the arguments of both attorneys.
      Verb <u>listened</u>
  2. According to the prosecutor, the judge did not listen to his case.
      Verb <u>did listen</u>
  3. The judge had already decided the issue.
      Verb <u>had decided</u>
  4. On the other hand, the defense attorney was not pleased either.
      Verb <u>was pleased</u>
  5. He was not convinced of the judge's objectivity.
      Verb <u>was convinced</u>
  6. The judge was used to such opposing viewpoints.
      Verb <u>was used</u>
  7. He had heard it all before.
      Verb <u>had heard</u>
  8. In fact, the judge did not know anything about the case.
      Verb <u>did know</u>
  9. He had been out of town for three weeks before the trial.
      Verb <u>had been</u>
  10. To him the two lawyers had just been actors on a stage.
      Verb <u>had been</u>

PRACTICE SENTENCES 1-6
  1. <u>He</u> owns several books about furniture styles and periods.
  2. Recently <u>he</u> developed an interest in the construction of furniture.
  3. This <u>interest</u> led to an interest in woodworking equipment.
  4. Now his <u>basement</u> contains numerous tools.
  5. Unfortunately his <u>shop</u> has poor ventilation.
  6. <u>Sawdust</u> covers everything, including the washer and dryer.
  7. His <u>wife</u> prefers to buy her furniture from a store.
  8. <u>Curt</u> built a beautiful oak cabinet.
  9. The <u>cabinet</u> cost him over $300 to make.
  10. His <u>wife</u> saw one just like it in a display window for $195.

PRACTICE SENTENCES 1-7
  1. Nearly every <u>model</u> is a classic.
  2. The <u>lines</u> of the car are sleek.

3. The <u>interior</u> is usually leather.
4. For years now the <u>body</u> has been fiberglass.
5. The <u>car</u> is famous for its speed.
6. <u>Owners</u> are in love with the car's power.
7. Is the <u>Corvette</u> a true sports car?
8. <u>It</u> probably is not.
9. <u>It</u> is too big and too heavy.
10. Proud <u>owners</u> are not into such labels, however.

PRACTICE SENTENCES 1-8

1. My <u>family</u> was raised in the city.
2. Pickup <u>trucks</u> were not common.
3. My <u>sister</u> once owned a sports car.
4. My <u>brother</u> had a V-8 Jeep.
5. My favorite <u>vehicle</u> had been a VW van.
6. So why did <u>I</u> decide to purchase a pickup?
7. My <u>family</u> moved to a rural area several years ago.
8. <u>Pickups</u> were more common than Cadillacs.
9. A truck <u>bed</u> comes in handy for hauling lumber and other things.
10. My <u>smile</u> broadens at the envy of my neighbor.

PRACTICE SENTENCES 1-9

1. Every day she can be found with a car full of children.
   subject: <u>she</u>   verb: <u>can be found</u>
2. She has been selected the neighborhood chauffeur.
   subject: <u>She</u>   verb: <u>has been selected</u>
3. The job was fun at first.
   subject: <u>job</u>   verb: <u>was</u>
4. Now she does not have time for it.
   subject: <u>she</u>   verb: <u>does have</u>
5. She is working eight hours a day in an accounting firm.
   subject: <u>she</u>   verb: <u>is working</u>
6. She was recently hired as a junior accountant.
   subject: <u>she</u>   verb: <u>was hired</u>
7. In addition, she has registered for three night classes.
   subject: <u>she</u>   verb: <u>has registered</u>
8. Her husband has been helping her.
   subject: <u>husband</u>   verb: <u>has been helping</u>
9. Still, many of the home and family responsibilities fall on her.
   subject: <u>many</u>   verb: <u>fall</u>
10. Obviously Rhonda has made a busy life for herself.
    subject: <u>Rhonda</u>   verb: <u>has made</u>

PRACTICE SENTENCES 1-10

1. Cindy <u>practices</u> dentistry and <u>works</u> with local civic clubs.
2. Last semester <u>I</u> <u>read</u> twelve books and <u>wrote</u> three papers.
3. Samantha <u>makes</u> good money and <u>saves</u> nearly half of it.
4. John <u>visited</u> his father and <u>gave</u> him a nice recliner.
5. Carmen <u>completed</u> her nursing program and now <u>makes</u> good money.

6. The children <u>went</u> to the amusement park and <u>played</u> all day.
7. Randy <u>bought</u> a new radio and <u>tuned</u> it to his favorite stations.
8. Nikki <u>has</u> thirteen Barbie dolls and <u>wants</u> seven more.
9. The hunter <u>went</u> to the woods before sunrise and <u>stayed</u> until noon.
10. My sister <u>plays</u> the clarinet in the local orchestra and <u>teaches</u> elementary school.

PRACTICE SENTENCES 1-11

1. A <u>Monet</u> and a <u>Manet</u> are two of their favorite paintings.
2. <u>Kareem</u> and <u>Antonia</u> recently purchased two Edsels.
3. The red <u>sedan</u> and the blue <u>convertible</u> are quite noticeable in their front yard.
4. A golden <u>vase</u> and a silver <u>ladle</u> are their newest additions.
5. The <u>vase</u> and the <u>ladle</u> were purchased from an estate sale.
6. Several years ago <u>Kareem</u> and <u>Antonia</u> went to a gun show.
7. An antique <u>pistol</u> and a collectible <u>rifle</u> were two of their purchases.
8. Pearl <u>handles</u> and an engraved <u>barrel</u> are the characteristics of the Colt pistol.
9. The lever <u>action</u> and the tube <u>magazine</u> identify the Winchester rifle.
10. <u>Kareem</u> and <u>Antonia</u> are still looking for collectible pairs that interest them.

PRACTICE SENTENCES 1-12

1. Tom drives the ball a long way off the tee.
   <small>d.o.</small> (above *ball*)
2. Unfortunately, his ball often misses the fairway.
   <small>d.o.</small> (above *fairway*)
3. His fairway irons, however, are quite accurate.
4. Tom does not chip the ball well around the greens.
   <small>d.o.</small> (above *ball*)
5. But he loves his putter.
   <small>d.o.</small> (above *putter*)
6. From ten feet in he putts the ball consistently well.
   <small>d.o.</small> (above *ball*)
7. Susan, on the other hand, hits her driver accurately.
   <small>d.o.</small> (above *driver*)
8. She is a good irons player also.
9. However, she cannot putt the ball well outside two feet.
   <small>d.o.</small> (above *ball*)
10. Together, though, she and Tom make a good team.
    <small>d.o.</small> (above *team*)

PRACTICE SENTENCES 1-13

1. Carla gave Lope a big hug.
   <small>i.o.</small> (above *Lope*)
2. He received the hug gladly.
3. Then the florist delivered Carla two dozen roses.
   <small>i.o.</small> (above *Carla*)
4. Carla was amazed at the gifts.
5. She prepared Lope a dinner.
   <small>i.o.</small> (above *Lope*)

6. She fixed him **i.o.** his favorite meal.

7. Carla did not understand Lope's motives.

8. Did Lope give **i.o.** her the ring as a proposal?

9. He gave **i.o.** her tokens of his affection.

10. However, he was not interested in marriage.

PRACTICE SENTENCES 1–14

1. She has always been an active <u>individual</u>.
2. She is a <u>jogger</u> and a weight <u>lifter</u>.
3. She became a tennis <u>champion</u> at thirteen.
4. Joyce is <u>one</u> of the top three women golfers in the state.
5. But to her, golf seems too tame.
6. She is now into basketball.
7. She practices four hours a day.
8. She is the top <u>scorer</u> for her team.
9. Joyce is also the only <u>woman</u> on her team.
10. Her teammates are her biggest <u>fans</u>.

PRACTICE SENTENCES 1–15

1. It is also very <u>valuable</u>.
2. The pearl handle is <u>genuine</u>.
3. The tang is stamped "Case Bros. Cut. Co., Little Valley, N.Y."
4. Knife collectors are <u>aware</u> of its value.
5. But they must be <u>careful</u>.
6. Older Case knives are often not <u>genuine</u>.
7. Some people in the knife business are not <u>honest</u>.
8. Fortunately, most dealers are very <u>reputable</u>.
9. This knife seems <u>genuine</u> to me.
10. I bought it for $850.

CHAPTER 2

PRACTICE SENTENCES 2–1

1. The <u>origins</u> go way back in <u>history</u>.
2. The <u>pieces</u> have taken many <u>shapes</u> over the <u>years</u>.
3. Some old <u>sets</u> are valuable.
4. Through the <u>years</u> <u>chess</u> has been a <u>game</u> of <u>strategy</u>.
5. Many <u>experts</u> say to move the <u>pawns</u> in the <u>center</u> first.
6. Next, the <u>knights</u> should be put into <u>play</u>.
7. Perhaps the <u>bishops</u> should be put into <u>play</u> after the <u>knights</u>.
8. Good <u>players</u> try to dominate the <u>center</u> of the <u>board</u>.
9. They do not move the <u>queen</u> too early in the <u>game</u>.
10. The <u>object</u>, naturally, is to capture the opponent's <u>king</u>.

PRACTICE SENTENCES 2-2

1. <u>She</u> gave an uncle in Phoenix a beautiful sweater.
2. The American Indian designs on <u>it</u> just seemed to suit <u>him</u>.
3. <u>She</u> gave <u>each</u> of <u>his</u> children a pair of slippers.
4. Sherrie gave <u>everyone</u> in the family a poinsettia.
5. Aunt Leda received a vase with Greek markings on <u>it</u>.
6. John Keats would have been proud of <u>it</u>.
7. <u>Sherrie</u> shopped in <u>all</u> of the stores in town for <u>her</u> brother's present.
8. <u>Several</u> of the clerks thought <u>she</u> was crazy.
9. "What is a Hula Hoop?" <u>they</u> asked <u>her</u>.
10. The hoop <u>she</u> found was listed as a football-throwing target.

EDITING PRACTICE 2-3

Dr. Jones has a daughter named Mary. She is the apple of his eye. When she was four years old, he gave her a sixty-four-piece tea set and an expensive Lionel electric train. When she was sixteen, he gave her a brand-new Lexus. Unfortunately, he was disappointed in Mary. She let one of her friends drive the car, and the friend wrecked it. Fortunately, no one was hurt. Mary has learned to be more careful with her possessions and her father's feelings.

PRACTICE SENTENCES 2-4

1. The old place had <u>a wooden</u> floor.
2. There were <u>small</u> tables, <u>tall</u> shelves, and <u>entire corner</u> displays throughout <u>the</u> shop.
3. One pine table contained <u>antique</u> glass.
4. <u>Some</u> pieces were <u>valuable</u> while others could have come from <u>a local</u> landfill.
5. <u>One</u> set of shelves contained <u>many</u> radios.
6. <u>No</u> radio was <u>newer</u> than 1945.
7. <u>An amateur radio</u> operator would be in <u>seventh</u> heaven.
8. <u>One corner</u> display was composed entirely of <u>old</u> rifles.
9. There was everything from <u>an antique</u> matchlock to <u>an impeccable</u> flintlock.
10. <u>The antique</u> shop had objects of <u>diverse</u> quality, but it was <u>a fascinating</u> place to visit.

PRACTICE SENTENCES 2-5

1. The <u>rusty</u> machine barely runs.
2. There is <u>little</u> paint anywhere on <u>the</u> body.
3. The <u>plastic</u> seat has <u>many</u> holes in it.
4. But <u>the</u> Simplicity is <u>dependable</u> and <u>reliable</u>.
5. Besides that, Jasper is too <u>cheap</u> to purchase <u>a new</u> machine.

PRACTICE SENTENCES 2-6

1. He (<u>did</u>, done) everything his teacher assigned.
2. By the middle of the week, he had (complete, <u>completed</u>) the research.
3. Then he (begin, <u>began</u>) to write.
4. He was not (use, <u>used</u>) to putting so much time into a project.
5. He even (<u>drew</u>, drawed) several maps.
6. The projects were (suppose, <u>supposed</u>) to be due Tuesday.
7. But Juan had (did, <u>done</u>) everything by Friday.
8. On Monday he (<u>saw</u>, seen) another student's project.
9. Juan knew he had (wrote, <u>written</u>) a better paper.
10. In fact, the teacher said Juan had (did, <u>done</u>) the best work of anyone in the class.

EDITING PRACTICE 2-7

1. The newspaper boy threw the paper in the bushes.
2. Valerie drank a two-liter Coke with her pizza.
3. I have driven a hundred miles each week this quarter.
4. Jay blew up more than 150 balloons for the dance.
5. Van had eaten over thirty shrimps by 6:30.
6. Ruth brought three friends with her to the initiation ceremony.
7. By mid-morning Mrs. Covington had gone to the grocery and the bank.
8. The child had stolen three video games before being caught.
9. *Paradise Lost,* written by John Milton, is a great epic.
10. The scientist threw his notes to the floor in disgust.

PRACTICE SENTENCES 2-8

1. I once *took* a chemistry course. past
2. It *had been offered* before. past perfect
3. It *will be offered* again next spring. future tense, passive voice
4. I wish I *had* not *taken* it. past perfect
5. I *was* in lab two afternoons a week. past
6. The course *is* interesting and worthwhile. present
7. But afternoon labs *will* always *be* a problem for me. future
8. My employer *expects* me at work every day at 2:00. present
9. He *has made* it perfectly clear that I am to report for work. present perfect
10. Any more afternoon labs and I *will be* out of a job. future

EDITING PRACTICE 2-9

1. He cleans the upholstery first and then does the dash.
2. When he finished this, he vacuumed the carpets.
3. He then wets down the outside and washes it with soap.
4. Jerry then washes the tires and cleans them.
5. He takes several soft rags and dries the car.
6. He applies wax to about one-fourth of the car at a time and rubs it off.
7. This makes the car shine and looks good.
8. He worked for four hours and took the pretty car to a dealer.
9. The dealer looked at the car and talked with the manager.
10. The dealer offered Jerry four hundred dollars and showed him a newer model.

PRACTICE SENTENCES 2-10

1. The bat was made by the Louisville Slugger Company. passive
2. The girl outran the shortstop's throw. active
3. Michael Jordan played basketball for the Chicago Bulls. active
4. My mother works with an accounting firm in Atlanta. active
5. The company car was sold by the business manager. passive
6. Andrew drove his mother's car into the driver's door of my car. active
7. The bill was padded by the mechanic. passive
8. The batteries in the child's toy ran down in just one week. active
9. The teacher talked to the student about his sloppy work. active
10. The entire crew was blamed by the supervisor. passive

EDITING PRACTICE 2-11

1. The concrete for the museum steps was poured by Phil.
2. The CEO prepared the memo.
3. The network censored the television show.
4. The authorities were kept abreast of local conditions by the amateur radio operator.
5. The date of the next test was announced by the professor.
6. A twelve-month contract was requested by Margaret.
7. The gardener sprayed the roses.
8. The novel *Losing Battles* was written by Eudora Welty.
9. The plumber solved the problem.
10. The award was accepted by the actress.

EDITING PRACTICE 2-12

1. I ordered my wife's Christmas gift in July, but I have not received it yet.
2. Danny dunked the basketball, but he broke his finger on the rim.
3. Greg prepared many different dishes, but Maria ate only one.
4. The player declared his innocence, but he refused a drug test.
5. Heather said she really admired Jose, but she refused his ring.
6. The appraiser looked over the car carefully and declared it a total loss.
7. The Express Mail package was lost in Chicago, but it was delivered on time.
8. The company rejected the ad campaign, so Fred redesigned it.
9. Morris dropped the radio, and he repaired it.
10. The manager submitted the proper requisition form, but the boss took no action.

EDITING PRACTICE 2-13

1. Several students forgot their books.
2. The hairdresser posted a list of her charges.
3. He should contribute all that he can.
4. Sue and Terry got their art supplies in the bookstore.
5. Individuals should put a lot of thought into their majors.
6. The students studied hard for their history test.
7. The woman did all her laundry on Sunday afternoon.
8. The men cleaned their shotguns before the morning hunt.
9. If some individuals wish to join the group, they should sign up in A 216.
10. The roses died because they were diseased.

PRACTICE SENTENCES 2-14

1. She worked <u>diligently</u> at two jobs.
2. <u>Plus</u>, she <u>dedicatedly</u> worked on a college degree at the same time.
3. <u>On top of this</u>, she had two children she loved <u>deeply</u>.
4. She survived <u>well</u> under these conditions for over two years.
5. <u>However</u>, one day she collapsed <u>completely</u>.
6. She had a stroke that damaged her left arm and leg <u>severely</u>.
7. She was <u>completely</u> disoriented for months.
8. For some reason the doctors had difficulty diagnosing her problem <u>correctly</u>.
9. <u>Nevertheless</u>, she visited a physical therapist <u>regularly</u>.
10. In less than a year, Cecilia was <u>nearly</u> back to normal.

PRACTICE SENTENCES 2-15

1. She put the monitor <u>on</u> her desk.
2. The keyboard is <u>near</u> her hands <u>on</u> the desk.
3. The computer itself is <u>beside</u> the desk.
4. The manual is <u>on</u> a shelf <u>above</u> the monitor.
5. Everything is conveniently located <u>for</u> her.
6. Currently she is working <u>on</u> a word-processing program.
7. She has a spreadsheet program <u>on</u> the same disk.
8. Joan works <u>at</u> the computer <u>throughout</u> the day.
9. She is pleased <u>with</u> the work she can accomplish <u>with</u> the machine.
10. <u>But</u> a few minutes ago, she accidentally erased a thirty-page report due <u>in</u> three hours.

PRACTICE SENTENCES 2-16

Individual student answers to this exercise will vary.

PRACTICE SENTENCES 2-17

1. They had a nice time, <u>but</u> the weather was hot <u>and</u> humid.
2. They couldn't decide whether to concentrate on swimming <u>or</u> hiking.
3. Sherry <u>and</u> her son Jeff went swimming.
4. Her husband Chris <u>and</u> son Billy hit the hiking trails.
5. After two <u>and</u> a half hours Chris <u>and</u> Billy returned to the lake.
6. They were hot <u>and</u> tired <u>so</u> they hit the water ASAP.
7. After supper Jeff <u>and</u> Billy put the tent up.
8. They argued whether to put it in the shade <u>or</u> out in the open.
9. Jeff <u>and</u> Billy put the tent in a clear area near the lake.
10. Fortunately it rained <u>and</u> cooled things off, <u>but</u> unfortunately the tent leaked.

PRACTICE SENTENCES 2-18

1. He talked to some of the instructors first <u>because</u> he wanted to determine their attitudes toward students.
2. <u>After</u> he talked to the instructors, he conversed with some of the students to get their opinions.
3. <u>After</u> he completed these discussions, he decided the school looked pretty good.
4. He signed up for the electronics program <u>because</u> he liked the job opportunities.
5. He felt <u>that</u> there would be many possible jobs in the local area.
6. Pedro found <u>that</u> the instructors and students were all willing to help.
7. Pedro, <u>who</u> had a knack for electronics, performed quite well in the pursuit of his degree.
8. <u>When</u> he graduated, Pedro had a GPA of 3.6.
9. He applied only at Universal Electronics <u>when</u> he sought a job.
10. <u>After</u> Pedro had worked at Universal for three years, the company thanked the college for preparing Pedro so well.

PRACTICE SENTENCES 2-19

1. <u>Good heavens</u>, Bob, let me help you with that.
2. <u>Ouch!</u> I dropped a hammer on my sore toe!
3. <u>Good grief</u>, Ed, why don't you just ask her if she will go out with you?
4. At least pick up a drill and look as if you're doing something, <u>for heaven's sake!</u>
5. <u>Gee</u>, after three days of rain I hope we can finally have our picnic.

CHAPTER 3

PRACTICE SENTENCES 3-1

1. The Cardinals <u>from the east side</u> had an outstanding center.
2. He stood six feet nine inches <u>in his bare feet</u>.
3. The Eagles <u>from the south side</u> had two outstanding guards.
4. The main problem <u>for the Eagles</u> was rebounding.
5. <u>In the first half</u> the Cardinals had a fifteen-point lead.
6. The Eagle coach came up <u>with a plan</u>.
7. He played a triangle and two, <u>with his two biggest men on the Cardinal center</u>.
8. <u>With the Cardinal center pinned in</u>, the Eagle guards scored easily.
9. The Eagles had pulled <u>within one point</u>.
10. However, the Cardinal center won the game <u>with a sky hook</u>.

PRACTICE SENTENCES 3-2

1. The teacher wanted *to make a point to his class*. <u>noun</u>
2. The student wanted a job *to pay off some of his bills*. <u>adverb</u>
3. The monument *to be constructed* is still in the planning stage. <u>adjective</u>
4. The car *to be sold at the auction* is a Studebaker Hawk. <u>adjective</u>
5. *To be chosen a member of the school choir* was May's dream. <u>noun</u>
6. Bob wanted *to repair the car before* his trip to Denver. <u>noun</u>
7. Michael played well in the game *to impress Nancy*. <u>adverb</u>
8. The package *to be mailed* is certified. <u>adjective</u>
9. Dean wants *to complete the course on time*. <u>noun</u>
10. The grass *to be mowed was* over a foot tall. <u>adjective</u>

EDITING PRACTICE 3-3

1. Racing down the hill, the children stopped their sled against a tree.
2. Having studied diligently for the test, Craig had a good grade for his reward.
3. Sleeping outside on a cold January night, Angela still wasn't warm enough in the new sleeping bag.
4. Having purchased a new tennis racket, Jason showed no improvement in his game.
5. Having been married for six years, Adrian began to think the ring on her finger was a burden.
6. Finished with the test, the students turned the papers in.
7. Being scientists, the professors studied the white mice.
8. Repaired by the jeweler for forty-five dollars, the watch Mary owned still failed to keep good time.
9. Determined to do a good job, Paulette painted the house slowly.
10. Spayed at the local animal clinic, the pet Shannon owned was now "safe."

PRACTICE SENTENCES 3-4

1. *Studying the field of accounting for four years,* Violetta wasn't sure what area of accounting she wanted to go into. <u>Violetta</u>
2. *Looking through many journals that advertised job openings,* she found many openings in auditing. <u>she</u>
3. The journals *listing these job openings* indicated many cities where jobs were available. <u>journals</u>

4. *Selecting where she preferred to practice,* the new graduate was faced with numerous choices. <u>graduate</u>
5. San Francisco, *being the site Violetta selected,* had thirty-three openings in auditing. <u>San Francisco</u>
6. *Choosing among eighteen different companies,* she began to study the firms. <u>she</u>
7. *Comparing salary and location,* she eliminated eleven of the firms quickly. <u>she</u>
8. *Selecting the five firms with the finest reputations,* Violetta set up interviews with them. <u>Violetta</u>
9. Violetta, *having confidence in herself,* performed well at all of the interviews. <u>Violetta</u>
10. *Settling into her new job and new city,* she is now a happy, successful young woman. <u>she</u>

PRACTICE SENTENCES 3-5

1. The local civic groups helped the homeless by *sponsoring a charity bazaar.* <u>o.p.</u>
2. *Getting up early* is not part of my normal routine. <u>subj.</u>
3. By *turning in early tonight,* I may be ready for the day's activities. <u>o.p.</u>
4. Some women prefer *working in mills to fast-food restaurants.* <u>d.o.</u>
5. *Selecting a good camera* can take some study. <u>subj.</u>
6. The opponents won the election by *stuffing the ballot boxes.* <u>o.p.</u>
7. Upon *receiving a good credit rating,* Tom applied for six credit cards. <u>o.p.</u>
8. Emily likes *receiving praise and attention.* <u>d.o.</u>
9. *Driving at speeds over a hundred miles an hour* is a thrill and a challenge. <u>subj.</u>
10. *Doing laundry and cleaning house* can ruin a weekend. <u>subj.</u>

PRACTICE SENTENCES 3-6

1. *Washing his own clothes* was a new experience for him. <u>gerund</u>
2. *Looking at all those knobs on the washer and dryer,* Ramon thought about doing his laundry in the sink. <u>participle</u>
3. *Going to the grocery store* was also puzzling for him. <u>gerund</u>
4. Ramon, *standing in the store,* saw cleaning solutions for every item in his home. <u>participle</u>
5. *Confused by the unbelievable assortment of cleaners,* he just bought brand names he had heard of. <u>participle</u>
6. *Taking all the goodies home with him,* Ramon was ready to go to work. <u>participle</u>
7. *Deciding what part of the house he would clean first* was his first choice. <u>gerund</u>
8. He started *cleaning the kitchen.* <u>gerund</u>
9. The newly mopped kitchen floor, *being extremely sticky,* dampened his enthusiasm. <u>participle</u>
10. *Considering all the circumstances,* Ramon hired a cleaning service. <u>participle</u>

CHAPTER 4

PRACTICE SENTENCES 4-1

1. Although there were many to choose from, <u>I selected one in the eighteen-hundred-dollar price range.</u>
2. Because I do a lot of typing, <u>I was most interested in a good word processor.</u>
3. <u>Microsoft Word and Word Perfect were the programs</u> that I had heard the most about.
4. <u>I chose Microsoft Word for my system.</u>
5. <u>I had difficulty learning the program</u> because I had originally learned on another word-processing program.

6. After I was able to operate Microsoft Word, I <u>tackled Power Point</u>.
7. <u>The program was confusing</u> because I didn't even know what it was supposed to do.
8. <u>A friend suggested the Excel spreadsheet as my next task</u>.
9. Although I am not fascinated by numbers, <u>I found the program fun</u>.
10. <u>I may continue experimenting with the computer</u> if I keep discovering so many new things.

PRACTICE SENTENCES 4-2

1. <u>Although he has abused her for years</u>, she has not told anyone.
2. He would get better <u>if she didn't say anything</u>.
3. Some of her friends suspected <u>because they saw bruises on her face and arms</u>.
4. Many battered women are hesitant to mention abuse <u>because they are afraid</u>.
5. <u>Although it shouldn't be the case</u>, some are ashamed to admit abuse.
6. <u>Because his parents were alcoholics</u>, her husband had been an abused child.
7. <u>Although he had never harmed the children</u>, she was afraid of that possibility.
8. Molly studied spouse abuse <u>when she was in college</u>.
9. She decided to talk to her professor <u>when she recognized her situation</u>.
10. <u>Even though he sympathized with her</u>, the professor told her to confront the problem in a clinical setting.

PRACTICE SENTENCES 4-3

1. The bench, <u>which is covered in leather</u>, is five feet long.
2. All the attachment parts and accessories, <u>which are high-quality steel</u>, work together smoothly.
3. The base, <u>which is solid and level</u>, provides a good foundation for the entire machine.
4. The leg lift, <u>which can handle four hundred pounds</u>, is connected to the pile of weights at the front of the machine.
5. The lift bar, <u>which can be set at three different positions</u>, has comfortable hand grips.
6. The weights, <u>which are made of shiny steel</u>, range from twenty-five pounds to four hundred pounds.
7. I planned a daily schedule <u>that I intended to follow every day</u>.
8. After three weeks on the machine <u>that I had bought</u>, I could feel my body firming.
9. My body, <u>which was firming up nicely</u>, began to get lazy.
10. Now my fine machine, <u>which has so many good features</u>, rests undisturbed in the basement.

PRACTICE SENTENCES 4-4

1. We finally added a garage to the house twenty years <u>after the home was constructed</u>.
2. The garage protects us and the cars <u>whenever the weather is bad</u>.
3. The garage needed gutters, however, <u>because the roof spilled over right at the entrance</u>.
4. <u>When we had enough money</u>, the gutters were added.
5. <u>If we had it to do over again</u>, we would have the garage painted.
6. We thought we would paint the garage <u>when the construction was finished</u>.
7. <u>Although we had good intentions</u>, we did not finish the job.
8. <u>Even though the flat ceiling is easy to paint with rollers</u>, we didn't get it painted.
9. The peaks were not painted <u>because we did not have a ladder</u>.
10. <u>Whenever our neighbors speak of community pride</u>, we bow our heads in shame.
11. They may be glad <u>if our garage rots and collapses</u>.

PRACTICE SENTENCES 4–5

1. When the weather was nice, he carried a gas stove, an inflatable boat, inner tubes, and several friends.
2. Nathan and his friends usually stayed until it got dark.
3. The truck was easy to pack up since it didn't have a camper top.
4. Sometimes Nathan went camping by himself because he liked time alone by the river.
5. Once when he was there by himself, a violent thunderstorm came up.
6. Even though the road was muddy, the truck came through fine.
7. On another occasion Nathan went to the river while there was snow on the ground.
8. Although snow was up to the axle, the truck kept going.
9. Nathan returned home because he got cold.
10. He got stuck in his driveway because he could not see the ice under the snow.

PRACTICE SENTENCES 4–6

1. He felt that she was friendly and pretty. p.n.
2. But he didn't know who she was. d.o.
3. He wanted someone to introduce him to whoever this new girl in the neighborhood might be. o.p.
4. Someone told him that her name was Tomasina. d.o.
5. Roy Lee asked that she join him for a cup of coffee. d.o.
6. Whatever restaurant they attended was fine with him. s
7. He enjoyed her company and found out that her name was Tomasina. d.o.
8. Whatever her background might have been soon became unimportant. s
9. He believed that the relationship could never work. d.o.
10. Tomasina would not go out with whoever smoked cigarettes. o.p.

CHAPTER 5

PRACTICE SENTENCES 5–1

1. She (connects) the hose by herself.
2. She (attaches) the sprinkler and (turns) the faucet.
3. In no time, she (is soaking) wet and (having) fun.
4. Sometimes her brother Julio (joins) her.
5. Angel and Julio (turn) the sprinkler on each other.
6. Usually one of them (gets) mad.
7. The last time, Julio (squirted) his sister good.
8. Angel ran to Mommy and (told) on him.
9. Mommy and Angel (talked) to Julio and (warned) him.
10. With Mommy back in the house, Julio (gave) Angel a face full of water.

PRACTICE SENTENCES 5–2

1. He talked to some people(,) but everyone told him something different.
2. Some people prefer small dogs(,) yet many others like big dogs.

3. He looked through some books, but they didn't help him.
4. Finally, William went to a nearby pet store, and he looked at the varieties available.
5. He didn't like the thought of a dog in the house, and he preferred larger dogs anyway.
6. William got his girlfriend Jane to go with him to the pet store, but she was only going to provide advice.
7. At the store William fell in love with a beautiful Irish setter, and Jane liked the dog also.
8. William wanted to buy the dog, but the price was five hundred dollars.
9. He really wanted the dog, so he paid the price, and he and Jane took the dog to its new home.
10. The dog likes to get into other people's garbage and chase cars, but William has never regretted the five hundred dollars.

PRACTICE SENTENCES 5-3

1. The first thing [that she did] was till a spot of ground in her backyard.
2. [After she finished with the tilling,] she went to the local garden supply store and bought some seed.
3. She knew [that she had to plant the seeds the proper depth and the proper distance apart.]
4. She added some fertilizer to each hole [that she dug.]
5. Then Bella turned the sprinkler on the area [that she had prepared.]
6. [After she had done all this,] she waited for the plants to come up.
7. Three weeks later she saw [that nothing was growing in the garden.]
8. She decided [that she needed some help.]
9. A friend [who had tended a garden for years] came over to have a look.
10. Bella's friend told her [that she had added too much fertilizer to each plant.]

PRACTICE SENTENCES 5-4

1. Mort bought a new car, but he was dissatisfied with it [since it could go only 120 miles an hour on a racetrack.]
2. Sue got her pepperoni pizza, but she sent it back [when she saw anchovies on it.]
3. [Because he was not a very good dancer,] Alfred was uncomfortable at parties; in fact, he was even uncomfortable around girls.
4. Look [before you leap,] or you may regret your move for a long time.
5. The jury members entered the courtroom [when the judge called them,] but they still had not reached a decision.
6. The man said [that he did not agree with the new law;] furthermore, he intended to change it.
7. Arlene looked at houses for days, but she bought the one on Lowe Street [because she liked the floor plan and the location.]
8. William thought [his watch was broken,] but it only needed a battery.
9. Fred purchased a scientific calculator [since he was not good in math,] and his grades improved significantly
10. Lamont saw the most beautiful girl [he had ever seen,] but she was just a picture in a magazine.

EDITING PRACTICE 5-5
Individual student answers to this exercise will vary.

EDITING EXERCISE 5-6
Individual student answers to this exercise will vary.

CHAPTER 6

PRACTICE SENTENCES 6-1
1. The computers for the office (is, <u>are</u>) to arrive this afternoon.
2. The plants (is, <u>are</u>) guaranteed for one year.
3. The snow blower (<u>runs</u>, run) smoothly.
4. The rare coins (costs, <u>cost</u>) over seven thousand dollars.
5. Clarissa (<u>practices</u>, practice) the piano three hours each day.
6. The chain saws in the local hardware store (comes, <u>come</u>) with many accessories.
7. My cat (<u>eats</u>, eat) as if there will be no tomorrow.
8. The list of volunteers for the tornado relief (<u>is</u>, are) growing daily.
9. The maintenance staff (<u>puts</u>, put) in long hours.
10. The books on the shelf (is, <u>are</u>) in bad condition.

PRACTICE SENTENCES 6-2
1. Cass (appraise, <u>appraises</u>) diamonds for his father's jewelry store.
2. Psychologists (<u>say</u>, says) everyone has some mental hangups.
3. Mrs. Williams (celebrate, <u>celebrates</u>) the anniversary of her gall bladder surgery every year.
4. Statisticians (<u>say</u>, says) Americans are getting taller.
5. Iris (go, <u>goes</u>) to her aerobics class every Tuesday.
6. Scientists (<u>tell</u>, tells) us not to smoke.
7. Criminologists (<u>attend</u>, attends) all the meetings they can.
8. Bernice (see, <u>sees</u>) her father at least once a week.
9. Mr. and Mrs. Stevens (<u>send</u>, sends) their daughter off to school each morning.
10. Ernest (play, <u>plays</u>) the title role in *The Importance of Being Earnest*.

PRACTICE SENTENCES 6-3
1. The man with the three Honda motorcycles (<u>has</u>, have) a broken leg.
2. The boss, as well as his employees, (<u>expresses</u>, express) concern for the future of the company.
3. John's collection of records, tapes, and CDs (<u>is</u>, are) well known by the local radio stations.
4. Many homes in this country (has, <u>have</u>) more than one television set.
5. Becky, along with her children, Jason and Nikki, (wax, <u>waxes</u>) the cars every summer.
6. The three telephones in the house (is, <u>are</u>) all on the same line.
7. Many NASCAR fans, including Tonya, (follows, <u>follow</u>) every race.
8. All of the flowers in the garden (was, <u>were</u>) beautiful this year.
9. The runner with the expensive shoes, warm-up suit, and athletic bag (<u>finishes</u>, finish) last in every race.
10. The girls with a good attitude and a desire to learn (makes, <u>make</u>) the best grades in the class.

PRACTICE SENTENCES 6-4

1. The star guard and star center (averages, <u>average</u>) over eighteen points per game.
2. My roommate and I (spends, <u>spend</u>) much time together.
3. William Wordsworth's best friend and companion (<u>was</u>, were) his sister.
4. Bob, Ted, Carol, and Alice (participates, <u>participate</u>) in many community activities.
5. Both television sets in the house (needs, <u>need</u>) repairing.
6. The public and the law (is, <u>are</u>) beginning to crack down on drunk drivers.
7. Rupert's guns and knives (was, <u>were</u>) highly valued by an appraiser.
8. Lena's three cars all (needs, <u>need</u>) new paint jobs.
9. All types of handheld tape recorders (has, <u>have</u>) come down in price.
10. Mr. and Mrs. Orion (wants, <u>want</u>) to visit Hawaii.

PRACTICE SENTENCES 6-5

1. Both of the men (does, <u>do</u>) well when the pressure is on.
2. Somebody on the staff (<u>wants</u>, want) a new editor.
3. Everyone (<u>is</u>, are) convinced that an annual competition is worthwhile.
4. Some of the women (goes, <u>go</u>) to the track every morning.
5. Anything (<u>goes</u>, go) in the sport of rugby.
6. No one (<u>likes</u>, like) the aluminum bats used in college baseball.
7. Anyone who knows the rules (<u>thinks</u>, think) chess is a challenging game.
8. Some of the stolen bonds (was, <u>were</u>) recovered.
9. The coach said that anyone who hustles (<u>makes</u>, make) the team.
10. No one (<u>wants</u>, want) to do well more than Harvey.

PRACTICE SENTENCES 6-6

1. Either the managers or the employees (is, <u>are</u>) to receive pay increases.
2. Neither the gym nor the library (<u>is</u>, are) to be opened this year.
3. Neither the students nor the instructor (<u>is</u>, are) about to be satisfied with the grades on the last test.
4. Neither the city manager nor the board members (plans, <u>plan</u>) to vote for the proposal.
5. Either the players or the coaches (is, <u>are</u>) planning to demand newer equipment.
6. Either the dean or the nursing instructors (is, <u>are</u>) to redesign the program for next fall.
7. Either Janis or Sue (<u>is</u>, are) qualified for the position.
8. Neither the workers nor the managers (likes, <u>like</u>) the new government regulations.
9. Neither Cara nor her sisters (is, <u>are</u>) ready for the tournament.
10. Neither Leroy nor Michael (<u>enjoys</u>, enjoy) the competition between them.

PRACTICE SENTENCES 6-7

1. On the fence in the backyard (<u>is</u>, are) a tall stand of grass.
2. On the power lines over the driveway (is, <u>are</u>) more than a dozen birds.
3. There (<u>is</u>, are) a big mess in the kitchen.
4. In the park near the pond (<u>stands</u>, stand) a statue of Thomas Jefferson.
5. Behind the mirror on the wall (<u>is</u>, are) the looking-glass world.
6. There (is, <u>are</u>) three men and two women applying for the position.
7. There (<u>is</u>, are) a bat flying around the basement.
8. Under the bridge on Mockingbird Lane (is, <u>are</u>) seven or eight ducks.
9. There (<u>is</u>, are) a scar on the back of my right arm.
10. At the entrance into the park (<u>stands</u>, stand) a memorial to veterans.

PRACTICE SENTENCES 6-8

1. The class (is, are) deciding on its senior gift to the school.
2. The faculty (is, are) concerned about the shortage of time in its new exam schedule.
3. The number of freshmen elected at the last induction ceremony (is, are) small.
4. The board (has, have) to complete its budget by next Thursday.
5. The family always (studies, study) its vacation plans carefully.
6. A number of athletes on the team (was, were) suspended because of the drug test results.
7. The committee (is, are) thinking about reconsidering its findings.
8. The number of applicants for the scholarship (was, were) small.
9. The jury (orders, order) its meals at the same time each day.
10. The number of Hispanics attending medical school in Florida (increases, increase) each year.

PRACTICE SENTENCES 6-9

1. The students usually prefer the professors who (prepares, prepare) their lectures thoroughly.
2. Most people trust whoever (inspires, inspire) them the most.
3. He is the man who (defines, define) positive as "mistaken at the top of one's lungs."
4. The equipment that (was, were) purchased for the camping trip never arrived.
5. The students who (contributes, contribute) the most to the paper this year will receive the best staff positions next year.
6. The clothes on display at the yard sale are not the ones that (is, are) for sale.
7. The animal that wins the prizes at the dog shows is not necessarily the one that (makes, make) the best pet.
8. An electrical appliance that (has, have) a damaged cord should be repaired.
9. Putting a lot of money into a lawn that is not properly maintained (makes, make) little sense.
10. The conference recognizes the athletes who (does, do) the most for their schools.

PRACTICE SENTENCES 6-10

1. Practicing with a slingshot (relaxes, relax) me.
2. Watching too much television (becomes, become) a habit after a while.
3. Playing a musical instrument (requires, require) much time, patience, and practice.
4. Riding a motorcycle alone in the woods (is, are) not a good idea.
5. Practicing the Morse code (is, are) relaxing to some people.

PRACTICE SENTENCES 6-11

1. The news (does, do) not come on until 6:30 P.M.
2. Measles (is, are) nothing to take lightly.
3. *The Life and Times of Judge Roy Bean* (is, are) interesting reading.
4. At higher levels economics (gets, get) very mathematical.
5. Athletics (is, are) a lucrative business these days.
6. *U.S. News & World Report* (is, are) a good source of information.
7. Aeronautics (is, are) an area of study for car designers.
8. *Gulliver's Travels* (is, are) Swift's best-known work.
9. Ham and eggs (is, are) a popular breakfast dish.
10. *The Chicago-Sun Times* (is, are) a famous newspaper.

PRACTICE SENTENCES 6-12

1. (That, <u>Those</u>) types of tomatoes are the best.
2. Each man is expected to keep up with (<u>his</u>, their) own equipment.
3. Everyone can keep (<u>his/her</u>, their) weight down if necessary.
4. The article said (this, <u>those</u>) aluminum baseball bats hit the ball fifteen to twenty feet farther than the wooden ones.
5. Each of the women had (<u>her</u>, their) own views about marriage.
6. Someone forgot to turn off (<u>his/her</u>, their) bath water.
7. Each person contributed what (<u>he/she</u>, they) could afford.
8. (These, <u>This</u>) kind of rose produces a small flower.
9. Every member of the faculty expressed (<u>his/her</u>, their) opinion concerning the new attendance policy.
10. It should be easy for either of the two women to prove (<u>her</u>, their) qualifications for the job.

PRACTICE SENTENCES 6-13

1. Monica and her parents were not able to agree on where to spend (her, <u>their</u>) vacation.
2. Corey and Kathleen are both having trouble in (her, <u>their</u>) math course.
3. The administrators from the vocational area and the deans from the technical area are discussing contract provisions for (his, <u>their</u>) areas.
4. Eva and Marlena are glad to speak out about (her, <u>their</u>) views on the topic of abortion.
5. The lawyers for the defense team and the prosecutors were unable to decide on how to handle (his, <u>their</u>) cases.

PRACTICE SENTENCES 6-14

1. Either Aluna or Idi will attend the conference if (<u>she</u>, they) gets elected.
2. Neither the managers nor the employees would speak up for (his/her, <u>their</u>) suggested salary raises.
3. Either the astronauts or the NASA manager will get (<u>his/her</u>, their) way.
4. Neither the bank manager nor the bank customers understand (his/her, <u>their</u>) view about the new manager.
5. Either Robert or Juan will win the contract for the plans that (<u>he</u>, they) proposed.
6. Neither the show's star nor its producers cared for the script that (he/she, <u>they</u>) were given.
7. Neither the students nor the student government were pleased with the new regulations that (<u>they</u>, it) received.
8. Neither the shipmates nor the captain could confirm (<u>his/her</u>, their) reservations on the boat.
9. Either the golfers or the club professional will determine the rules for the tournament (<u>he/she</u>, they) want to arrange.
10. Either Gabriella or Maria will attend the meeting if (<u>she</u>, they) can.

PRACTICE SENTENCES 6-15

1. The Board of Trustees is considering what (<u>its</u> their) new drug policy will include.
2. The class of '98 is pleased with the gift (<u>it</u>, they) will make to the school.
3. The General Assembly are debating (its, <u>their</u>) own salary increase.
4. The committee feels it must make a decision soon if (<u>its</u>, their) credibility is to be maintained.
5. The team supports (<u>its</u>, their) coach.

6. The group are not in agreement on many of the issues (it, <u>they</u>) discuss.
7. The Arts Council is a tax-deductible contribution for (<u>its</u>, their) supporters.
8. The jury is not sure (<u>it</u>, they) can reach a decision today.
9. The Academic Council is considering adding a policy on academic probation to the student handbook (<u>it</u>, they) publishes.
10. The herd is resting peacefully in (<u>its</u>, their) pen.

PRACTICE SENTENCES 6-16

1. Anyone (<u>who</u>, which) wants to succeed should learn self discipline.
2. The animal (who, <u>which</u>) was injured was taken to the veterinarian.
3. The man (<u>that</u>, which) won the car race used illegal equipment.
4. She loaned her horse to a boy (<u>who</u>, which) had never ridden before.
5. The businessman (<u>who</u>, which) lost the contract also lost his job.

CHAPTER 7

PRACTICE SENTENCES 7-1

1. Does the press have the right to investigate the private lives of public figures? <u>sentence</u>
2. Seeking out any information available. <u>phrase</u>
3. Printing rumors as readily as facts. <u>phrase</u>
4. Many members of the general public resent such invasion of privacy. <u>sentence</u>
5. On the other hand some people hang on every word. <u>sentence</u>
6. All citizens reacting in an individual way. <u>phrase</u>
7. The problem can become serious. <u>sentence</u>
8. Some people around the world blaming the press for the death of Princess Di. <u>phrase</u>
9. Some limits must be set. <u>sentence</u>
10. But being qualified to set the new procedures. <u>phrase</u>

PRACTICE SENTENCES 7-2

1. He was excited about the upcoming car show. <u>complete sentence</u>
2. Which was to be held in May at the fairgrounds. <u>subordinate clause</u>
3. He had built the car from the chassis up. <u>complete sentence</u>
4. Although a few finishing touches were needed on the bodywork. <u>subordinate clause</u>
5. The car was just about ready to be shown. <u>complete sentence</u>

EDITING PRACTICE 7-3

Individual student answers to this exercise will vary.

CHAPTER 8

PRACTICE SENTENCES 8-1

1. She talked with the owner of a studio in a nearby town ◯ he gave her some advice.
2. He suggested she purchase a good 35-mm Nikon camera ◯ it is good for most general-use purposes.
3. He further recommended she purchase a Rolleflex ◯ this camera is better for more specific purposes.

4. He told her she would need some studio lighting ◯ he suggested several kinds of lights.

5. He reminded her of the importance of backdrops ◯ she would need at least three.

6. He recommended that she keep plenty of film ◯ for best results it should be kept in the refrigerator.

7. She couldn't afford to purchase all this equipment at one time ◯ she decided to open her studio with what she had.

8. She made her own backdrops ◯ they were more imaginative than ones in the supply stores.

9. Her customers came slowly at first ◯ her reputation spread, however.

10. Now her studio is making a profit ◯ she is happy and independent.

EDITING PRACTICE 8-2

1. She originally had trouble with cartilage damage; this problem resulted in arthritis in her knee.
2. Her doctor performed arthroscopic surgery; unfortunately, the surgery did not solve her problem.
3. The arthritis continued to get worse; Jeannie was no better off.
4. She consulted three other orthopedic surgeons; each agreed to try to help her.
5. One of the surgeons operated on her knee; he removed as much of the affected area as possible.
6. He explained the procedure to her; he indicated he would remove all damaged or diseased portions he saw.
7. But he informed her of a potential problem; sometimes it takes many surgeries to remedy the problem.
8. Sometimes the problem is never corrected; it is only alleviated temporarily.
9. Jeannie was feeling down; in fact, she was getting downright depressed.
10. Now, after seven knee operations, she does not like the situation with her knee; she is, however, glad that she can walk unassisted.

EDITING PRACTICE 8-3

1. Many of the stories are said to be based on fact, <u>and</u> there are people who have witnessed the events.
2. The Devil's Tramping Ground is a huge, bare circle in which no vegetation will grow, <u>and</u> it is located in the central part of the state.
3. In the legend of the Devil's Tramping Ground, it is said the Devil removes any objects placed in the bare spot, <u>but</u> no one has ever proved that it is actually the Devil who removes them.
4. Another story, the legend of the Brown Mountain Light, has many explanations, <u>and</u> each one differs in its interpretation of the meaning of the mysterious light.
5. In the mountains of North Carolina, a mysterious light appears, <u>yet</u> there is no apparent reason for the light.
6. Some people say an old slave has come back from his grave carrying a lantern and looking for his master, <u>and</u> a song called "The Brown Mountain Light" relates that version, although that is not the most popular explanation.
7. Another popular legend is of a young girl who hitches a ride with strangers and disappears from their car, <u>yet</u> she always appears on dark, foggy nights and wears a white gown.

8. Apparently, a young girl was killed on a bridge near Chapel Hill many years ago, <u>and</u> ever since that foggy night, she has been trying to get someone to take her home.

9. Many people say they have stopped to pick her up and take her home, <u>but</u> she always disappears without a trace before they reach her home.

10. You should never tell a North Carolinian that these stories are not true, <u>for</u> you may be speaking to someone who has witnessed one of these mysteries.

PRACTICE SENTENCES 8-4

1. The body seemed to be in good shape; there were no bad dents anywhere.

2. He took it for a test run; everything seemed to work well.

3. The interior had a few rough areas; he thought he could repair them.

4. Then one day a fleck of paint fell off; under the paint there was nothing but rust.

5. On a trip to the repair shop the engine quit running; Chilo was stranded.

6. The mechanic told Chilo that the engine had frozen up; it couldn't be repaired.

7. Rebuilding the engine would not help; the block was cracked.

8. The mechanic gave him bad news; it would cost three thousand dollars to repair.

9. Chilo was quite angry; he consulted a lawyer.

10. The lawyer told Chilo there was little that could be done; the term he used was *caveat emptor.*

PRACTICE SENTENCES 8-5

1. Some of the movies were made in the 1930s, 1940s, and 1950s; Christine was not born until 1971.

2. One of her favorites is *The African Queen*; it stars Humphrey Bogart and Katharine Hepburn.

3. Her father told her about the movie before they watched it; he thought she would enjoy it.

4. It is about a man and a woman on a dangerous boating excursion; the man and woman have very different personalities.

5. The woman is quite religious and conservative; the man is a gin-drinking capitalist with few convictions.

6. She convinces him to support Britain's war effort; he agrees just to humor her.

7. The woman demonstrates that she has courage and determination; she surprises her male companion.

8. As the movie progresses, a mutual admiration develops between the two; they fall in love.

9. In the end the two are willing to give their lives for each other; they wish to be married first.

10. Christine's father asked if she thought such romances actually existed in real life; she said she certainly hoped so.

CHAPTER 9

PRACTICE SENTENCES 9-1

1. <u>She</u> has an innate talent.
2. Nevertheless, <u>she</u> practices rigorously every day.
3. <u>She</u> feels that a great athlete is made as well as born.
4. Because <u>she</u> is as dedicated as <u>she</u> is, her coach doesn't push her.
5. Her coach knows <u>she</u> is an athlete who will do her best.

PRACTICE SENTENCES 9-2

1. The vice president promoted <u>her</u> to the position of sales manager.
2. The coach told <u>us</u> to hustle.
3. Mother told <u>us</u> girls to get quiet.
4. The man <u>whom</u> he most admired died in an accident.
5. Mrs. Terrill gave <u>me</u> a nice Christmas bonus.

EDITING PRACTICE 9-3

1. C
2. All of his former teachers feel he is a man <u>who</u> can be trusted.
3. C
4. He offered his assistance to those <u>who</u> he thought could be of help to him.
5. He married a woman <u>who</u> could help him with his goals.
6. C
7. C
8. But when he began to see that some attorneys <u>who</u> he knew were getting in trouble with the courts, he decided to put ethics above ambition.
9. C
10. He is serving his fourth term in the Senate, and many constituents feel he is the man <u>who</u> should be nominated for the presidency in the next election.

EDITING PRACTICE 9-4

1. C
2. I appreciate <u>your</u> helping me with the project.
3. <u>His</u> raking the lawn was a nice contribution to the wedding.
4. C
5. <u>My</u> arguing with the police officer did not help my case.

PRACTICE SENTENCES 9-5

1. Sara, the store owner, said Sue had expensive tastes.
2. Mr. Joyce was informed by Mr. Adams that his stress level was too high.
3. Sally was told by her mother to go to the store.
4. The teacher told the student, "You are too tired to perform at your best."
5. The gardener told his boss, "You need more money for the landscape to be developed as originally drawn."

PRACTICE SENTENCES 9-6

Individual student answers to this exercise will vary.

PRACTICE SENTENCES 9-7

Individual student answers to this exercise will vary.

PRACTICE SENTENCES 9-8
Individual student answers to this exercise will vary.

PRACTICE SENTENCES 9-9
Individual student answers to this exercise will vary.

PRACTICE SENTENCES 9-10
Individual student answers to this exercise will vary.

CHAPTER 10

PRACTICE SENTENCES 10-1
1. Hwan drove carelessly into the tree on the side of the road.
2. Mary uses her fax machine frequently.
3. The FBI agents opened the package carefully.
4. Bruce Lee handled his martial arts weapons flawlessly.
5. Ambrose combed his hair frequently.
6. Antonio's tape recorder did not work properly.
7. The astronomer studied his charts closely.
8. The teacher graded the term papers quickly.
9. Jasper used his credit card a little too frequently.
10. Tammy's stomach pained her terribly.

PRACTICE SENTENCES 10-2
1. Grady's electric sander was expensive.
2. Ralph's dog is ready for the dog show this weekend.
3. The coffee in the cafeteria was bitter this morning.
4. Geraldo's hair looks nice.
5. Beatrice appeared confident after her interview.
6. The project has been ready for nearly two weeks.
7. Benny's new woodcarving was different.
8. The flowers on the table smelled fresh.
9. Sidney seems happy at this college
10. Mia became enthusiastic about her new job after the first paycheck.

PRACTICE SENTENCES 10-3
1. The old coffee tastes (bitter, bitterly).
2. Rick, not feeling well, ran the race (slow, slowly).
3. Corey did not perform (good, well) on the test.
4. The golfer studied the putt (careful, carefully).
5. Donna's hair looks (good, well) today.
6. Colin stroked the ball (smooth, smoothly).
7. Lenny looks (careful, carefully) at wood before he buys it.
8. Darrell talked (rapid, rapidly) during his job interview.
9. Phil responded (angry, angrily) to his friend's insult.
10. The violinist performed (admirable, admirably) at the concert.

PRACTICE SENTENCES 10-4

1. He has the (harder, <u>hardest</u>) serve of all the players on the team.
2. He is also the (more accurate, <u>most accurate</u>) server.
3. However, his teammate Raul is the (better, <u>best</u>) at hitting volleys.
4. Roberto, though, has the (better, <u>best</u>) baseline game in the conference.
5. He is also the (better, <u>best</u>) at hitting lob shots.
6. Roberto and his friend Julius used to play (equal, <u>equally</u>) well.
7. But Roberto practiced (more diligent, <u>more diligently</u>).
8. Eventually Julius took up golf since Roberto beat him so (consistent, <u>consistently</u>) in tennis.
9. Roberto (enthusiastic, <u>enthusiastically</u>) entered the conference tournament.
10. He accomplished the (better, <u>best</u>) record of anyone who had ever entered.

EDITING PRACTICE 10-5

1. The **gubernatorial** candidate passed the lie detector test.
2. The **judicial** branch of the government is perhaps the one citizens understand the least.
3. The high school teacher reprimanded a student for his **childish** behavior.
4. The United States has a long history of **racial** prejudice.
5. The candidate was having trouble getting donations for his **senatorial** campaign.
6. Some adults are not serious enough about their **parental** responsibilities.
7. Sergeant Preston was a member of the Royal **Canadian** Mounted Police.
8. Suzy got a job as a **medical** technologist.
9. The **mayoral** candidate filed for the election this morning.
10. For three years now, the dentist has operated his office without a **dental** assistant.

CHAPTER 11

EDITING PRACTICE 11-1

1. Some teachers strongly encourage students to write journals, but most students don't like the idea at first.
2. Eugene wanted to become a police officer, yet he didn't have time to go through the training program.
3. The moon will be full tomorrow night, so it should be perfect for camping.
4. The flat roofs on the buildings are interesting, but they leak.
5. Nadine got interested in playing chess, and she apparently has an aptitude for it.
6. Eric went with his wife to a yard sale, and he was surprised at some of the bargains.
7. The horticulturalist drew up landscape plans for Jim's yard, but he was not satisfied with them.
8. Mariano thought that the coin he had purchased was valuable, but he was disappointed when he found out it wasn't.
9. Mikail wants to get married and settle down, but he hasn't found the right woman yet.
10. Ted Bundy claimed that pornography caused him to commit his crimes, yet most people feel he was just trying to delay the death penalty.

EDITING PRACTICE 11-2

1. Although I studied for the test, I did not do well.
2. The plane having already taken off, I had to reschedule my flight.
3. Not many hours before, the polls closed.
4. Interestingly enough, everything we planned went off without a hitch.
5. On graduation day Yvette threw her cap in the air and yelled, "I made it."
6. If I can get the parts by Wednesday, I will have your car ready Friday.
7. Nanette, did you get the new outfit you wanted?
8. Yes, I think Howard would be perfect for the job.
9. In the center of the pet store, we found the cat we wanted.
10. Gluing the vase as carefully as possible, I was able to repair it adequately.

EDITING PRACTICE 11-3

1. The customer wanted a good, dependable truck.
2. Tommy, Jason, and Lewis were the three winners.
3. All he had in his pockets were two quarters and a pocketknife.
4. The company hired an intelligent, charming manager.
5. If you cannot sleep, get out of bed, read a book, or watch television.
6. The students said it was an unfair, even tricky test.
7. The new Spanish teacher spoke with a southern accent.
8. Drive the car to the shop, park it in front of the service door, and explain the problem to the service manager.
9. Sue Ellen is a graceful, versatile athlete.
10. Anne told Julian that he was rude to his parents, crude to women, and generally obnoxious to everyone.

EDITING PRACTICE 11-4

1. The store's owner, a self-made man, is proud of his accomplishments.
2. One actress that I really enjoy watching is Jessica Tandy.
3. Drive the truck across the field, through the creek, and up the muddy slope.
4. The challenging, motivational telecourse was popular with most students.
5. In 1998, 153 people were killed in the mudslide.
6. Lauren's daughter Susie refused to vote for the same candidates as her parents.
7. Tommy said, "I feel as if everyone depends on me."
8. Camille, please sort your own laundry.
9. Interestingly enough, the cheaper blender was the better one.
10. Keats's poem "On First Looking into Chapman's Homer" is one of his most famous.

EDITING PRACTICE 11-5

1. John visited Portland, Maine, during the middle of winter.
2. Beth Westbrook, President of the College, attended the Governor's Ball.
3. Meredith celebrated her graduation on May 21, 1995.
4. Richard Kildare, M.D., is popular with his patients.
5. William McKinnon, Vice President of Marketing, has been ill all week.
6. On Monday, August 14, 1995, the largest factory in town closed down.
7. Brenda Davenport, D.D.S., has an office in the Nalle Clinic.
8. The meeting is to be in Dallas, Texas, on April 21, 1995.
9. Walker Barnett, Chairman of the Board, does not tolerate dissenstion.
10. On Wednesday, November 15, 1995, the new stretch of highway will be opened.

EDITING PRACTICE 11-6

1. The woman(,) who is responsible for the accident, cannot be found.
2. Voters(,) that take their citizenship seriously, are well-informed about every election.
3. Carl is both a good athlete(,) and a good student.
4. At dinner(,) Jeremy always serves a fine wine.
5. Roseanne believes(,) that her plan will work.
6. Bob is an intelligent, polite, and handsome(,) administrator.
7. The man tried hard to be heard(,) and spoke as loudly as he could.
8. The young instructor with the air cast on his leg(,) broke his ankle last week.
9. The local postal supervisor says(,) that the mail is distributed quickly, but carefully.
10. The employees(,) gathering in the break room, are circulating a petition.

CHAPTER 12

There are no practice sentences in this chapter.

CHAPTER 13

EDITING PRACTICE 13-1
1. Sophocles' play *Antigone* is in many freshman English anthologies.
2. The show's star was difficult to get along with during the filming.
3. Sherrie and Dianne's apartment is quite expensive.
4. Someone's mail-order purchase was left on the front lawn.
5. The dining-room table's finish is in poor condition.
6. The Alexanders' home has been vandalized.
7. Samuel Johnson's *Rasselas* is an enjoyable book to read.
8. The faculty members' vote clearly showed their support for the proposal.
9. Ladies' watches are not as small as they used to be.
10. Margaret's helping the injured child was a humane response to an unfortunate situation.

EDITING PRACTICE 13-2
1. I don't think I can afford the house I had planned to build.
2. They're available to everyone that wants to attend the meeting.
3. It's not expected to be a big media event.
4. Who's expected to attend the convention in Washington, D.C.?
5. The CEO is expected to arrive at nine o'clock.

EDITING PRACTICE 13-3
1. The mathematics department was searching for candidates with M.A.'s in physics and astronomy.
2. The division secretary said my *play*'s looked like *ploy*'s.
3. The 7's and 9's in the manuscript looked similar.
4. The words *son*'s and *sun*'s sound alike.

5. The *g*'s on the printer did not print properly.
6. Tommy made three *A*'s and two *B*'s last semester.
7. The *i*'s and the *l*'s looked too much alike.
8. My handwriting does not distinguish well between *a*'s and *o*'s.
9. The University of Minnesota granted 286 M.A.'s last semester.
10. On my computer keyboard I often strike *q*'s for *w*'s.

CHAPTER 14

EDITING PRACTICE 14-1
1. The golfer said to his caddy, "Hand me the nine iron."
2. "I would like to take some lessons in music theory," I told my mom, "and then take some piano lessons."
3. "Did you know that there are only three computers available in the Writing Center?" said one student to another.
4. The instructor of the electrical applications class told the students, "Be sure to turn off the power source before starting to work."
5. "The timer for the bomb," the bomb squad leader said, "was a simple drugstore alarm."
6. "I need a new car," Tom said, "but I don't know what kind I want."
7. Jorge knew that his company's bid would not be accepted.
8. "Only three members of the team will be able to make the trip to New York," the debate coach told his squad.
9. "The steaks are a little crisp," Blanche told her neighbors.
10. "Willie, you must practice at least an hour a day if you expect to maintain and improve your skills," his coach told him.

EDITING PRACTICE 14-2
1. *The Washington Post* ran an article entitled "Watergate Revisited."
2. Many readers are fond of Robert Frost's short poem "Home Burial."
3. Ernest Hemingway wrote a short story about abortion called "Hills like White Elephants."
4. "I Am Born" is the title of the first chapter of Dickens' novel *David Copperfield*.
5. Emily Brontë's novel *Wuthering Heights* is a classic.

EDITING PRACTICE 14-3
1. Erwin asked, "Will the new sandwich shop open on time?"
2. Jean yelled in pain, "I think I broke my leg!"
3. "Young Goodman Brown" is a well-known short story by Nathaniel Hawthorne.
4. The teacher, who was nearly in a panic himself, shouted to the students, "Don't panic."
5. A "hertz" is a unit of frequency.
6. Sari yelled, "Turn off the power!"
7. Ernie said, "Do you really think the new parking proposal will pass?"
8. John asked, "Do you know the words to the famous western song 'The Streets of Laredo'?"
9. The drivers' license examiner told the group, "Bring your test papers to the front of the room when you finish."
10. "Ozymandias" is a fine short poem by Shelley.

CHAPTER 15

EDITING PRACTICE 15-1

1. Churchill Downs in Louisville, Kentucky, is the site of the Kentucky Derby.
2. The United States entered World War II in 1941.
3. Christmas Day is a sad time for many lonely people.
4. In 55 B.C. Julius Caesar invaded England.
5. It was F.D.R. who said, "We have nothing to fear but fear itself."
6. The Lincoln Memorial in Washington is very impressive.
7. The meeting will begin promptly at 10:00 A.M.
8. The temperature was 3°F this morning.
9. Steve's mother said, "Please close the door."
10. Dry Wells is a ghost town.

EDITING PRACTICE 15-2

1. The Masters is a famous golf tournament.
2. Andrew Jackson was the American general at the Battle of New Orleans.
3. Highway 21 has a hugh pothole about two miles from Stokesbury.
4. I have studied *Wuthering Heights* at least three times.
5. The Mitchell River is perhaps the cleanest river in Surry County.
6. Lauren studied German at Syracuse University.
7. I named my boat the *Suzy Q.*
8. My aunt lives in Racine, Wisconsin.
9. Stone Mountain is an interesting place to visit.
10. Huan subscribes to *People, Life,* and *Time* magazines.

EDITING PRACTICE 15-3

1. Herman Wouk scored two hits with *The Winds of War* and *War and Remembrance.*
2. I like the Morning Flower pattern for everyday china.
3. The Oakland A's are trying to get into the playoffs.
4. *Invisible Man* is a fine novel by Ralph Ellison.
5. The woman thought Death stalked her constantly.
6. "The Cask of Amontillado" is a short story by Poe.
7. Eliot Ness worked for the Treasury Department.
8. Michael Jordan was a star for the Chicago Bulls.
9. Have you ever read the book *My Brother Was an Only Child?*
10. Carla thinks Professor Reece is an excellent teacher.

CHAPTER 16

EDITING PRACTICE 16-1

1. The Reverend Miller will conduct services at 11:00 P.M. Sunday.
2. George Washington served the country well as the first president.
3. Captain Adams is from Helena, Mont.
4. Columbus discovered America in A.D. 1492.
5. The United States is in good shape economically.
6. Victor Hugo was a famous French novelist.

7. Mary and Jane spent all day at the fair.
8. Raleigh is the capital of North Carolina.
9. Julius Caesar invaded England in 55 B.C.
10. Clark has a CB radio in his car as well as a ham radio.

EDITING PRACTICE 16-2

1. Tammy is a patient at Charter Hospital.
2. The radio station's call letters are WAYS.
3. The chemical symbol for salt is NaCl.
4. The bag of kitty litter weighed over twenty pounds.
5. The stockholders' meeting is planned for Tuesday, September 6, 1999.
6. The abortion clinic on East Boulevard was bombed last Thursday.
7. The bag of fertilizer weighed over eighty pounds.
8. The young soldier went AWOL.
9. The committee headquarters is on Fifth Avenue.
10. Page 4 of Chapter 5 has a famous misprint.

EDITING PRACTICE 16-3

1. The address of the courthouse is 5314 Main Street.
2. The project took 3 men, 2 women, 5 typewriters, and 5,653 sheets of paper.
3. Sam Duff decided not to run for reelection as representative from the Eighth District.
4. Theodore was born on September 25, 1977.
5. Alfred Norton has already had five wives.
6. Chapter 12 needs to be rewritten.
7. The Mustangs defeated the Greyhounds 86 to 73.
8. Highway 462 is nearly complete.
9. The committee met regularly from 1986 to 1992.
10. Over 62 percent of those solicited responded to the questionnaire.

EDITING PRACTICE 16-4

1. One mile is 1,760 yards.
2. The Forty-second Regiment is ready to go.
3. The fire started at eight o'clock at night.
4. The offices of Flagler & Sharp are located on Seventh Avenue.
5. Norbert is to meet the preacher at the First Baptist Church tonight.
6. There were 2,523 suggestions in the suggestion box.
7. Ninety-three percent of the women favored the new maternity leave policy.
8. The Ninety-ninth Congress was embroiled in controversy.
9. Fifteen couples returned from their vacation early.
10. The concert is scheduled to begin in the park at two o'clock.

CHAPTER 17

EDITING PRACTICE 17-1

1. Penny asked me if she could borrow ten dollars.
2. Please leave the room.
3. Will you please credit my account for the returned merchandise.
4. Evening classes at the college begin at 7:00 P.M.

5. Dr. Jackson can see you today at 10:00 A.M.
6. The receipt for twenty-eight dollars and thirty cents should be written as $28.30.
7. Did you have a chance to visit with your sister in Richmond, Va.?
8. Please close the window, Charles.
9. Rev. Van Ringold is supposed to drop by today at 2:00 P.M.
10. Rick asked the coach if the team had been selected yet.

EDITING PRACTICE 17-2

1. The critic wrote, "She [Emily Dickinson] was the finest American poet of the nineteenth century."
2. "Ernest Hemmingway [*sic*] won the Nobel Prize for literature," the article said.
3. The professor wrote, "He [William Shakespeare] is the finest dramatist the world has ever known."
4. The book stated, "It took some time before William Falkner [*sic*] was appreciated by the public."
5. The hostess left a note for her staff that said, "Their [*sic*] are not enough wine glasses."

EDITING PRACTICE 17-3

1. Please listen for the following broadcasts: the morning one at 8:00, the afternoon one at 1:00, and the evening one at 6:00.
2. *Thinking Critically: A Beginner's Guide* was not a best-seller.
3. John 3:16 is a very popular passage from the Bible.
4. My English class meets from 10:00 A.M. to 11:20 A.M.
5. *Byron: A Collection of Critical Essays* is a book of collected essays on the works of the poet Byron.
6. Be sure to follow these steps: disconnect electrical appliances, raise windows slightly, go to a safe place in basement away from all windows.
7. I set the VCR to begin taping at 8:15 P.M.
8. *Relativity: An Introduction to Einstein* provides a useful introduction to relativity.
9. The meeting is scheduled to last from 10:00 A.M. to 11:30 A.M.
10. *Generations: An Introduction to Drama* is a good beginning text on the subject.

EDITING PRACTICE 17-4

1. Do you think Tammy is emotionally stable?
2. Don't drop that sheet of glass!
3. Did you notice that the flag was at half mast?
4. Be quiet!
5. Will the senator get the bill drafted on time?

EDITING PRACTICE 17-5

1. Jodie, Jackie, Burt, and Ned—these are the most promising students in this year's class.
2. The project—thank heavens it was funded—will employ many people.
3. Hector stuttered, "P—P—Please give m—m—me a ch—ch—chance."
4. I have only one more paper to grade—the one on genetic experimentation.
5. Clive—or was it Joel?—made the best score of anyone ever to have taken the test.
6. The student speaker began, "I—uh—wish to talk to you—uh—about a matter of—um—great importance."
7. Judge K— did not wish to be identified.
8. Three women—Joan, Susan, and Alice—decided to run for the office.

9. Otto asked Vivian, "Would you l—l—like a p—p—piece of c—c—candy?"
10. The wooden object—or was it plastic?—was found in the wreckage.

EDITING PRACTICE 17-6

1. The report (see the enclosed photos) covers the subject adequately.
2. Clarence Darrow (1857–1938) defended John Scopes.
3. Please consider three things: (1) cost, (2) location, and (3) reputation.
4. Mark Twain (see also Samuel Langhorne Clemens) is America's most noted humorist.
5. Members of the NCTE (National Council of Teachers of English) will meet in Denver this year.
6. I paid two hundred dollars ($200) for the watch.
7. John Calvin (1509–1564) was a famous religious reformer.
8. The car my son wanted was (a) too expensive, (b) too old, and (c) too impractical.
9. The portfolio (notice the oil paintings in particular) represents three years' work.
10. Wyatt Earp (1848–1929) lived a long life during dangerous times.

EDITING PRACTICE 17-7

1. Emily Dickinson said, "The soul selects her own society, / Then shuts the door; On her divine majority, / Obtrude no more."
2. My friend Williard took electronics on the pass / fail system.
3. The female cadets and / or the administration will take the matter to court.
4. Ralph Waldo Emerson wrote, "Rhodora! If the Sages ask thee why / This charm is wasted on the earth and sky, / Tell them, dear, that if eyes were made for seeing, / Then Beauty is its own excuse for being."
5. The job requires knowledge of the Microsoft Word and / or the Word Perfect word-processing system.

PRACTICE SENTENCES 17-8

1. There are at least twenty-five ways to complete that project.
2. The verb is spelled d-e-v-i-s-e, the noun, d-e-v-i-c-e.
3. The team had a pre-game meeting in the locker room.
4. The nineteen-eighties was a time of political conservatism.
5. Ninety-seven people applied for one job opening at the bank.
6. I read pages 491–543 in my history text last night.
7. The man-made virus was barely contained.
8. There is much pro-Israeli sentiment in the American government.
9. Joel Barlow (1754–1812) is a little-known American poet.
10. The day-to-day figures looked good for the new company.

Index